For my parents

Industrial Redundancies

A comparative analysis of the chemical and
clothing industries in the UK and Italy

LIDIA GRECO
University of Lecce, Italy
and
Employment Research Centre
Trinity College, Dublin

ASHGATE

Published by
Ashgate Publishing Limited
Gower House
Croft Road
Aldershot
Hampshire GU11 3HR
England

Ashgate Publishing Company
131 Main Street
Burlington, VT 05401-5600 USA

Ashgate website: http://www.ashgate.com

British Library Cataloguing in Publication Data
Greco, Lidia
    Industrial redundancies : a comparative analysis of the
    chemical and clothing industries in the UK and Italy. -
    (The dynamics of economic space)
    1. Structural unemployment - England - Teesside 2. Structural
    unemployment - Italy - Brindisi 3. Chemical industry -
    England - Teesside 4. Chemical industry - Italy - Brindisi
    5. Clothing trade - England - Teesside 6. Clothing trade -
    Italy - Brindisi
    I. Title
    331.1'3786'0941

Library of Congress Cataloging-in-Publication Data
Greco, Lidia, 1969-
    Industrial redundancies : a comparative analysis of the chemical and clothing industries
    in the UK and Italy / Lidia Greco.
        p. cm. -- (The dynamics of economic space series)
    Includes bibliographical references and index.
    ISBN 0-7546-0964-2
        1. Employees--Dismissal of--England--Teesside. 2. Employees--Dismissal
    of--Italy--Brindisi. 3. Chemical industries--England--Teesside. 4. Chemical
    industries--Italy--Brindisi. 5. Clothing trade--England--Teesside. 6. Clothing
    trade--Italy--Brindisi. I. Title. II. Dynamics of economic space.

    HF5549.5.D55 G74 2002
    331.12'5--dc21
                                                                    2002024925
ISBN 0 7546 0964 2

Printed and bound by Athenaeum Press, Ltd.,
Gateshead, Tyne & Wear.

Contents

List of Figures

List of Tables

Preface

This book has its immediate origins in the research that I conducted for my Ph.D. in the Department of Geography at the University of Durham during the period 1997-2000. It is a study about industrial and employment change over space. It examines processes of redundancies and restructuring in the chemical and clothing sectors of two industrial areas, Teesside (UK) and Brindisi (Italy) and seeks to explain why they occur in the way they do.

It became clear to me, as I was exploring these issues, that the central theoretical and methodological apparatus of mainstream economistic literature on such phenomena was inadequate. The conceptualisation of redundancies in terms of economic rationality and market competition simply failed to consider the particular nature of the wage relation and the unique manner in which companies assess situations and set objectives to pursue profitability. It is claimed, in fact, that it is the rigidity of the cost of labour and the institutional regulation of the employment relation which compromize the competitive nature of the labour market and force companies to adjust to adverse market conditions by reducing employment rather than real wages. Similarly, from a methodological perspective, the emphasis placed on economic factors alone implied the uniformity of adjustment patterns and their mono-causal determinants.

The limits of orthodox theory, unable to explain the crisis of the traditional model of waged labour as well as to propose effective policy prescriptions, suggested to reflect on the evolution of capitalist economies and institutional change, that is, the change of social forms that provide a stable framework to economic behaviour and activities. The work adopts therefore an institutionalist perspective; its contribution lies in an understanding of the extent and manner in which processes of restructuring and redundancies are shaped and mediated by specific institutions and the processes through which they take place. It has put the wage relation and institutions that regulate it at the centre of analysis. In accordance with the insights of pioneer old institutionalists such as Veblen, Commons and Clark, it has assumed that the quality of labour and its contribution to production are not reducible to the labour contract and, therefore, cannot be subjected exclusively to monetary exchange. It follows that the formal and informal institutions of labour, a reflection of wider societal arrangements, constitute the critical factors for explaining corporate performance and change. They influence the pursuit of profitability and efficiency as they affect the definition of what is rational according to a specific institutional configuration and compatible with the values that a given society considers socially and economically legitimate. Redundancies and restructuring come to be conceptualised as institutionally constructed processes and, as such, geographically situated. In other words, besides the causes of different nature that lead to restructuring and redundancies, such an approach allows us to account for the institutional framework that governs the relationships between capital and labour and, therefore, the evolution of economic processes in the contemporary phase of capitalist development. Furthermore, it does not simply allow us to acknowledge the salience of institutional configuration on restructuring and redundancies but, more importantly, it helps to explain such processes in the light of the changing societal values that guide economic action. This work does not offer a theory of institutions; it rather seeks to contribute to a conceptualisation of industrial unemployment which is sensitive to the complexity of this phenomenon, to the role of agency and to the inherently geographical nature of processes of industrial and employment change. These are precisely the dimensions that conventional economic analyses do not explain. Two important implications can be drawn from the analysis. First, it allows us to transcend the debate that, in the last two decades, has revolved around the dichotomy rigidity versus flexibility. By the end of the work it will be apparent that the emphasis of this debate is misplaced and concretely misleading. It is misplaced because the key issue for industrial unemployment and restructuring relates to the regulatory solutions that allow certain economic and labour performances to be consistent with the values of a given society. It is misleading because deregulation does not necessarily enhance the free working of productive and market forces; it surely moves the problem of industrial unemployment (the problem of labour) from a collective to an individual level. Second, this perspective puts the theme of the social value attributed to labour back into the theoretical and political debate. The willingness to consider the cost of labour as a variable rather than a fixed cost of production raises questions about new ways of reproducing labour.

The work behind this book has benefited from the help and presence of numerous people that I wish to thank. My gratitude is primarily for Ash

Amin and Ray Hudson, my supervisors in Durham, whose critical insights have helped me to refine the theme of this research. Many thanks also to Jamie Peck, and especially to Franco Chiarello and David Sadler for their guidance and encouragement in undertaking the publication of this work. Obviously, it could not have succeeded without the co-operation of the people of Teesside and Brindisi who have been involved in the research. They offered me their help by answering my queries and providing data; their standpoints have been of great value for the work. In Durham, in the Department of Geography, I found a friendly and collaborative environment that has been extremely important in the development of my research; I fondly recall especially Javier Pineda to whom I owe a lot. I would like also to mention Undala Alam and Tariq Elamin Bakheit for their sincere affection over the years. Finally, my thanks go to the editor Valerie Rose and to the Ashgate staff for their professional support.

List of Abbreviations

BSC	British Steel Corporation
CENSIS	Centro Studi Investimenti Sociali
CGIL	Confederazione Generale Italiana del Lavoro
CIG	Cassa Integrazione Guadagni
CISL	Confederazione Italiana Sindacati dei Lavoratori
CNA	Confederazione Nazionale Artigiani
DC	Democrazia Cristiana
ENI	Ente Nazionale Idrocarburi
EVC	European Vynil Corporation
GMB	General Municipal and Boilermakers
ICE	Istituto per il Commercio Estero
ICI	Imperial Chemical Industries
INPS	Istituto Nazionale della Previdenza Sociale
IRI	Istituto per la Ricostruzione Industriale
M&S	Marks and Spencer
MDI	Methl Diphenyl Di-Isocyanate
PP.SS.	Partecipazioni Statali
TCI	Teesside Chemical Initiative
TEC	Training and Enterprise Council
TVJSU	Tees Valley Joint Strategy Unit
VCM	Vinyl Chloride Monomer

Chapter 1

Introduction

Facing redundancies seems to be a recurrent problem for industrial areas. Businesses seem to have entered a regime of continuous restructuring[1] in which the re-organization of production and labour is no longer a cyclical occurrence in the context of economic hardship or paradigmatic change; restructuring is an integral part of normal corporate activity (Carabelli and Tronti, 1999). Primarily because of the dominance of neo-liberal rhetoric, the perspective that has monopolized the economic debate on industrial redundancies is one rooted in neo-classical economics and its core variable is the cost of labour.[2] Whenever a negative economic situation requires it, companies, as profit maximising agents, must radically reduce input costs and output prices to bring the organization's operation into alignment with market expectations (Usui and Colignon, 1996). In pure form, such an adjustment is unproblematic given perfect information of markets and prices. In practice, the rigidity of the cost of labour and various forms of institutional regulation of the wage relation are said to compromize company profitability and to determine a greater increase in industrial unemployment.[3] Profit squeezes are said to ensue when, during a phase of economic downturn, wages remain above the marginal product of labour at full employment (Bruno and Sachs, 1985). In other words, a reduction in aggregate demand pushes companies into more radical adjustment centred upon the reduction of their employment base as they are unable to modify a disequilibrated wage dynamic relative to output.

The "wage rigidity" argument has gained widespread acceptance outside the academic domain. Among policy makers it is argued that an efficient organization of work requires the provision of flexible and cheap labour and its swift adjustment to demand; as indicated by Carabelli and Tronti (1999), this is deemed possible primarily through the use of flexible work contracts and the outsourcing of services and intermediate production processes. A consensus has therefore emerged in Europe around the position expressed by the Organization for Economic Co-operation and Development (OECD). While designing a strategy of intervention for the labour market envisaging a wide range of policies, such an organization has attributed a special emphasis on micro-economic policies and on the mechanisms regulating the labour market; for industry to increase its competitiveness in international markets, to react to shocks in aggregate demand and to avoid serious implications for the employment base, it is necessary to slacken labour legislation and allow the free working of the labour market (OECD, 1999; 1997; 1994; CEPR, 1995; Artis, 1998; Jackman, 1999). Conversely, macro-economic and structural policies, aiming to favour for instance technological innovation, are attributed a role of pure support. In the prevailing view, therefore, restructuring paths should be nested within a new socio-economic paradigm, which replaces collective bargaining and state-mediation with corporate-driven flexibility and entrepreneurialism.

In this work, it is argued that the insights provided by the new orthodoxy on redundancies are theoretically and methodologically flawed. By defining the price of a special commodity (labour), that contrary to others needs to be reproduced, the definition of the wage cannot merely respond to economic laws (Marx, 1977; Polanyi, 1944; Peck, 1996; Picchio, 1992). Second, the thesis that rational behaviour is compromized by the system of employment relations, as it reduces the company's capacity of being cost effective, depicts a highly stylised economic scenario. In this view, any company, regardless of size, sector, location, etc. would assess and respond in a predictable way, through restructuring and redundancies, to wage pressure on profits. The argument here is that not only may the causes compromising profitability levels have a variety of origins, but in many cases companies do not find it profitable to enforce a reduction of the wage level because of its possible negative effects on workers' productivity (see, among others, Akerlof and Yellen, 1986). Profitability is a relative measure: it varies according to sectors (Silva, 1995) and, within them, between companies, and its definition is concretely mediated by a series of non-economic factors, e.g. ethical norms of behaviour. Similarly, a labour retention strategy can be just as market rational and cost efficient if it leads to higher productivity, e.g. the "high route" labour strategies (Streeck, 1992; Sabel, 1994). From a methodological perspective, the emphasis of the new orthodoxy falls upon economic determinants alone. Company patterns of adjustment are uniform, definable a-priori and centred almost exclusively upon the labour dimension; their role as that of workers or other collective agencies (e.g. trade unions) becomes of reaction or perhaps of support. Indeed, restructuring processes and employment change are seen as events that happen to people whose strategies cannot affect them. By the same token, redundancies are accounted for as the inevitable result of the company's attempt to return to profitability, treated as unproblematic and discrete events. This work reconsiders therefore other explanations of industrial unemployment, which seem to have been silenced by the mainstream interpretation. The insights of Keynesian economic theory, of Marxian political economy and of Schumpeterian theory are deemed important in the understanding of macro-economic dynamics concerning wage determination, restructuring and employment change. Other accounts of industrial unemployment have been provided, from a micro-economic perspective, by the efficiency wage models. Departing from the conventional neo-classical approach, such models have emphasized how firms tend to set wages at a higher level than the market clearing one, precisely to ensure above-average levels of productivity. The interpretation of industrial unemployment provided by the old institutionalist tradition as well as by recent developments within this stream of literature, namely the regulation and convention theories, significantly distinguishes itself from conventional economic analyses. Industrial unemployment is explained as the result of regulatory deficits that emerge from the failure of institutions to compose the divergent interests between capital and labour expressed in the wage relationship. The alternative stances sketched above offer important counter-explanations of the phenomenon of industrial unemployment and, in their light, this work seeks to develop an alternative approach to redundancies. It focuses on the intermediate institutions of the wage relation to reconcile the macro-economic perspectives and the preference models. The approach is nested primarily in the old institutionalist tradition of Thorstein Veblen, John Commons and John Clark. In this tradition, institutions, understood as formal and informal consolidated behaviour, are not simply seen as influencing and regulating actors' action but also as affecting their cognitive schemes. Accordingly, the understanding of redundancies and restructuring processes centres around the institutions that enter the process of wage determination. The latter comes to be treated as an institution itself and, as such, the outcome of corporate culture, of the embeddedness of firms action in national and local institutional set-ups, of the instrumental and symbolic relations firms entertain with their external environment. The emphasis of an institutionalist approach lies therefore less in the claim that organizational action adapts to the conditions of the market or is independent, but that organizations behave as part of specific institutional systems. Such systems influence company decisions as they do the definition of what is rational according to the particular institutional configuration. No economic action can therefore be read apart from a determined institutional framework which reflects specific historical and spatial features. From a sociological perspective, an attempt to overcome the polarization between macro and micro sociological approaches and to account for the role of institutions on organizational practices and labour market dynamics has been put forward by the new economic sociology represented, among others, by authors such as Granovetter, Zukin, Powell and DiMaggio.

The conceptualization of industrial redundancies and restructuring within an institutionalist perspective could constitute a potential breakthrough in industrial geography, overcoming the major shortcomings of conventional economic views on the theme and opening new prospects for further research. The crisis of the traditional model of waged labour, as well as of an industrial system that does not produce jobs in relation to its growth, represent a challenge to traditional models of economic analysis and especially to current debates centred on the dichotomy "flexibility-rigidity".

The Focus of the Work

The work investigates both the sectoral determinants and the place-specific variables that determine processes of employment and industrial change. By accounting for the formal and informal institutions, spatially and historically embodied, that find expression in the wage relation, it also seeks to highlight the various elements that frame the actions and strategies of companies, workers and other socio-economic groups (e.g. unions) to affect industrial restructuring and unemployment. The main argument advanced is that industrial restructuring and redundancies are institutional constructions and geographically situated as such. This means first to acknowledge the irreducibility of economic transformation to pure market forces and to emphasize the salience of corporate practices in the explanation of the way in which profitability is pursued through adjustment dynamics and the employment change. Rather than considering industrial restructuring and redundancies as events caused by exogenous factors, this work investigates them as processes which account for the interplay of individual and group actions, in a particular moment and place. In so doing, second, such a conceptualization highlights the spatial specificity of restructuring processes and redundancies. In addition, by bringing back into account the role of agency in institutionally and spatially specific contexts, this interpretation acknowledges it as the outcome of open and indeterminate processes which are subject to political struggles, to societal values and norms that do not act neutrally. Third, on the role of wages, it argues that it is the ensemble of relationships influencing wage determination to provide companies with the stability necessary for their economic activity and allow them to respond to external perturbations while preserving their unity.

This work explores processes of corporate restructuring and employment change in two industrial areas, Teesside (in the north-east of England) and Brindisi (in south-east of Italy), by drawing upon the evidence from two industries: the chemical and the clothing sectors. Teesside and Brindisi are both facing, although with different intensity, similar challenges of industrial restructuring and employment change following the crisis of their dominant industries. Nevertheless, they have different institutional set-ups. Teesside is characterized by a culture of compliance and co-operation between employers and workers and by a weak trade union movement; these are the legacies of the pervasive paternalistic influence of iron and steel and chemical industries on industrial relations, strategies and policies of the local labour market. In Brindisi, the corporatist model of governance regulates labour market dynamics. However, the presence of informal economic activities implies that the micro-regulation of labour market dynamics is widely diffused and co-exists with the formal one. The chemical and the clothing sectors display a difference in terms of the role of the cost of labour on the total cost of production. Whilst clothing is wage sensitive, technological characteristics assume a primary importance in determining performance in the chemical sector. Such a diversity impacts also on the quality and quantity of the workforce required. In addition, the diverse features of the production process of the two industries influence the character of industrial relations and, therefore, the process of wage determination. Contrary, thus, to market-centred analyses, which envisage the convergence of firms towards a single, uniform form of restructuring, synonymous with redundancy, the approach suggested here implies that restructuring is the outcome of a specific alchemy of internal corporation relations and interactions with the outside world. Concretely, the findings show that the response to similar economic pressures has generated in the two areas different patterns of adjustment producing diverse effects on company employment base. Yet, by focusing on the local environment in which companies are embedded, it is revealed how place-specific social and historical practices represent important variables to explain redundancy processes in the two areas.

The Structure of the Book

The next chapter develops the alternative approach to industrial unemployment. It first offers a critique of the wage rigidity argument rooted in the neo-classical paradigm. Then it develops a sympathetic critique of other macro-economic conceptualizations, of preference models, and of the institutionalist perspectives. By focusing on the formal and informal institutions that enter the process of wage determination, such an approach claims that industrial unemployment and restructuring are institutionally and spatially constructed.

Chapters 3 and 4 present the details of restructuring in the two regional contexts. Each chapter is divided into three parts: the first presents a background analysis of the economic and employment trends in the area examined, while parts two and three are devoted to sectoral analysis. The aim of these two chapters is to provide an explanation of chemical and clothing company adjustment paths in each region; to shed light on the processes through which these have been pursued; to consider their implications on the sectoral relations of production and employment.

Chapter 5 is a comparative chapter. First, it highlights the sectoral determinants of the processes of employment change in the two case-study areas. It also points out the significance of geographical context: place-specific economic and social features contribute to explain the variety of corporate adjustments and their diverse impact on company employment base. In the light of these findings the chapter then engages with the theoretical debate on industrial unemployment and processes of corporate restructuring. Rather than endorsing the convergence of corporations towards uniform patterns of industrial and employment restructuring, as suggested by market-centred analyses, it claims the complexity of the phenomena under investigation as well as their geographical specificity. Finally, chapter 6 draws together the strands of my argument and identifies some of the crucial theoretical and political issues related to it.

The methodology behind the empirical work is discussed in the appendix. It indicates the sort of questions and methods to be pursued within an institutionalist interpretation of redundancies and industrial restructuring. It then explains how the two case studies were studied.

Notes

[1] This term is ambiguous. Business and organizational literature may refer to it to indicate: re-organization of production (elimination of product lines, plant closures) and/or re-organization of work. In general, the term indicates all the strategies undertaken to relieve corporate cost burdens (Usui and Colignon, 1996), and as such is used in this work.

[2] This is the initial argument of a wider debate developed especially during the 1990s. It focuses on the factors (e.g. unemployment benefits, welfare protection) that, by affecting the supply side of the labour market, alter the level at which the wage clears it and, therefore, the free working of demand and supply of labour (Sestito, 1997).

[3] It is a popular argument within much of the most recent economistic literature, for instance, to contrast the performances of the USA and European labour markets and to attribute the lower levels of unemployment of the former to the lighter institutional regulation of the labour market (Layard et al., 1994).

Chapter 2

Theorizing Industrial Unemployment

The Wage Rigidity Argument and Industrial Unemployment

The interpretation of industrial redundancies that has gained prevalence in the economic and policy debate, principally on the crest of neo-liberal political rhetoric,[1] is rooted into the neo-classical tradition and focuses upon the relevance of wage rigidity on company costs in explaining the rise and the persistence of the phenomenon.[2] The neo-classical paradigm holds that the labour market is a competitive market, characterized, like any other market, by perfectly rational economic actors (individuals and firms) and it is self-regulating: changes in the price of labour (wages) and the geographical mobility of workers are deemed to be the mechanisms that clear the temporary excess of labour demand over labour supply, and vice-versa (Armstrong and Taylor, 1993). It is not assumed that the labour market works perfectly, e.g. at zero costs of mobility or with perfect information: the existence of imperfections is in fact acknowledged (Friedman and Friedman, 1979; Layard et al., 1994). The contention instead is that such imperfections, due to ignorance of and friction around opportunities, are relatively unimportant and can be eliminated if the perfectly competitive model is pursued. In particular, as synthesized by Winter:

> [in this view] firms are characterized by the technological transformations of which they are capable – formally by production sets or production functions. Like consumers, firms are unitary actors and are economically rational; more specifically, they maximize profit or present value (Winter, 1993, p.180).

This is rationalized as reflecting company interests under the prevailing assumptions of competitive markets, perfect contracts and optimal adaptation of organizational and production practices to the prevailing market price (Usui and Colignon, 1996; Williamson and Winter, 1993; Best, 1990). Although uncertainty in company decision-making process is contemplated, it is deemed unable to alter the actual outcomes in the market which benefits ultimately a situation of perfect information

(Kaufman, 1994). During phases of market recession, input costs and output prices need to be modified to bring the organization's operation into alignment with market rationality and to return to a state of equilibrium. In pure form, the nature of such an adjustment is unproblematic. In reality, it is claimed that a major restriction of the last two decades has been the inability of the industrial system to adjust to the changes required at the macro-economic level. Competitiveness is said to require flexibility in the adjustment of production to demand, and in the provision of labour at the lowest cost; however, the regulation of the labour market and, specifically, of the wage relation, compromizing the link between wages and productivity, implies that a reduction in aggregate demand carries a greater increase in unemployment (Artis, 1998; Jackman, 1999).[3] In other words, the institutional regulation of wages, which during economic downturn remain above the marginal product of labour at full employment, produces profit squeezes and forces companies to introduce more radical adjustment mechanisms, including making workers redundant (Bruno and Sachs, 1985). Wage rigidity, with its negative effects on employment levels, is to be attributed mainly, although not exclusively, to employment relations regulating wages and conditions of labour. Specifically, union power has prevented workers from acknowledging that a real wage problem existed. As explained by Bruno and Sachs:

> ... it is one thing to understand the ramifications of higher [costs of raw material], however, and another to convey them credibly to workers in the course of wage negotiations. Since firms have a natural incentive to overstate the need for real wage reduction, pronouncements by firms about a profit squeeze fall on sceptical ears. The result is that real wages do not fall as sharply as they would under full information ... (Bruno and Sachs, 1985, p.196).

As a consequence, companies are obliged to adjust to adverse market conditions by reducing employment rather than real wages and the nature of the layoff process is random (Layard et al., 1994). Following the same line of argument, Grossman and Hart (1981) have shown that workers are more likely to accept real wage cuts only in the context of layoffs: they tend to underestimate employer requests as these are believed to obtain wage concessions by falsely claiming an adverse shock. This stream of neo-classical literature therefore conceptualizes redundancies in terms of economic rationality and market competition. It implies, on one hand, the uniformity of the adjustment paths and, on the other, "isomorphic employment practices" (Usui and Colignon, 1996, p.552). Job losses are the necessary outcome of processes of restructuring or plant closure dictated by levels of profitability jeopardized by institutional interference in the market. Context has no relevance in such dynamics; indeed, it is treated as a residual factor in addition to other variables. Following this theoretical position, prevailing policy views have emphasised the key importance of micro-economic measures for a better working of the labour market.[4] The indications suggested in the OECD Job Study (1994) and in all its subsequent publications encourage particularly the reform of the mechanisms regulating the labour market towards a greater flexibility; this concerns working times, wages and wage negotiation which should reflect market conditions. Specifically, aggregate wage flexibility is deemed crucial for the ability of an economy to adjust to economic shocks.

The wage rigidity argument has several shortcomings. First, from a historical perspective, to blame industrial relations for the upward pressure of wages is flawed. During the last two decades, the bargaining capacity of trade unions has decreased consistently in all industrialized countries (Sestito, 1997). In addition, countries that were more heavily unionised (Sweden and Finland) have not performed worse than those where unionism has shown a marked decline (e.g. Britain, France, the Netherlands) (Nolan, 1994). Perhaps, it is because of such factors that, on the base of internationally equivalent micro-economic data sets, Blanchflower and Oswald (1994) suggest that wages are negatively related to the level of unemployment and that, indeed, the wage curve presents a downward-sloping shape (see figure 2.1). Their work indicates four possible theoretical explanations for the interpretation of the curve. First, when the wage rate is high, it is in the interest of both firms and workers to ensure that as many as possible of those in the labour pool have jobs (contract models). A second explanation is that a high degree of joblessness tends to reduce workers' capacity to claim wage benefits (bargaining models). A third explanation is provided by appealing to the efficiency wage models (see infra). Finally, the negative relation between wage and unemployment has been explained using the so-called idea of "persistent dis-equilibrium". Within a labour market that adjusts slowly, non-equilibrium states may repeat over time: depressive or recession phases may consequently have a negative influence on both pay and job opportunities.

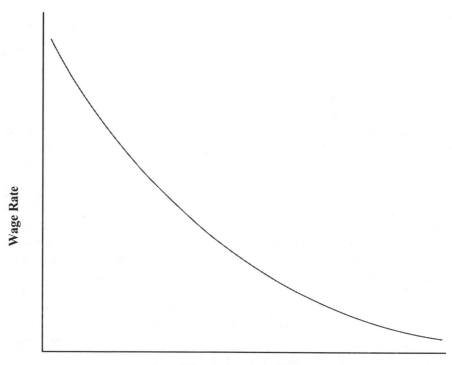

Local Unemployment Rate

Figure 2.1: The wage curve

Concretely, not only may the causes compromising profitability levels have a variety of origins but, as will be shown later, most companies do not find it profitable to enforce a reduction of the wage level because of the possible negative effects on workers' productivity. In addition, profitability is a relative measure. Indeed, what an adequate rate of profit is varies widely between sectors and, within sectors, between companies. As explained by Silva (1995), the link between wages and employment is not the same in all sectors, as it depends on production techniques whose evaluation is largely independent from wage dynamics. Yet, it is shown that decisions about restructuring necessarily involve neither loss of profit (e.g. in cases of rationalization) nor redundancies (e.g. in cases of intensification). Second, this account theorises corporate restructuring in terms of profit maximising behaviour; as indicated by Winter (1993, p.188), profit is expressed in terms of "the mathematics of optimisation". Profitability is deemed not to be affected by any external condition and the costs associated with the cognitive operations to achieve optimization are omitted. Indeed, company decisions are believed to be based on information available in the market, so that their path of adjustment consists in the mere search for equilibrium between costs and prices. In contrast, Winter notes that rather than profit-making, companies are typically profit-seeking whose rationality is bounded (Winter, 1993): there are limits to the capacity to receive, store and process information. Uncertainty about the economic environment and its complexity make company decision-making processes difficult, characterized by variety which reflects the unique manner in which they assess situations and set objectives. Yet, by assuming the mechanical nature of the formation of company preferences, the neo-classical conceptualization underestimates such a process (Levine, 1998) as well as the salience of context. Company and individual decisions and actions do not occur in neutral environments, independently from the socio-economic structure in which they are embedded. The interaction of structures and institutions, affecting the way in which decisions are made and different answers to stimuli provided, assumes a unique, distinguishing feature, dependent on particular contingent and sedimented conditions that vary according to time and space (Harvey, 1969; Gregory and Urry, 1985).

Macro-Economic Alternatives

The Keynesian Interpretation of Industrial Unemployment

The understanding of the economic relations between wages and unemployment dynamics provided by the Keynesian theoretical apparatus contrasts with that of the neo-classical tradition. At a micro-economic level, it is recognized that a relation exists between wages and employment but of a reverse nature to the interpretation provided by neo-classics through the Phillips' curve (Cahuc and Kempf, 1993).[5] In the neo-classical perspective, profitability gains are reduced by inflation. As this is provoked by an increase in prices due to an increase in wages, the reduction in the level of wages is deemed to be beneficial for a temporary reduction in unemployment as companies are more willing to hire unemployed workers (Hoang-Ngoc, 1996). In the Keynesian interpretation, instead, it is not the wage that determines the level of employment but it is the level of employment that determines the wage. As explained by Hoang-Ngoc (ibid.), the decrease in nominal wages does not necessarily provoke a parallel decrease in real wages, as the level of prices depends on factors connected to the uncertainty of adjustments between demand and supply: indeed, nominal wages and prices could vary in the same direction. In such a perspective, therefore, the major source of employment change is the entrepreneurs anticipation of their decisions concerning investment. At the macro level, again in contrast with the neo-classical perspective, the Keynesian theoretical framework conceptualizes the economic system as a system that does not move spontaneously to equilibrium. Indeed, it is its irregular growth, determined by demand fluctuations, unforeseeable situations or erroneous economic calculations, that affects company decisions about investments which, in turn, determine unemployment dynamics and the level of wages (Hobson, 1922). Rather than being the labour market clearing mechanism, the wage represents one of the factors contributing to the instability of the economic dynamic: indeed, the economic system is characterized by the slow reaction with which wages and prices respond to demand fluctuations. The stability of wages in case of a fall in product demand will determine a reduction of labour demand; conversely, a fall in labour demand will lead to a reduction of product demand, if prices stay stable.

The combination of the micro and macro-dimension of the Keynesian analysis suggests that company profitability is seen as a function of the level of demand for products which individual firms and plants can do little to influence since it depends on overall demand. When demand falls, capacity may be rationalized and plant closures may occur (Fothergill and Guy, 1990). Contrary to the neo-classical position, the Keynesian conceptualization leaves room for institutional intervention, namely demand-side policies which, by stimulating industrial activity, would positively affect employment dynamics (Matzner and Streeck, 1991). In these views, the real limit to the growth of job opportunities lies in the fact that the productive potential of industrial systems is unable to ensure an appropriate level of investment. The main contribution of the Keynesian theory on industrial unemployment lies in its emphasis on the strict relation between the growth of the economy and the growth of productive forces or, in other words, on the influence of demand-side conditions on both company performance and on the overall employment level. By pointing out the link between investment and employment levels, whereby the former becomes a function of the level of demand for products, this theory has "opened up the need for explanations of wage levels beyond marginal productivity ... and thus reserved an area for the impact of institutional and other social factors" (Kerr, 1994, p.73). Indeed, it leaves room for the influence of exogenous factors (principally expansionary measures) on wages. However, the exclusive focus on the level of effective demand as the source of employment growth leads this conceptualization to neglect the analysis of the supply-side elements of the labour market (e.g. workforce characteristics, union presence, regulatory frameworks) that influence company behaviour and, consequently, their position in the market. In addition, by interpreting redundancies and restructuring as the outcome of a disequilibrated working of the economic system, it fails to acknowledge that job losses, like any other economic phenomenon, are also determined by economic dynamics at a supra-national scale (e.g. situations of over-capacity affecting a particular sector on international markets) and at a sub-national level (e.g. the profitability of a specific plant within corporate strategies). Also within this view, contextual specificity is neglected. Finally, from a policy perspective, the Keynesian interpretation is dominated by demand-side, state-centred, interventions; it underestimates, for instance, the possibility that local policies to enhance the mobilization of endogenous potential affect employment dynamics.

The Marxist Perspective on Redundancies

Within Marxian political economy, emphasising the conflicting relationship between capital and labour, industrial unemployment is explained as a structural condition of capitalist societies, even though its fluctuation is seen as the result of short-term dynamics related to the cycles of capitalist growth (Mandel, 1995). For Baran and Sweezy (1966), the capitalist search for profit gives rise to intense rivalry and competition between firms. This is pursued in part through technological innovation and parallel reduction of costs, resulting in the intensification of work (Sayer, 1989). This process, however, can ultimately lead to the under-utilization of capacity if the surplus cannot be absorbed by consumption. Restructuring and redundancies follow as a consequence. Despite the centrality of the wage relation in the Marxist theory, wages alone are attributed a marginal role in explaining unemployment. It is the level of unemployment instead that has consistent effects on wages. According to Marx, wages represent a harnessing of power to labour, "promising to expend labour in the interest of and under the direction of purchaser, in exchange for a sum of money, the wage" (Bottomore, 1984, p.265). Yet, the level of wages varies according to the demand and supply conditions of the market. The existence of almost permanent excess of labour supply over labour demand translates into a greater pressure on wages, whose level is depressed by the great quantity of people available in the market.

Within the Marxian tradition, job losses are connected to the intrinsic logic of capitalist accumulation. In the long term, redundancies are ultimately the consequence of capital and labour competition through which capital manages to appropriate consistent shares of profit, given its pre-eminence within the relation. Marxian political economy thus emphasizes the primary asymmetry of power within the labour market, considered the terrain of political struggle between capital and labour. It highlights the flaw of the neo-classical conceptualization in ignoring the fundamentally political nature of economic processes. Marxism fails, however, to acknowledge that other, secondary, asymmetries exist among employers (e.g. between monopoly and competitive firms) and workers (e.g. unionised or non-unionised workers, gender or ethnic groups). In addition, no short-term condition is supposed to influence unemployment dynamics. Moreover, despite claims of historicity, the holistic conceptualization of the capitalist system proposed by the early Marxist approach becomes both trans-historical and a-historical and, as such, substantially insensitive to context specificity and spatial differentiation; redundancies and restructuring are therefore deemed to be disentangled from spatial factors.

During the 1970s, attempts to develop a less deterministic conceptualization of industrial unemployment and restructuring emerged within the Marxian tradition. One strand recognized the importance of spatial differentiation for the labour process and of political practices connected to it (Harvey, 1989; Massey, 1995; Massey and Meegan, 1982; 1985; Herod, 1991; Cox and Mair, 1988). All these contributions have stressed that a key to understanding employment dynamics is the geography of the relations of production. In their view, the spatial distribution of jobs, their availability and their features is related to the way in which production is organized over space. Redundancies and employment change are conceptualized as the outcome of a ceaseless de-valorization of capital which entails specific implications for the geography of industry and labour. For example, in a well-known study, Massey and Meegan (1982) identified three forms of corporate restructuring: intensification, investment and technical change and rationalization. Confined to the existing geography of plants, intensification implies an increase in productivity achieved mainly through the re-organization of work. Job losses occur when productivity grows faster than output.

Investment and technological change consists in new productive capacity and may imply new plants and locations. In stagnant or declining industries, this combines with the layoff of workers. Finally, the third form of corporate restructuring is rationalization. Undertaken to reduce capacity, rationalization is associated with plant closure, dis-investment and capital shift with their legacy of job losses. According to these authors, behind these patterns of restructuring lie the production processes which, recognized as social processes, help to explain employment decline. Following this line of reasoning, and focusing specifically on rationalization, Bluestone and Harrison explain how:

> buying and selling entire businesses and transferring capital from one sector to another, relocate facilities to different parts of the country and to different areas of the globe and [especially] shift capital out of older industrial areas bringing about large scale redundancies should be read as the outcome of corporations active strategies to escape having to live with a labour force that, through the previous industrialization process itself, has become costly (Bluestone and Harrison, 1982, pp.164-5).

In the field of economic geography, these neo-Marxist positions provide a less deterministic account of industrial unemployment. By rejecting that company behaviour responds mechanistically to the logic of capital accumulation, they illustrate that the analysis of employment must be set in the context of broader social processes, both inside and outside the firm. The key issue is to understand the reproduction over space of the social relations of production. Here too, however, there are some deficits. Paradoxically, the taxonomy of restructuring forms identified by Massey and Meegan, to which much literature has referred, ends up delineating a rigid framework of restructuring paths into which companies seem to fall as scapegoats of market dynamics. Despite recognising the production process as a social process, there is a tendency to emphasize the supremacy of market dynamics over the variety of adjustment paths that can be concretely undertaken by single companies and resulting from interactive processes involving also other individual (workers) and collective actors (e.g. unions, local institutions).[6] In addition, market circumstances are not properly stressed. As pointed out by MacLachlan (1992), different types of market stimuli involve different restructuring paths.

Business Cycles and the Labour-Saving Effects of Technological Innovation

A different reading of industrial restructuring and employment change emerges from the interpretation of the Schumpeterian theory of business cycles. Here, changes in the labour market are associated with particular technological transformations (Schumpeter, 1968). Specifically, industrial unemployment is regarded as the effect of the downward phases of the economic cycle linked to the obsolescence of technological endowments. In contrast to equilibrium economics, Schumpeter proposes a disequilibrated model of economic growth characterized by partial crises and business cycles. A process of technological change, indicated as creative destruction, affects economic structure from within, and the firm is the principal agent of such transformations. Accordingly, rather than being considered as mere "black boxes" (Pitelis and Wahl, 1998), firms are conceptualized as active actors seeking to take advantage of resources and opportunities, to compete on the basis of new commodities, technologies and types of organization rather than on prices. In this theoretical framework, also the concept of profit undergoes a re-configuration; it ceases to be a return to capital, becoming a return to successful innovation (Best, 1990). In this framework an industrial sector is more than a collection of individual firms producing substitute products. Indeed, the demise of an individual firm may be part of the process of creative destruction:

> a perfectly competitive industry that allocates efficiently in line with the neo-classical ideal is vulnerable to complete destruction (Best, 1990, p.121).

Employment change is consequently connected to industrial cycles: the ability of entrepreneurs to create and exploit new opportunities for profit, generates the conditions for full employment, ensuring rising output and real wages (Goodwin, 1991). The work of neo-Schumpeterian scholars has both complemented and partially revisited Schumpeter's initial theorization (Hicks, 1973; Freeman et al., 1982; Dosi, 1982). Schumpeter did not explicitly discuss the possibility that displacing effects connected to technologies could generate industrial unemployment. As new industries and technologies are implemented, economies of scale can be exploited and the pressure shifts to cost-saving innovations. Neo-Schumpeterian analysis has therefore focused on the market mechanisms that allow the system to re-absorb job losses. These are mainly of two types: mechanisms based on prices and on income. In the first case, the labour saving effect of technological innovation gives the opportunity to sell goods for a lower price, with the consequent increase in demand generating more employment. In the second case, increased profits associated with technological change produces more investments and more employment.

Neglected both by neo-classical and Keynesian economics,[7] the study of structural change and technical innovation has provided a valuable account of the processes of change that relate industries and firms to specific employment/unemployment dynamics. The Schumpeterians point out that aggregate statistics tend to ignore the growth of certain industries and technologies and the decline of others, and also that, within the same industry, differences exist between firms that manage to adopt and exploit new technologies and those that lag behind. The understanding of industrial employment change suggested by this perspective faces two major criticisms. First, the conceptual framework is dominated by a deterministic vision of economic events. On the one hand, companies turn to be trapped into the mechanical phases of business cycles which become the only parameters constraining or enhancing entrepreneurial action and restructuring processes (Best, 1990) and, on the other, job losses are the inevitable result of their reaction to external economic dynamics which urge them to continuous adaptive paths. Second, it has been remarked that a more appropriate analysis of the effect of technological progress on employment cannot be limited to the labour market as it also affects the market of the factors of production (Vivarelli and Gatti, 1995; Vivarelli, 1991).

The approaches reviewed above have in common a macro understanding of economic action. In these views, redundancies and restructuring processes are understood as the inevitable outcome of economic structures, impinging on micro-economic circumstances that the action of individuals can neither affect nor modify. All have a prevalence of structure over agency. In addition, instead of being the expression of specificity, context is considered as the container in which economic events take place.

Micro-Economic Perspectives: Preference Models

The approaches reviewed in this section focus on the wage setting process and place it in the arena where capital and labour relations historically take place, that is to say, in the firm. They hold that the determination of wages is based on conventionally neglected factors, such as beliefs, convention-based norms of behaviour, habits, etc., which reflect preferences and regulate actor action. The efficiency wage models reject the conceptualization of the labour market as a perfectly competitive and self-regulating market where wages are determined by the spontaneous adjustment of demand and supply of labour. They acknowledge instead that actor decisions are influenced by preferences which, in the context of wage determination, are only partially driven by maximising behaviour. The main contention common to all the efficiency wage models is that to ensure particular levels of productivity, companies tend to fix the wage at a higher level than the market clearing one. Behind this act lie economic and social motivations; whilst the ultimate objective of companies is to obtain adequate levels of profitability and productivity, achievement hinges upon specific internal dynamics such as norms and codes of behaviour, control of the production process, stability of the workforce base, etc. Such models are therefore concerned with factors that explain why firms often find it unprofitable to cut wages and industrial unemployment, even in adverse labour market circumstances, tends to stabilize (Akerlof and Yellen, 1986; Kaufman, 1994).

The models presented below have been gathered into three main groups, distinguished by the methodological tradition to which they belong, although they share common arguments (Costabile, 1995).

Approaches Based on Methodological Individualism

Methodological individualism holds that individual agents have predetermined needs and tastes and are driven by the desire to satisfy them, whilst social institutions and norms of behaviour emerge out of their interaction and only regulate the conflicts between individual and collective rationality. Capitalist firms thus represent an efficient solution to individuals' natural tendency to free ride: their profit maximising strategy is dictated by the need to control such a tendency (Shapiro and Stiglitz, 1985). Similarly, the rule excluding undercutting among workers emerges as a solution to their egoistic behaviour and to its disruptive consequences (Solow, 1980;1990).

A shirking model The model elaborated by Shapiro and Stiglitz (1985) assumes the existence of an information asymmetry between employers and employees at the workplace. As the process of monitoring work is imperfect and the workers have some discretion in their job effort, it follows that they may have the tendency to shirk, for instance, by reducing their effort. To avoid this occurrence, firms are induced to raise the wage level; therefore, workers receive wages that are higher than the market clearing level in order to increase their productivity. At this stage, they fear being fired and they do not shirk. At the aggregate level, higher wages will tend to reduce labour demand and, in consequence, the resulting equilibrium envisages industrial unemployment. Those who are unemployed involuntarily and who would be ready to work for lower wages are not taken into consideration by firms because they will have an incentive to shirk.

A fairness-based model Solow's contribution has sought to shed light on the reason that prevents unemployed workers from offering their work for a lower wage, especially when the rate of unemployment is high (Solow, 1980; 1990). According to Solow, the rejection of undercutting is due to a social norm that excludes it as a strategy in the labour market on the basis of fair behaviour among workers, employed and unemployed. The generation of the social norm derives from a process that is very similar to the prisoner's dilemma: after a first game that will give a sub-optimal result for each player, who seeks to maximize their result, a strategy of co-operation arises as a solution. Fair play is dictated by a preference to maximization which, however, may lead individuals to internalize new social norms.[8] Firms may accept wage undercutting if there are workers ready to do so but if a worker undercuts, he/she might get the reservation wage for future periods.[9] It is for this reason that the strategy of undercutting may reveal counterproductive.

Approaches Based on the Social Nature of Preferences

The approaches gathered in this second group assume the social nature of preferences.[10] First, institutional arrangements and social dimensions are seen to influence the formation of individual preferences. Second, economic rationality does not dominate individual behaviour. By internalising the norms and values of the society or system in which they live, individuals accept them as framework rules influencing their preferences. It follows that worker attitudes towards work are affected by their participation in workplace dynamics (Bowles, 1985) or by their perception of the fairness with which they are treated by the management (Akerlof, 1982; 1984; Akerlof and Yellen, 1986).

A shirking model The contribution proposed by Bowles (1985) is based on the shirking model.[11] Nevertheless, it differs from the one analysed above in that it attributes the existence of market imperfections to the prevailing institutional arrangements and to the conflicts arising among economic agents; the utility functions and preferences have a social rather than an individualistic foundation. According to Bowles, the firm is constrained not only by costs but also by the conflict of interests between employers and employees. These conflicts oblige the firm to a non-market clearing strategy. The presence of unemployment is therefore functional to retaining employer power, since a wage strategy that clears the market would make workers indifferent to being employed or unemployed. Contrary to the Shapiro and Stiglitz model of unemployment as the undesirable cost of keeping under control human nature, in the Bowles model, industrial unemployment contributes to the maintenance of the prevailing institutional arrangements, preserving class distinction.

A fairness-based model Akerlof's fairness-based model explains the failure of the wage mechanism to clear the labour market because of the existence of social norms, conventions and rules of conduct that, at the workplace, guide human behaviour according to principles that cannot be reduced to maximization and instrumental rationality. On the basis of empirical research, Akerlof has shown that, contrary to any rational, economic calculation, employees can work more than that actually required by the firm following an "effort norm", generated by a sentiment of trust and solidarity (Akerlof, 1982; 1984; Akerlof and Yellen, 1986). In return, they expect an appropriate, fair wage. This is why firms, for example, do not accept the offer of unemployed workers to work for the market clearing wage. This would, in fact, affect the solidaristic relationships existing in the firm. In other words, it is a social norm, in this specific case, the effort norm, that regulates workers' behaviour and that makes the minimum wage a sub-optimal strategy for the firms.

Approaches Based on Competitive Group Strategies

The approaches below explain industrial unemployment as the outcome of opposing competitive groups in the labour market. Its presence is due to a firm's decision to leave their wage levels unaltered.

The participation model According to Weitzman (1986), the labour market is governed by a sort of agreement between firms and workers whose main elements tend to change very slowly. Contrary to the neo-classical position, the predominant situation in the labour market is wage rigidity. In a buoyant economy, wage rigidity does not constitute a problem. In the opposite situation, instead, when for instance there is a contraction in aggregate demand, unemployment is largely due to the decision to fire workers: a reduction in wages is in fact deemed to achieve only a short-term equilibrium. In the long run, it will constrain spending capacity, with downward pressure on the whole economy. By contrast, it is argued that a reduction in the level of unemployment is possible by transforming the wage-based model into a system of worker participation. Then, workers come to be considered, and consider themselves, as affiliated to the firms: during periods of expansion, profits are shared among them and more workers are employed. While the expansion in demand and workforce may reduce the share of profits for the existing workforce in some firms, the production system at aggregate level will tend towards a higher level of employment.

Insider-outsider models The "insider-outsider" models explain unemployment as the outcome of the capacity of the supply of labour to influence wage levels and employment (Lindbeck and Snower, 1986). The basic assumption of these models is that employers usually face higher costs when substituting more expensive workers with cheaper workers, because new employees require a certain amount of training and time before they reach the optimal level of productivity. This is why employers do not often find it profitable to hire less expensive workers (outsiders), and offer higher wages to existing workers (insiders). This allows the insiders to maintain a level of wage that is higher than the market clearing one, despite the existence of a reserve of workers ready to work for less.

The efficiency wage models have opened important perspectives of analysis for the labour market. By highlighting different corporate strategies in the pursuit of profit through the definition of wages, all the models contrast with the traditional neo-classical approach which, instead, assumes that "firms do not really exist"[12] and that wage determination is achieved through market mechanisms. In general, however, the main shortcoming of these models is that their analysis of economic dynamics is confined to company level. This is especially true for the models based on methodological individualism which tend to provide an account of a firm's wage setting process completely dis-embedded from the wider economic and social context. In reality, neither profitability nor the wage level can be considered as the outcome of merely internal decisions. Profits are largely dependent on the specific economic conditions affecting a particular industry, while the wage level is sensitive to policy decisions concerning directly (e.g. the categories of workers called to participate to the labour market, such as young people, women, etc.) and/or indirectly (e.g. financial discounts for firms) labour market dynamics (Saint-Paul, 1995, 1996). It is for these reasons that approaches assuming the social nature of preferences as well as those pointing out the dis-homogeneity of the labour market provide a better understanding of the wider institutional arrangements and influences that affect a company's internal behaviour. However, a fuller account of the institutions influencing economic behaviour is needed in order to identify which of them are significant for the wage relation and how they influence it.

Institutionalist Interpretations

Institutionalist Economics

The study of the institutions of industrial unemployment has a long, but neglected, history. It lies at the core of the theoretical apparatus advanced by pioneering old institutionalists such as Veblen, Commons, Mitchell and Clark during the thirties.[13] Institutionalist thought is profoundly anti-methodological individualism as it sees the institutionalization of economic activity as the crucial category for economic analysis. Defined as "way[s] of thought or action of some prevalence and permanence, which [are] embedded in the habits of a group or the customs of a people" (Hamilton, 1932, quoted in Hodgson, 1998, p.179), institutions are deemed to shape the economy and make it an instituted process. They are formal (e.g. rules, laws and organizations) as well as informal or tacit (e.g. habits, routines, social norms or values). The alternative conception of human agency is based on habits and routines that are believed to affect not only individual behaviour, but especially cognitive processes as well as perceptions (Veblen, 1919). As explained by Hodgson (1998), habits are non-deliberative forms of behaviour that arise in repetitive situations and come to explain individual rational choices. It is through the imitation and emulation of behaviour that habits enter the cognitive frame of individuals. Then, acceptance and consolidation within a group or society lead to the emergence or reinforcement of institutions. As expressed by Commons:

Instead of isolated individuals in a state of nature they are always participants in transactions, members of a concern in which they come and go, citizens of an institution that lived before them and will live after them (Commons, 1934, pp.73-4).

It follows that institutions are regarded as imposing social coherence upon human activity through the continuing production and reproduction of habits of thought and action. In a context dominated by information asymmetry, market uncertainty and knowledge boundedness, individual decisions and actions need stable and mutual anticipation. Institutions provide the appropriate stability, by giving a solution to the limited rationality that characterizes individual action in the market. The institutionalist perspective also emphasizes the unpredictable and evolutionary character of social and economic relations. Institutional transformation occurs as the consequence of unanticipated consequences; the loss of efficiency of the established institutional framework leaves room for other institutions to emerge in a process of mutual adjustment. Clearly, institutional change is the outcome of individuals' action within groups which pursue objectives that are shaped by present institutions (Hodgson, 1992). This theoretical framework sharply contrasts with neo-classical thought. For the latter, individuals are rational and maximising agents. A cognitive framework, which does not contemplate uncertainty, drives their utility function: actors are portrayed as having a complete overview of all possible choices and understanding of their consequences. Institutions are seen as market imperfections, as distortions to equilibrium.

The Wage Relation and the Problem of Industrial Capitalism

The labour contract and the institutions of labour   The framework advanced by the old institutionalist scholars clearly implies a radical re-consideration of the concept of market. Rather than the realm of economic transactions occurring independently from societal institutional arrangements, the market comes to be considered as an institution in itself where exchanges are organized around, and based on, economic, legislative and ethical rules, all historically determined. With respect to the labour market, the point of departure of institutionalism lies in the recognition that labour differs from true commodities. Commons (1924), whose work has had a major impact on the development of the institutionalist perspective in labour economics, insists on seeing labour as a human action, a human power that synthesizes worker willingness to work and the institutions regulating it. Thus, whilst, like other transactions, the exchange of labour is based on worker and company freedom to engage and disengage, the qualitative difference lies in the fact that the human capacity – goodwill, the willingness to work – has no exchange value. Indeed, as indicated in this passage:

> what he sells when he sells his labour is his willingness to use his faculties according to a purpose that had been pointed out to him. He sells his promise to obey commands. He sells his goodwill. But even this promise has no exchange value (Commons, 1924, p.284).

The institutions that regulate the relationship between labour and capital become therefore central in the institutionalist analysis of labour relations and industrial performance. They are defined as determining the content and coherence of labour provision and are not independent from the other institutions of society (Rodgers 1992 quoted in Bazzoli, 1994). Wage bargaining is the most immediate expression of the institutions of labour as it synthesizes a contractual relation in which capital and labour divergences may find a balance. Indeed, the contract concerning the economic value of the exchange crystallizes nothing else than individual willingness (Hodgson, 1988). In the institutionalist conceptualization, wage bargaining does not account simply for the monetary exchange value of labour, but above all for the ensemble of the conditions of labour. Specifically, the employment relation is seen as a process of continuous negotiation which links the efficiency of labour to a non-contractual factor, that is, goodwill. The latter is the result of relations of mutual trust between employers and workers that cannot be specified when the contract is stipulated but that can be obtained only through mediation.

A typology of the institutions influencing wage bargaining can be delineated from Commons (1924; 1934) who identifies three types of institutions of labour that intersect to obtain goodwill (table 2.1). The first type, whose underlying economic principle is rarity, addresses the exchange between individual actors. The second type of institutions regulate the production between hierarchical actors following the principle of efficiency. Finally, there are institutions that regulate collective action: the underlying economic principle responds to futuribility or security of anticipations. According to Bazzoli (1994), these institutions can be distinguished at two levels: on the one hand, institutions where transactions take place (the market, the enterprise, the state); on the other, institutions that regulate the transactions (rules of exchange, use and distribution).

Table 2.1 The institutions of labour according to the taxonomy indicated by Commons

Institutions Transactions	Institutions where transactions take place	Formal and informal institutions regulating transactions
BARGAINING TRANSACTIONS	MARKET	RULES OF EXCHANGE
	Resource allocation	Institutions recording the contract
Exchange	Organization of the exchange of labour force	Institutions of the labour contract (e.g. rules to fix wages, rules to access/exit jobs)
MANAGERIAL TRANSACTIONS	ENTERPRISE	RULES OF USE
Production	Resources creation	Organizational principles and rules (hierarchy, performance evaluation)
	Organization of the labour process	Rules of co-ordination, control and mobilization of the workforce
RATIONING TRANSACTIONS	STATE	RULES OF DISTRIBUTION
Collective negotiation and Regulation	Division of costs and benefits of economic activity	Field, competence and mode of public intervention
	Bargaining organization at central and local level	Institutions regulating professional relations and conflicts, institutions produced by collective negotiations

Source: Adapted from Bazzoli, 1994. Adapted by permission

It follows that the rules of exchange and the norms that protect labour emerge from exchange transactions. This constitutes the dimension related to the labour contract. Transactions concerning the organization refer to the rules of direction that define the labour process. Finally, rules of participation and distribution define a specific way of governing industrial relations (this concerns the sphere of transactions concerning collective regulation). To each of these constituting dimensions of wage bargaining, a series of formal and informal institutions is attached which reflect the economic system and the social organization of production, historically determined. The enterprise constitutes the locus in which such dynamics take place. As indicated by Perroux (quoted in Bazzoli, 1994), the enterprise is the place where an organized process contributes to create wealth; it is the heart of the historical dynamics of capitalism and of the social relations upon which it relies. However, the enterprise is also at the centre of problems. It is the place where the conflicting and divergent dynamics of capital and labour occur and manifest themselves, primarily in the definition of production and efficiency.

Unemployment as the problem of industrial capitalism The problem of labour is therefore essentially an industrial problem and the generation of unemployment constitutes its major paradox. Unemployment is the dimension that reveals the existence of a problem within the traditional industrial organization of labour and raises questions about its economic viability – as a source of economic efficiency and its institutional viability – in its capacity to evolve and ensure social cohesion. In Commons' view, but also in Clark's work (1923), at the heart of capitalism and its evolution lies the conflict between social institutions and forms of production. Specifically, the divergence between capital and labour, manifesting primarily in the enterprise, lies in the definition of the production process and its efficiency, and in the way in which profit is pursued. Commons distinguishes two ways of obtaining profit: one is through scarcity, the other through efficiency (Commons, 1924). In the first case, profit is made by increasing market prices or reducing wages: it is obtained principally through effectiveness in bargaining. The second way of making profit lies in the efficiency of production, whereby profit is obtained through increases in productivity or the reduction of product costs, without raising prices. It is the pursuit of profit through scarcity, dominating capitalist enterprises, and the incomplete nature of the contract, regulating the pure exchange of labour, that lead to a conflicting organization of work and a lack of democratization in the economic system. As explained, the labour contract lies in an ambivalent relation which is not considered in the legislation (Bazzoli, 1994). On the one hand, there exists the legal relation in which employers and employees have the same bargaining capacity: the freedom to engage or not in the contract, although bargaining power is uneven.[14] On the other hand, the contract sanctions nothing else than an agreement with which the worker sells his capacities and their utilization by the employers in the organization of production.

It is for this reason that both Commons and Clark stress the centrality of wage negotiations which, by affecting the willingness to work, impinge upon the process of accumulation and labour conditions. Industrial goodwill is the dimension without which the other factors of production cannot work efficiently; it follows that the problem of labour, hence the problem of industrial capitalism, cannot be avoided simply by increasing productive capacities and without enhancing the willingness to work. The transformation of relations within enterprises towards the account of the social costs of labour could, in Commons' view, overcome the conflicts related to the pursuit of profit through scarcity and lack of co-operation in the workplace. This poses the question of the social value attributed to labour. It appears clear that, in contrast to conventional understanding, the institutionalist perspective treats the cost of labour not as a variable but as a fixed cost. The continuity and stability of its provision affect the efficiency of the organization and, in such a way, labour becomes a social cost. For entrepreneurs, however, it is merely a variable cost which is not accounted for at firm level but passed onto society. In the capitalist organization of production, therefore, the cost of labour catalyzes the fracture between the individual and collective dimension. With his emphasis on negotiation, Commons also suggests the institutionalization of trade unions. These are neither agents accepting the definition of the organization of production dictated by capitalist enterprises nor revolutionary forces aiming to reverse industrial and societal principles. Rather, trade unions are conceived as economic and political institutions contributing to the regulation of the disputes arising in the economic realm: therefore, they are seen in pragmatic terms (Bazzoli, 1994). In Commons' view, trade unionism is the institutional and counterbalancing force within the capitalist organization of economy and society that contributes primarily to the achievement of better work conditions through the process of negotiation. Industrial relations are therefore characterized by a continuum of conflicting and common interests in the definition of the "rules of the game". Specifically, collective bargaining is a process of negotiation whose regulatory outcome represents the compromise that, in a determined historical moment, becomes the macro-rule governing industry. Such a process is clearly influenced by the multiple interests existing in the economic and social realms. Yet, in contrast with the Marxist perspective, institutionalism denies the existence of two classes struggling for the control of the means of production. Instead, society is articulated into a variety of different groups, all bearing equal values and rules, which could become a legitimate institutional framework. Rather than by exploitation, their relationships are dominated by power relations which are the main determinants of institutional change.

The originality of the institutionalist tradition with respect to the positions reviewed previously lies in the fact that it approaches industrial unemployment as the outcome of processes of institutionalization and regulation. Industrial unemployment is conceived as the result of institutional shortcomings whose primary explanation lies in the complex dynamics concerning the wage relation. For instance, institutions governing the production process affect corporate performance as they regulate, among other things, the understanding of production habits. Conflicts on the way in which resources are managed and work organized may lead to mistrust and disputes which impinge on the efficiency of labour. However, whilst interpreting industrial unemployment as an institutionally constructed phenomenon, the institutionalist tradition fails to acknowledge that processes of wage determination and, ultimately, the regulation of the employment relation assumes a significant geographical component. That is, industrial unemployment is institutionally constructed and is such in geographically distinctive ways. Indeed, institutional inter-dependences are geographically situated; institutional interaction is the expression of interests, constraints and opportunities of individuals and social groups that are embedded in contexts and respond to sedimented practices.

The Current Debate: Regulation Theory and the Theory of Conventions

The problem of labour is at the centre of the analysis of two other streams of thought whose theoretical apparatuses show clear points of convergence with the old institutionalist tradition. Both regulation theory and the theory of conventions concentrate on it through the investigation of the wage relation and labour institutions and their transformation over time.

Regulation theory Rooted into Aglietta's work of the end of the 1970s (1978; 1979) and fully developed by Boyer (1988; 1993), the project of regulation theory includes investigating the problem of labour: it focuses on institutions, conceived as systemic regularities that channel economic activity and its reproduction, and, in particular, on the institutions of labour. Regulation theory holds the existence of a strict relation between the *rapport salarial*, or wage relation, and the overall pattern of regulation of a socio-economic system. Specifically, the wage relation is deemed to subsume a regime of growth through the regulation of contradictions and conflicts emerging between the limits of the economic system and the strategies of social groups (Bazzoli, 1994; Peck, 1996; Boyer, 1993). The wage relation represents that concrete institution in which the relation between capital and labour is stabilized and the necessary coherence between the accumulation system and the mode of social regulation is concretely ensured.[15] It follows, therefore, that institutions have a meaning only in relation to accumulation; they are subject to crises and, therefore, assume historical and evolutionary forms. As the concept of regulation takes form at the macro-economic level, the employment relationship becomes the key macro-historic form to investigate and understand capitalist dynamics. Indeed as indicated by Boyer:

> [the regulation approach] is sufficiently broad for us to be able to anticipate a priori close linkages between the form of wage/labour relations and the method of regulation ... [to a considerable extent] economic crisis and change and change in the wage/labour relations determine one another (Boyer, 1988, p.10).

The crisis of Fordism, according to Boyer, is the crisis of the employment relationship that dominated capital–labour relations after the war. It was during the 1970s that the archetypal pattern of regulation, associating the Fordist model of employment relations[16] to the Keynesian management of economy, entered a deep crisis. The end of the phase of intense accumulation, that had benefited companies from the post-war period until the beginning of the 1970s, based on mass production, and that had been sustained by national expansionary policies, signalled both the transformation of the canons for economic competitiveness and the mode of social regulation. As competitiveness started to be ensured by an increasing variety of products on shorter time scales, in smaller quantities and at lower prices (e.g. Sabel and Piore, 1984), a debate emerged about the need for different institutions of labour which would second such production needs (see Gorz, 1999); from the mid-1980s onwards, labour economics and sociology of work have been characterized by the debate claiming the flexibilization of wages and employment relations (Jessop et al., 1991; Peck, 1996). What is at the core of this transformation is clearly indicated:

the debate about flexibility and its methods is assuming the traits of a proper challenge which does not refer to the simple adjustment in the economy but it will carry to a total redefinition of wage-labour relations and other forms of organization (Boyer, 1988, p.252).

The problem of industrial unemployment derives, therefore, from a paradigmatic crisis that has emerged from the mismatch between regime of accumulation and mode of social regulation. Specifically, it is the modification of the institutions regulating the employment relationship and, therefore the primary relations between capital and labour, to promote the modification of the overall social rules connected to them. The contribution of regulation theory lies in the consideration that institutions and the regulation of the asymmetric relationships between capital and labour are at the core of the analysis of capitalist economy and its transformation. By focusing upon the macro-dimension of the analysis, neglected by the old institutionalist tradition, regulation theory holds the centrality of the role of the wage relation in the economy as, in the long-run, it conditions its dynamics. Nonetheless, its conceptualization of the employment relationship has some shortcomings. First, the macro significance of the wage relation allows little account of the processes of collective negotiation underlying it, the compromises emerging from it in a specific historical period. Indeed, regulation theory is neither a theory of collective action nor a theory of negotiation. The categories of analysis are such that they end up hiding both the plurality of economic actors and the logic driving their actions which, in fact, disappear behind macro-economic processes. As argued by Bazzoli (1994), regulation theory lacks a substantial theory of institutions; it proposes them in relation to what they do rather than analysing them for what they are. Thus, questions arise about the capacity of this theory to endogenize institutional change and historicize economy. Second, regulation theory reduces institutions to differences between national social formations (Michon, 1992, Peck and Tickell, 1995). In addition, intra-national variability is seen as a contingent variability around dominant historical-national models. What is pointed out by critics is that what matters is not simply that institutions have effects, but to evaluate their effects. Peck (1996), for example, argues for the importance of accounting for the sub-national level of regulation to understand what national systems are constituted of.

The theory of conventions The theory of conventions has achieved a major role in the economic analysis of institutions and labour starting from the work of Boltanski and Thevenot (1987).[17] Its aim is twofold: on the one hand, to provide a theory accounting for human action in the economy as the neo-classical attempt to explain it through universal intentions and rationality is rejected, and, on the other, to build a general model taking into account the different forms of co-ordination existing in the economy and provided by conventions. The analysis is centred on the understanding of actor action in an economic context that is assumed to be characterized by uncertainty with respect to the performances and expectations of other actors. As Storper and Salais put it:

> the different pragmatic tasks of any economy require co-ordination between the individuals who engage in them and this co-ordination can only come about when their interpretations lead to a sort of "agreement" about what is to be done in the sense that what each person does meets the expectations of the others on whom he or she depends (Storper and Salais, 1997, p.16).

Within this view, co-ordination is achieved when actors define a set of common references, indicated as conventions, that go beyond the actors as individuals, but which they nonetheless build and understand in the course of their actions. Conventions emerge as definitions of, and responses to, uncertainty; they are attempts "to order the economic process in a way that allows production and exchange to take place according to expectations which define efficiency" (Storper and Salais, 1997, p.16). Conventions are accepted because of the routinised nature of relationships that then favours their collective legitimization. Specifically, convention theory maintains that work is characterized by uncertainty; this is because of the nature of labour and of the employment relationship. This composes two divergent interests (capital and labour) in three different moments (hiring, use and dismissal of labour). The objective is therefore to understand the social forms that reduce the uncertainty connected to the wage relation and that allow its efficient regulation. The wage relation comes consequently to be re-interpreted in terms of conventions of labour. Salais (1989; 1991; 1992) distinguishes two major labour conventions: one concerning productivity levels, the other the quantity of labour employed or unemployed. The convention of productivity, involving work routines, customs, shared skills, etc., concerns workers' acceptance of making concrete efforts in return for a wage. However, when expectations are not met and the product remains unsold, a second labour convention emerges, the one of unemployment. Such a convention implies an ex-post adjustment of the number of workers but also the modification of working time or expectations, without compromising the convention of productivity of those workers who maintain their jobs. Within this conceptualization, therefore, the wage relation and unemployment become the instruments regulating the activity and the quality of labour.

Like the old institutionalist tradition, convention theory emphasizes the cognitive processes connected to social interaction. This focus allows, on the one hand, the understanding of the limits of actor behaviour and, on the other, the process of rationalization operated by institutions. In this sense, conventions represent the mechanisms that allow a micro-coordination of economic behaviour and gives coherence to the employment relation. The major deficit of this theory lies instead in its account of the evolution of economic systems. Thus, while acknowledging the inherently temporal nature of conventions,

> [convention theory] remains a vision where the change of convention occurs because of the incapacity of the previous one to interpret the "noises" coming from the outside (Bazzoli, 1994, p.357).

It follows that the stimulus to change assumes an exogenous nature and conventions are deemed not to have any internal contradiction. Yet, with concern to the scale of analysis, convention theory is "comfortable with plant-, industry-, and (sometimes) regional-level of analysis" (Peck, 1996, p.102), while remaining sceptical about generalizations referring to national models. In a parallel fashion to the regulation theory, but due to an opposite theoretical apparatus, convention theory seems to fail to acknowledge the salience of the changing relations within and between scales.

The originality of the stances presented above lies in the interpretation of industrial unemployment as an institutionally constructed process. In contrast to the neo-classical view, for which the wage relation exclusively regulates the monetary exchange of labour, all three positions reviewed above hold the centrality of the employment relation in determining labour market dynamics and, specifically, the employment/unemployment balance. The problem of labour is therefore interpreted as the outcome of regulatory shortcomings unable to compose and mediate the divergent, asymmetric tensions afflicting capital and labour within capitalism. At company level, an efficient organization and co-ordination of the labour process needs the deployment of willingness, knowledge and productive habits. As labour is action, and, therefore, judgement, discretionary choices and control, and production is an institutional process of creation of knowledge and goods, the central issue is to mobilize resources and worker co-operation. The rules governing the production process and employment relations impinge upon the efficiency of labour as they produce knowledge, regulate the understanding of collective norms and the management of the factors of production. It follows that, for instance, the lack of co-operation between employers and workers, of sedimented practices affecting the transmission of technical knowledge, of representation of worker rights, are all factors influencing the non-contractual conditions of the employment relation that are, however, important for corporate performance and employment/unemployment dynamics. The compromise of company performance and its impact on employment levels can also derive from the way in which the employment relation is conceived at collective level. The processes of negotiation, expression of social processes creating rules, are central both to employers, as they condition the process of accumulation, and to workers, as they allow the amelioration of their conditions. Lack of regulation or uneven power relations in the bargaining process amplify conflicts between capital and labour and their impact on company performance. Also the institutions that come before, such as the educational system, and that follow the employment relation, such as arrangements for retired workers, are important in defining the relations between capital and labour. At collective level too, relations of confidence are a social construction that depends on the institutional framework constituting a mediation of divergent values and interests among social groups.

The focus on institutions paves the way for an interpretation of industrial unemployment characterized by complexity (accounting for the action) and evolution (accounting for transformations). These dimensions are precisely the ones that the conventional economic analysis cannot explain: the structuration of society, the role of groups, as well as the underlying power relations for the imposition of divergent interests, cannot find an account within such theories that, by being interested exclusively in the dynamics of market forces, consider them as given. The three institutionalist positions reviewed also share a common limitation. Whilst the analysis of the wage relation within the old institutionalist theoretical apparatus neglects the spatial specificity of institutional interaction, regulation theory and theory convention tend to situate themselves virtually at the opposite end of the spectrum with respect to the issue. On the one hand, the conceptualization advanced by regulation theory leads to the effacement of intra-national variability as institutional arrangements, crystallising the social pact between economic actors, provide the necessary stability to the national system of accumulation; variability underlying institutional interaction at diverse local levels is deemed to be a mere reflection of the national model. On the other hand, by maintaining a more contextual orientation, the theory of conventions is less able to produce a more comprehensive theoretical framework.

The Insights of Economic Sociology

The dissatisfaction towards the dominant economistic explanation of processes of redundancies and restructuring and the recognition of the role of institutions in explaining them lead the institutionalist perspective towards the debate on institutions and the employment relation that, from a sociological perspective, has been developed by the new economic sociology. It is appropriate in this context to remember that, although undertaking different research paths, both the approach centred on social networks and sociological neo-institutionalism move a strong critique of the methodological individualism underlying the neo-classical conceptualisation as well as of the approach developed by the new institutionalists.

Despite their dissatisfaction towards the abstractions of the prevalent micro-economic analysis, the latter failed to elaborate a theory which did not assume actors' rational behaviour. New institutionalist economics, represented primarily by Williamson, Coase, North, Aoki, Alchian, Demsetz, Schotter, accepts the existence of an initial state of nature without institutional arrangements. However, uncertainty and lack of information imply transaction costs which can be reduced if contractual arrangements are set up. The move from individuals, taken as given, to a variety of institutions is, therefore, dictated by the enhancement of economic efficiency; the state, the market, the firms are economic institutions (or webs of contracts) among actors aiming to maximise their interests; they also end up influencing individual preferences and shaping their interaction. Institutions are therefore seen as ex-post co-ordinating mechanisms (COREI, 1995).

Both the social networks approach (or structural approach) and sociological neo-institutionalism theorize human action as a socially-oriented action which, therefore, cannot be explained solely on the base of individual motivations. The structural approach assumes that human action is intrinsically influenced by the collocation of actors in the webs of relations in which they are involved.

In alternative to both an "undersocialised" conception of human action (prevalent in classical and neo-classical economics) and an "oversocialised" one (which has been prominent for decades in the sociological realm), Granovetter, the most influential scholar of this stream of thought, suggests the notion of embeddedness (1985). Accordingly, personal relations and networks have a key role in generating trust and discouraging malfeasance among social actors. Ongoing social relations constrain institutions and actors' behaviour: therefore, to construct them as independent is "a grievous misunderstanding" (Granovetter, 1985, p.482). It is the embeddedness of actors in these relations and networks that allows the dissemination of information and the control of behaviour. Rather than having a functionalist explanation – they emerge spontaneously as efficient solutions to face co-ordination problems – institutions are socially constructed, in the sense that they reflect the conditioning of the networks and webs of relations on individuals' choices; efficient solutions may not emerge automatically. In a pioneer work, Granovetter (1973) revealed not only the influence of social networks and informal relations on finding a job, but also that individuals embedded in weak social networks have greater access to a greater number of opportunities and information.

In contrast to the structuralist view, for which social networks and links condition the rational pursuing of actors' interests, sociological neo-institutionalists emphasize the role of cultural variables in defining primarily actors' interests and then the ways in which they are pursued. Therefore, besides structural embeddedness, they propose considering cognitive, cultural and political embeddedness. In situations of uncertainty and lack of information, individual and collective actors can rely neither on rational behaviour leading to optimal choices, nor completely on the networks of relations in which they are embedded. Indeed, their behaviour is also driven by the solutions that are considered more appropriate and legitimate in the environment in which they interact; this explains the persistence and inertia of institutions even when they lose their efficiency.

The work of Powell and DiMaggio on isomorphism (1991) seeks to explain precisely the homogeneity of models of behaviour in a given organizational field. Starting from the critique of the theory of organizations suggested by Hannan and Freeman which, following a darwinian conception, assumes that the homogeneity of a production system implies the selection of the most efficient production units, Powell and DiMaggio show that the homogeneity of a model is more likely to be determined by institutional isomorphism (e.g. labour regulations, industrial relations), legal isomorphism (e.g. universities and specialised schools) and even mimetic isomorphism. These isomorphisms tend to establish binding behaviour among individual and collective actors which also emerge as the outcome of the influence of strong organizations on others depending on them (e.g. the relationships between core and subcontracting firms).

These streams of literature help to acknowledge that the outcomes of economic action can vary substantially according to the social structure, the institutional history, collective action, etc. However, these positions run the risk of emphasizing historically-specific analytical systems and of diminishing the specific contribution of economic factors.

Conclusions

The chapter has built towards an institutionalist framework for understanding industrial unemployment (see table 2.2 for a summary of the diverse theoretical positions). The approach proposed distances itself particularly from the orthodox model and its interpretation of industrial unemployment centred upon the negative role of wages on company profitability and efficiency. It considers the contribution of the macro-approaches reviewed above, with their insights on the macro-economic dynamics affecting the employment relation, and of preference models assuming the social nature of preferences that, from a micro-economic perspective, shed light on company active wage strategies. In addition, following the institutionalist tradition, the alternative framework suggested approaches industrial unemployment by looking at the processes of institutional regulation that affect economic action. It has conceptualized industrial unemployment and restructuring as institutionally constructed processes. It emphasized the role of intermediate formal and informal institutions that, through individual and collective action, affect the process of wage determination within companies. Analytically, this implies taking into consideration the divergent economic and social interests embodied by different actors (companies, workers, trade unions and also other socio-economic organizations) as well as the values underlying strategies and the wage relation. But, in this identification of specific institutions, some complementarity between macro-economic perspectives and the preference models is desirable, in order to shed light on the complexity and interdependency between structure and agency in the determination of employment change. There is the need to consider the influence of both demand-side and supply-side factors in the labour market. Fluctuations in the aggregate demand represent important elements in determining an expansion or contraction of the overall level of market demand for labour. Its salience lies in the fact that it is the area where job structures are shaped and the level and nature of demand is determined (Doeringer and Piore, 1971; Labour Studies Group, 1985; Reich et al., 1973). Labour demand is therefore important in affecting company position in the market and also in determining the type of labour requirements. Both dimensions are crucial in the definition of the levels of wages as well as in the delineation of the power relations marking capital and labour dynamics which, in turn, are determinant for the wage setting process.

Table 2.2 Theoretical positions and causal bases of industrial unemployment

Theoretical positions	Causal bases of industrial unemployment
Wage-rigidity argument	Wage rigidity, institutional regulation of the employment relation, trade union power, welfare system
Keynesian interpretation	Employer investment decisions, level of aggregate demand
Marxism	Conflicting relations between capital and labour, under-utilisation of capacity determined by surplus not absorbed by consumption
Neo-Marxists	Social relations of production, organisation of production over space
Schumpeterian theory	Business cycles determined by technological transformation
Preference models: Based on methodological individualism	Shirking model: Wages higher than the market clearing level because of information asymmetries between employers and workers at the workplace Fairness model: Rejection of undercutting by unemployed workers

(cont.)

(table 2.2 cont.)

Theoretical positions	Causal bases of industrial unemployment
Based on the social nature of preferences	Shirking model: Wages higher than the market clearing level because of the conflict between employers and workers at the workplace
	Fairness model: Wages higher than the market clearing level because of solidaristic relationships between employers and workers at the workplace
Based on competitive group strategies	Participation model: Wage-based model hinged upon divergent interests between employers and workers
	Insiders/outsiders model: The costs for the substitution of insiders are higher than the savings obtained hiring outsiders
Old institutionalism	Divergence between capital and labour in the definition of the production process and efficiency, failure of the traditional wage relation to consider the institutions that allow to obtain goodwill
Regulation theory	Mismatch between regime of accumulation and mode of social regulation
Theory of conventions	Ex-post adjustment when expectations concerning production are not met, means to regulate the activity and the quality of labour

However, the factors indicated above are not directly relevant to decisions on redundancies and restructuring and to the type of process of adjustment to be undertaken. For instance, an expansionary phase in a particular company/industry does not exclude restructuring nor does it imply an expansion of employment. What is important to note is that these factors themselves are intertwined with specific supply-side conditions in the labour market. Company technical and work dynamics reflect (and affect) the strategies pursued by families, by trade unions and other socio-economic organizations, by the state and so on (Offe and Hinrichs, 1985; Picchio, 1992; Rubery, 1978; Saint-Paul, 1996). These strategies shape labour market participation through the division of labour in the household, through processes of occupational socialization, through the preference given to certain occupations, etc. State policies also influence industrial relations and labour contract systems as well as the system of welfare protection. By highlighting the processes underlying individual and collective action, the perspective advanced here argues that redundancies are historically contingent and geographically situated. They are not the outcome of market forces responding to the principles of rational choice/profit maximization, efficiency and perfect competition in a system tending towards a state of equilibrium. They are the historical and spatial expression of capitalism the adequate analysis of which cannot avoid its historicisation and the recognition of its spatial heterogeneity. Also the institutions and the social and economic actors affecting redundancies hold contingency and spatial specificity. As the "geography of enterprises", conceived as non-identical capitals, is recognized (Dicken and Thrift, 1992), there is also the need to recognize the ways in which institutional forms, expressed at the company level, are both geographically distinctive and embedded into wider (national and international) institutional contexts, as are their outcomes. Concretely, the process of wage determination and the interpretation of labour and its associated costs assume spatially specific connotations. Wage determination is the outcome of unique interactive processes involving primarily companies, trade unions and workers and reflecting their strategies; these are continuously reshaped by external factors, by mutual interaction, by cultural conditions that are contextually embedded and respond, therefore, to sedimented practices. The interpretation of labour responds to socially and culturally constructed configurations that, at different levels, affect actor knowledge and decisions. Yet, what is relevant is not simply to identify which levels and geographies become relevant in explaining processes of restructuring and redundancies, but especially to understand the changing relations and influences between and within scales.

Notes

[1] Refer, among others, to Gamble, 1988.
[2] Refer to note 2 Introduction.

[3] Conversely, when demand rises, it is wages that benefit from productivity gains and this prevents a quantitative expansion in labour demand.

[4] As explained by Sestito, 1997, much of the OECD economic recommendations are based on economic analyses that refer to the demand and supply curves of neo-classical tradition.

[5] This curve, used to explain inflation, relates the variations of wages and unemployment.

[6] In the wake of Braverman's study (1974), labour process studies have acknowledged the importance of workers' struggles in labour process dynamics. They also emphasize the need to account for the diverse regimes of labour control and the subjects of it (refer to Peck, 1996).

[7] As Freeman et al. (1982) put it, economic analyses acknowledge the great importance of technology. However, its complexity and diversity often lead them to treat it as given.

[8] A social norm is internalized when it becomes a rule of behaviour among workers who act in relation to an expected action. Individual strategies and self-interest guide human behaviour, but social norms create the harmony between individual and social rationality.

[9] This is the level of wage at which a worker is not willing to accept a job.

[10] This methodological approach should be distinguished from the more radical expression of methodological holism, according to which individual behaviour is completely conditioned by social institutions (Costabile, 1995).

[11] This model constitutes an attempt to complement, from a micro-economic perspective, the macro analysis put forward by Marxian political economy.

[12] Coase quoted in Costabile, 1995, p.612.

[13] As Barbash (1994, p.59), quoting Dorfman, put it: "Veblen furnished the theoretical stimulus for the development of the thirties, ... Mitchell supplied the statistics [but] it was Commons and his group in Wisconsin who ... invented institutions".

[14] This is because their economic freedom does not have the same nature; by alienating their "property" through the sale of their labour, workers are dependent on their employment.

[15] The regime of accumulation is comprised of two elements: an accumulation system (a production-consumption relationship) and a mode of social regulation. An accumulation system is defined as a way of dividing and systematically re-allocating the social product. The mode of social regulation is an ensemble of regulatory mechanisms (habits, norms, customs) that allow a regime of accumulation to be realized (Peck and Tickell, 1992).

[16] This model attempted to unify the collective interests of capital and labour around a programme of full (male) employment and universal welfare. The wage relation, left to collective bargaining, acted as a source of domestic consumer demand (Peck, 1996).

[17] As clarified by Bazzoli (1994), different currents of research refer to this theory. Its main scholars are Thevenot, Salais, Orlean, Favereau.

Chapter 3

Corporate Restructuring and Redundancies on Teesside

Introduction

The last decade has been a period of major industrial change for the chemical and clothing sectors on Teesside: processes of restructuring have involved a great number of local companies and redundancies have accompanied them. Both industries have become more labour-cost sensitive; nonetheless, an explanation of redundancies centred on the cost of labour fails to capture important other dimensions. Redundancies in the chemical sector have been mainly due to the process of business re-organization and re-configuration of the employment relationship undertaken by Imperial Chemical Industries (ICI), following the end of the period of demand-led growth that had led the company to achieve market dominance and, with it, of a particular way of making profits. Job losses in the clothing industry have very different causes. To fulfil retailer pressure on prices, local producers have chosen to move their production (or part of it) to low labour costs countries; this has led to downsizing and job loss.

PART 1 FROM INDUSTRIAL OUTPOST TO UNEMPLOYMENT BLACKSPOT:[1] ECONOMIC AND LABOUR MARKET CHANGES ON TEESSIDE

Economy, Labour Market and Local Industrial Culture in the Period of Growth – From the Beginning of the Century to the 1950s

Recent economic literature points out that on Teesside[2] (figure 3.1) the highest proportion of employees work in service industries and that the economy of the area is becoming increasingly diversified (Tees Valley Joint Strategy Unit (TVJSU), 1999 also for sub-regional data). As is well-known, until two decades ago, the economy of Teesside was dominated by heavy industries. Two major expansionary phases contributed to the process of industrialization of this rural area.

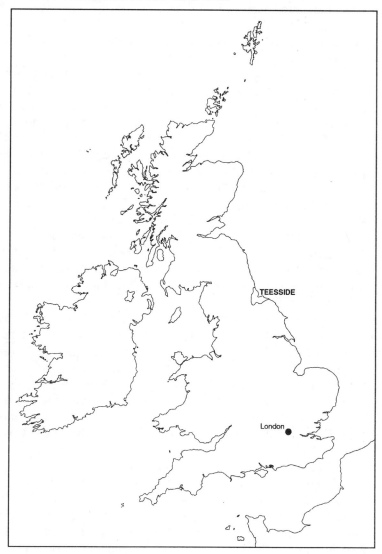

Figure 3.1: Teesside in the UK

The existence of coal and iron ore led to the growth and development of the first industries during the 19th century around iron and steel as well as shipbuilding. It is only in a second phase, at the beginning of the last century, that the area witnessed the growth of the chemical industry (Beynon et al., 1994); Teesside became a place of national and international significance for its role in British capitalist expansion, a centre of engineering, steel and chemicals.

As the process of industrialization occurred in an area where industrial activity was previously absent, the major companies located there came to define its social and labour market characteristics and to mould the cultural aspects that marked the specificity of Teesside's industrial history. First, the increasing centrality of the industry in the area led concerns and interests of private capital to sweep away the ones carried by land owners and to become dominant within the area's governing structures. Local government adapted to the demands of capital, contributing to the policy of consensus that characterized Teesside's political life. Second, industry specialization in base sectors sharply defined the gender division of labour and the occupational structure of the local labour market. Men were completely absorbed by the industries in manual and semi-skilled jobs. The influx of migrant workers from elsewhere in the North and Ireland satisfied industry's further needs, while women were confined to non waged work in the home (Beynon et al., 1986). It is only during the post-war period that political and socio-economic forces, committed to avoid the transformation of the local labour market, favoured the settlement of the first female-employing activities in the area as they were considered complementary and non-competitive with the existing heavy industries. The model of industrialization also shaped the future of class relations. Indeed, "an embryonic" working class began to establish itself only over the subsequent years when private capital interests had already been consolidated and resulted prevalent with respect to those of labour (Hudson, 1994, p.196). The existence of a few big firms gave rise to a culture of dependency: companies provided wages, housing and other consumption artefacts. Big companies deliberately pursued a strategy of compliance and co-operation with the workers and presented it as the only possible form of industrial relations (ibid.). This social construction revealed all its importance for the management of workplace dynamics, for the reproduction of labour provision as well as for the management of redundancies when economic downturns compelled restructuring processes. The conditions of compliance set by local companies for the reproduction of labour satisfied a twofold objective: they were functional to the realization of surplus and they became the central mechanism to dominate local society. Paternalistic relationships inside and outside the workplace constituted the means through which working-class needs were channelled as well as the reproduction of labour power. The competition between capital and labour assumed the traits of a tacit pact aiming to reduce the level and restrain the fields of confrontation and to achieve the harmonization of mutual interests. The company need for a stable workforce led to good work conditions and a wider commitment to the community. Similarly, trade unions ensured worker co-operation and collaboration within the workplace and accepted "the legitimacy of the market as an economic steering mechanism" (Hudson, 1989, p.9). On Teesside, therefore, a class consciousness against capitalist interests did not emerge as it did in other similar industrial areas such as Wales.

Labour Market Trends on Teesside from 1960s to 1980s

Only after the end of the war economy did it become clear that for heavy manufacturing a secular decline was underway and that for Teesside such specialization would penalize it (Hudson, 1994). By the mid-1960s, a political consensus emerged that the industrial apparatus needed modernising. Investment on Teesside concentrated heavily in the chemical sector, with considerable fixed capital investment,[3] and in the steel industry which was nationalized. The chosen policy programme favoured neither employment creation in local industries nor the diversification of the local industrial fabric whose job creation was not sufficient to compensate the decline of Teesside's traditional industrial activities.

The local labour market started to suffer employment decline and a rise in unemployment. These trends reflected a local economy facing both the effects of major de-industrialization and of a delayed industrial policy of restructuring (Martin and Rowthorn, 1986; Martin, 1989; Massey and Allen, 1988; Pollard, 1992).[4] There was a sharp decline in manufacturing employment (over the period 1965-1978, for instance, employment in the chemicals, metals and engineering dropped by 22 per cent), which was not balanced by the increase in employment – mainly confined to women – in the service sector. Unemployment (figure 3.2) started to increase in the first half of the 1970s. In 1977 it was double that in 1974 (8.2 per cent and 4.1 per cent respectively) and, in the period 1979-81, it doubled again from 9.3 to 18 per cent. In absolute terms, this meant that the number of unemployed people climbed from less than 21,000 to more than 40,000.

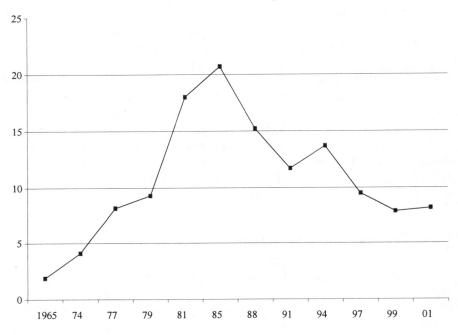

Source: Nomis

Figure 3.2: Unemployment rate on Teesside: the historical trend

As indicated by Foord et al. (1985, p.36), "few industries (indeed a few employers) have accounted for the bulk of Teesside's redundancies". Long-term unemployment became one of the principal characteristics of the local labour market (table 3.1). By 1986 the long-term unemployed represented over half of all unemployed people on Teesside with peaks of 55 per cent in Stockton. As a consequence, Teesside experienced the creation of surplus of manpower both male and female, part of which ended up swelling the ranks of those who preferred to leave the region for areas of growing labour demand.

Table 3.1 Long-term unemployment on Teesside during the second half of the 1980s

	Male	Female	Total
July 1985	54.9	37.4	50.3
July 1986	56.7	38.8	51.9
July 1987	53.8	37.9	49.8
July 1988	49.1	33.9	45.2
July 1989	45.5	32.9	42.3

Source: Nomis

At the same time, however, the area started to become attractive for a new round of investment.[5] With the end of regional financial incentives[6] and an increasing commitment towards attracting foreign investment, urged by the Conservative Government, local authorities were encouraged to promote economic programmes favouring inward investment as the major source of economic and employment opportunities. Trade unions too, after the failure to safeguard the major manufacturing plants, spread the culture of worker adaptability and flexibility to enhance the area's locational attractiveness. The north-east became the region for capital intensive plants[7] and for branch plants of global corporations. However, expectations linked to the new economic activities were frustrated as they were not able to absorb the quantity of people previously laid-off. Corporate relations and employment practices progressively responded to the principles of work flexibilization; with new management philosophies, workplaces witnessed a shift from standard to non-standard contracts (part-time, temporary contracts, subcontracting, etc.) and an increase in functional flexibility through skill polyvalence and job rotation.[8] As a consequence, the external labour market started to be characterized by soaring causalization and insecurity, leading to a growing percentage of people involved in black and informal economy (Hudson, 1988).[9]

Current Labour Market Trends

The process of industrial restructuring has continued on Teesside during the 1990s and the local labour market has consolidated the traits of the previous decade. First, plant rationalizations continued to maintain a high level of unemployment. Figure 3.3 shows the unemployment trend which, until 1996, was well above 10 per cent of the workforce, with a peak of 14 per cent in 1993. It is only in the second half of the 1990s, due to the combination of a general economic recovery and implementation of the New Deal schemes,[10] that the rate tends to decrease reaching 7.9 per cent by the end of the decade.[11] The male unemployment rate peaked in 1993 (19.5 per cent) while, although decreasing, it remained above 11 per cent at the end of 1999. The number of people seeking a job on Teesside is the highest in Great Britain (figure 3.4).

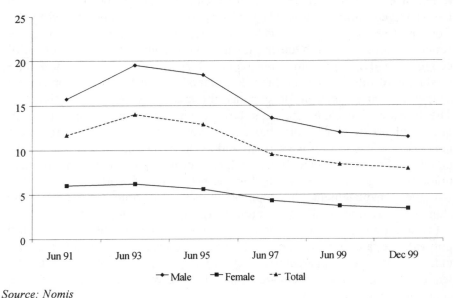

Source: Nomis

Figure 3.3: Unemployment rates on Teesside during the 1990s

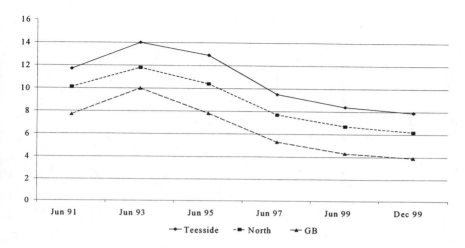

Source: Nomis

Figure 3.4: Unemployment rates during the 1990s: a geographical comparison

The rate of people who had been out of work for 12 months or more was 25 per cent at the end of the 1990s, but it was above 35 per cent at the beginning and peaked in 1996 at 41.3 per cent (figure 3.5). Again, long-term unemployment affects mainly men, although in the last few years the trend has declined substantially. Second, overall employment is declining in the area. On the basis of data provided by TVJSU, during the period 1991-1996, it fell by 5.4 per cent due to the further decline in the manufacturing sector and construction. The major negative change was recorded for Middlesbrough (-10.3 per cent), the decline was more contained in Stockton (-4.9 per cent) while Redcar and Cleveland maintained its employment levels practically unaltered (0.2 per cent) (table 3.2). Employment fell in the manufacturing sector and in construction especially in Stockton and in Redcar and Cleveland, while it increased slightly in Middlesbrough.[12] Almost 70 per cent of employment on Teesside is in the service sector while manufacturing absorbs 23.5 per cent (table 3.3). Service industries dominate employment opportunities for both men and women but through non-standard contracts (TVJSU, 1995).

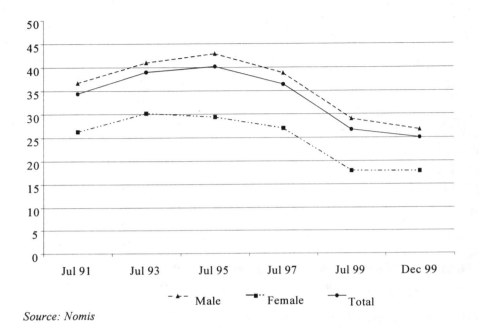

Source: Nomis

Figure 3.5: Long-term unemployment on Teesside during the 1990s

Table 3.2 Employment change by sector and borough, 1991-1996

	Middles-brough	Redcar & Cleveland	Stockton on Tees	Teesside
Agriculture, fishing, energy, water	170	-25	390	535
Manufacturing	570	-1,840	-6,090	-7,360
Construction	-30	-50	-1,560	-1,640
Services	-6,490	1,990	3,760	-740
Total	**-5,780**	**75**	**-3,500**	**-9,205**
	(-10.3%)	(0.2%)	(-4.9%)	(-5.4%)

Source: TVJSU

Table 3.3 Employees in employment by sector and borough, 1996 (%)

	Middles-brough	Redcar & Cleveland	Stockton on Tees	Teesside
Agriculture, fishing, energy, water	1.3	2.6	1.8	1.9
Manufacturing	10.5	33.6	26.5	23.5
Construction	5.6	5.5	6.0	5.7
Services	82.6	58.3	65.7	68.9
Total	**100.0**	**100.0**	**100.0**	**100.0**

Source: TVJSU

Table 3.4 shows that male full-time employment has decreased substantially in all the boroughs on Teesside in favour of part-time occupations. Female full-time employment by contrast has increased, possibly due to employment opportunities in the public sector, in light manufacturing activities, and women association with lower costs of labour.

Table 3.4 Employment change by borough and type of occupation, 1991-1996 (%)

	Male full-time	Male part-time	Female full-time	Female part-time
Middlesbrough	-9.5	21.4	-15.2	-11
Redcar & Cleveland	-5.4	10.7	17.4	-0.7
Stockton	-16	54.9	11.9	0.6

Source: TVJSU

During recent years, the work culture of the area has lost its original specificity to become increasingly attuned to the transformation of employment relations at national level. Functional and numerical[13] flexibility have become the main principles governing employment relationships on Teesside where, due to the limited job opportunities, workers are expected to adapt to market demands. According to the projections by the TVJSU (1999), the trends in employment highlighted above will characterize the local labour market until 2006. Accordingly, a net increase in jobs is likely to be recorded in the service sector (approximately 18,000), with a slight rise in employment in construction, while employment in manufacturing is expected to fall (-3,500 jobs). Part-time employment will characterize the new job creation (80 per cent of new jobs will be on the basis of part-time or fixed contracts), while the number of people with two or more jobs is also likely to increase (+2,000). Yet, the changing structure of the local economy and the persistence of wide pools of unemployed people seem also to have delineated other categories of workers. Indeed, during the 1990s besides people with two or more jobs and those in casual employment, the local labour market progressively witnessed an increase in people working on fixed-term contracts (jobs are created for the duration of a specific project) and in the black economy, although no official statistics are available for the area (ibid.).

In summary, the end of full male employment on Teesside has resulted from the interaction of market and non-market forces and a major role has to be attributed to Teesside's specific industrial culture. This was based on a culture of consensus between capital and labour, whereby worker wage benefits were inextricably linked to company profitability gains, and on company commitment to the community through the production of profits in and through Teesside. Yet, the area's governing structures were attuned to the demand of capital. However, such a social pact could hardly be honoured when the convergence of economic events and policy interventions unfavourably affected local industrial performance. From the end of the 1970s, the local labour market saw a growing number of workers expelled from production processes and, for those still at work, a re-configuration of employment practices. At the same time, the shift from standard forms of employment to non-standard contracts has affected the local culture of work that is now based, as at wider level, upon the principle of flexibility.

PART 2 EXPLAINING INDUSTRIAL UNEMPLOYMENT IN THE CHEMICAL SECTOR

The Historical Development of the Chemical Industry on Teesside

The Development Years: From the Second Post-War Period to the Early 1970s

The location of the chemicals industry on Teesside dates back to the nineteenth century[14] but until the First World War the sector played a relatively small role in the area compared to the iron and steel industries, engineering and shipbuilding. The need to replace supplies from South America (specifically nitrogen) during the war boosted the development of a synthetic nitrate plant[15] at Billingham where, soon afterwards, a large deposit of anhydrite was discovered.[16] In the meantime, the area's locational advantages (deep sea port water, close access to the North Sea, cheap raw materials, etc.) started to be fully exploited by the first industrial settlements (North, 1975; Phillips, 1999). By the end of the Second World War, Billingham had become the largest chemical site in the world (Phillips, 1999; Northern Region Strategy Team, 1976). In 1926, ICI was founded from the merger of two firms with the aim of satisfying many of the chemical requirements of the British empire. The production of plastics started in the 1930s, while the production of petrochemicals, based on oil processing, substituted the use of coal around the end of the 1950s. This coincided with an international expansionary trend for chemical and plastic products lasting until the early 1970s, which, as pointed out by Hudson (1983), was determined by two related factors, namely the expansion of existing markets and the expansion of chemical products in markets previously belonging to traditional materials such as glass, paper, wood, etc. In addition, contrary to what happened for other manufacturing outputs, chemicals prices fell in this period. From 1963 to 1971, total sales for the most important Western chemical producers increased by 8.6 per cent, the value added by 8.7 and investments by 11.5 per cent. In the same period, employment grew by 3.5 per cent and productivity by 5.1 per cent (Northern Region Strategy Team, 1976).

In the period under examination, chemical production on Teesside is identified with its major firm, ICI, though five other large companies were also operating in the area.[17] The company developed its production in three sites: Billingham, which produced heavy inorganic chemicals,[18] Wilton whose plant specialized in organic chemicals[19] and polymers and North Tees, with the settlement in Seal Sands, which refined raw oil from the North Sea. It was ICI's technological breakthroughs that brought a consistent expansion of chemical production in the area, favouring increasing economies of scale and determining the conditions for the company's achievement of market dominance. The first of them involved Billingham and consisted of ICI's replacement of coal with natural gas as feedstock. The main implication of the process of innovation which led to the replacement of the coke-based process with the steam-reforming process was the achievement of a technological edge on international markets, allowing an increasing production at lower costs.[20] As indicated by Hudson, "the reduction from 11.6 to 0.3 man-hours in the quantity of socially necessary labour time required to produce one ton of ammonia is the most vivid indicator of the combination of increased scale of production and new technology" (Hudson, 1983, p.115). Furthermore, in 1966, the world's first commercial low-pressure methanol plant began its production in the site. Wilton too witnessed great technological advancements. The first cracker in 1951 had a nominal annual capacity of 30,000 tons; at the end of the 1950s, the annual capacity of the third cracker was 70,000 tons and a decade after the fifth cracker produced 450,000 tons per annum (North, 1975). The 1960s were therefore characterized by very high levels of industrial investment in the chemical sector symbolized also by the development of a new site along the north bank of the Tees. Seal Sands represented a privileged location for chemical companies seeking to expand their productive capacity. Undoubtedly, the decade represents a period of market-led growth in which Keynesian policies to support mass consumption coupled with consistent investment and technical advancements in the chemical sector to consolidate an upswing in the business cycle that lasted until the mid-1970s. ICI was at the time "the most modern petrochemical complex in the UK with few equals anywhere in the world" (Telfer, chairman of ICI Petrochemicals Division, quoted in Beynon et al., 1994, p.86) and "Wilton's pipelines ran in trenches rather than on pipe bridges, and its main roads were dual carriageway" (Phillips, 1999, p.6). The expansion of the firm maintained a steady pace until the mid-1970s but the economic conditions that had ensured full employment in the area were about to change. The circumstances for a period of reduction of labour inputs became apparent at the end of the 1970s and, for the first time, Teesside would experience redundancies.

The intense growth of the sector on Teesside was initially favoured by the combination of local, mainly physical, advantages and by a positive international conjuncture, characterized by soaring demand for chemicals manufacturing. These conditions certainly contributed to Teesside becoming one of the most important sites for chemicals production and to ICI assuming a dominant role in international chemicals production.

Industrial Culture in the Sector

An explanation of the success of the chemical industry on Teesside based on market conditions would offer only a partial account of the relevant processes. The extensive growth was facilitated by a well-defined industrial culture that was forged by the area's major company.

Industrial relations The development of Teesside around a few, but strong, companies led them not merely to influence the area's economic development but also to mark its industrial history. ICI, together with British Steel Corporation (BSC), monopolized the local labour market and found its strength and stability in the framework of its employment relationships. As a senior manager of the company put it:

> ... in Teesside, there is a long history of dependency on heavy industries. People have always relied upon their employers, which were supposed to provide a job for life, security, and continuous training.

A policy of formal co-participation of the workers in company's decisions concerning labour was carefully planned in the workplace through the establishment of Works Councils, Divisions Councils and a Central Council. However, this aimed at avoiding the diffusion of trade unionism rather than enforcing collaborative decision-making. Indeed, the efforts tended to produce a tacit alliance between the company and its workers and to socialize the belief that capital and labour interests could be harmonized. According to an ex-worker at ICI:

> Workers were institutionalized. There was a sense of family in the company. A person who got a job there [in ICI] was proud of this achievement.

Highly sophisticated work measurements aimed at tightening management control over work were introduced as well as means to reduce and control possible conflicts in the workplace. The introduction of Manpower Utilization and Payment Structures in 1965, substituted in 1969 by the Weekly Staff Agreement, favoured increasing productivity. As pointed out by Beynon et al. (1986), ICI's extensive control on its workforce was possible because of the combination of new management techniques and the limited experience of plant trade unions. Other devices to maintain a firm control on the workforce included selection recruitment, often based on passing jobs from generation to generation of the same family. There was also a strict hierarchy among workers in the workplace. Seniority and experience ordered work relations: skilled workers dominated over medium manual workers who, organized in teams, worked in shift patterns. Wage determination was based on the system of the sliding scales, which allowed flexible cost arrangements at time of reduced demand and strengthened the view that company's fortunes coincided with those of its workers (Beynon et al., 1994). The specificity of corporate relations in the industry therefore consisted of two dimensions. First, in line with the theoretical argument developed by some preference models, ICI adopted a model of industrial relations hinging upon high wages and good employment conditions, possible because of the firm's leadership and buoyancy in the market, in order to harmonize capital and labour interests (Akerlof's argument) and to reduce internal conflicts (Bowles' argument). The second dimension relates to the extension of company influence beyond the workplace, into the local community: "the company brought people together, at the company's expenses, on the company's beer, and in the company's comfortable surroundings" (ibid. 47) or "ICI was paying for the management's children to go to school, to university" (a local economic officer in interview).

The organization of work At the period of peak expansion during the mid-1960s, ICI employed around 30,000 workers who were engaged in a wide portfolio of business activities.[21] The three ICI sites created a huge single complex of interconnected inputs and outputs, constituting the perfect example of a vertically integrated company. ICI also developed a wide range of services which, functional to the production process itself, were retained in-house. Besides basic services such as maintenance, transport, catering, cleaning, etc., the company provided in-house engineering support and also training for newly hired personnel. As emerged in an interview with a senior manager of the company:

> The company was called pathfinder. It pioneered many different activities. When it was developing new processes, quite often there wasn't the service organization that would satisfy that, so what we had in the past was major workshops. We use to make our own equipment, we had our own design. We created the services.

The organization of work associated with ICI's gigantic organization of production hinged upon Tayloristic principles. These principles entailed the simplification and fragmentation of work processes that allowed a reduction in worker margins of discretion over execution and conception. Occupations were characterized by demarcation barriers between administrative and plant operators and, especially, among the latter. A profound division existed between process and craft workers, who lived completely different lives within the company: unlike craft workers, process workers were organized according to shift patterns to secure continuous flow. Although ICI offered favourable work conditions to all its workers in terms of wage levels and security of employment, the main division between plant and craft operators concerned earning levels. In contrast to craft workers, process operators could move upwards in the earning grades by increasing their wage levels. It is in consequence of demarcation that practices such as overtime started to be systematically used among craft workers with important implications for company costs.

The Decade of Transformation: From the Mid-1980s to the Mid-1990s

The General Economic Context: International and Local Trends

The 1980s opened with a situation of accentuated over-capacity that had started to afflict the international chemical market from the end of the 1970s. A series of circumstances explain this situation. First, the growth of the chemical industry was seriously halted by the rise in the price of oil following the two oil shocks. These impacted on the cost of raw materials and contributed to erode corporate profit margins.[22] Second, during the same period, many oil- and gas-producing countries, such as several Middle-East countries, developed technological capacities to enter processing operations, whereas other countries, such as Brazil or South Korea, entered the market with their own chemical and petrochemical products (Hudson, 1983). Third, it was apparent that the industry was approaching maturity. As indicated, "the difference between its growth and that of other sectors began to narrow. This was mainly due to the diminished opportunities for substitution and the onset of market saturation" (Chapman, 1986, p.40). Yet, 'the industry also failed to maintain the growth dynamics previously based upon product and process innovation' (ibid.). While a few new products had been introduced since the period of major expansion, the reduction of costs and the search for profit was mainly achieved through the intensification of economies of scale. As a result, the global chemical industry faced a downward slide characterized by falling prices and over-capacity, leading to stagnant demand and production throughout the 1980s and 1990s (Financial Times, 18-11-1997).

Teesside, as a major international centre for chemical production, was seriously affected by the new market conditions. The Wilton works especially were penalized by the increase in the cost of raw material. As a consequence, projects were made to replace naphtha (from oil) with ethane (from natural gas) as feedstock by exploiting the large deposits existing in the North Sea. It was increasingly evident in fact that the petrochemical and the plastics business were facing a period of low profitability due to excess ethylene production. Implications on employment dynamics became soon apparent. During the period 1971-1984, nearly 14,000 jobs were lost in the industry (-42.1 per cent) and the share of the sector as a proportion of total employment in the county fell during the period from 14.1 to 10.5 per cent (Chapman, 1986). The poor performance of the international economy however should not be counted as the only responsible factor for the decline of the chemical sector on Teesside and, more in general, in the country. UK productivity in the industry had consistently lagged behind the levels achieved elsewhere. Low levels of investment especially contributed to lower levels of output in the UK with respect to other European countries (ibid.). Furthermore in 1979 and 1980, the UK chemical industry suffered from a domestic economic policy leading to the over-evaluation of the pound against the US dollar and the Deutschmark (Pettigrew, 1985).

ICI's Strategy in a Changing Scenario

ICI's problems appeared to be even more complex. At the beginning of the 1980s, the company was trapped in a slowly growing domestic market[23] and it was extremely dependent on petrochemical products whose demand had consistently slowed (Arora et al., 1998). Its financial performance was soon affected: profits as percentage of sales dropped from 11.8 per cent in 1979 to 5.8 per cent in 1980 (figure 3.6). On Teesside, during the period 1977-1984, ICI's employment declined by 34.6 per cent (figure 3.7).

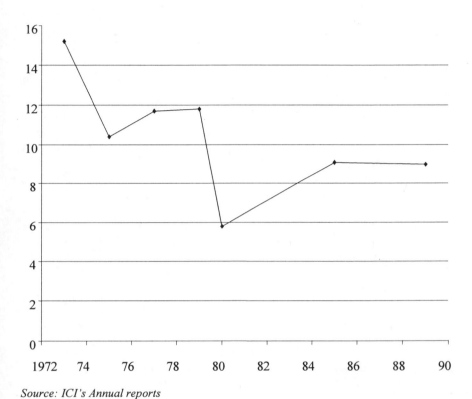

Source: ICI's Annual reports

Figure 3.6: ICI's profits as a percentage of sales during the 1970s and 1980s (selected years)

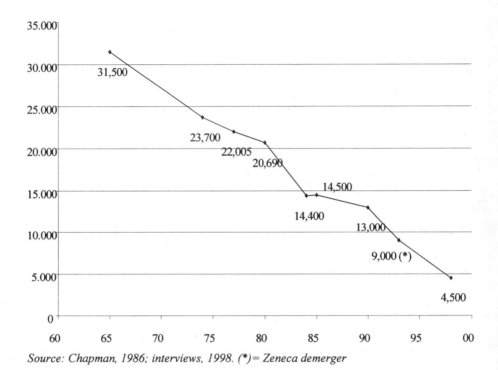

Source: Chapman, 1986; interviews, 1998. (*)= Zeneca demerger

Figure 3.7: ICI's employment trends on Teesside (selected years)

The other element that had contributed to penalizing ICI's position within
the chemical market during the late 1970s-early 1980s was the lack of an
adequate programme of investments. The company reacted to the changing
economic scenario by embarking on an extensive process of restructuring.
It soon became clear that a shift in its long-term strategy was occurring and
that the centrality of Teesside within it would be questioned. As
commented by a company's manager:

> The main board decided that ICI was going to specialize rather than have a
> wide business portfolio and to move away from heavy chemicals to speciality
> chemicals, with all that goes with it.

The new business strategy consisted of a more focused business
approach leading to the sell-off of businesses connected with the heavy end

of production (petrochemicals, halochemicals, etc.) and privileging the expansion of the more profitable light chemicals[24] (commodity chemicals). Whereas up to the mid-1980s, ICI had pursued a strategy of diversification, covering a wide range of products, the decade from the mid-1980s to the mid-1990s marks its search for niche and less volatile markets.[25] In less than two decades, ICI shifted "from diversity to focus, concentrating on core activities in global markets in which it has or can achieve a competitive advantage to become a world leader", through selective acquisitions, divestments of weaker activities and asset swaps with its competitors (Cleveland County Council, 1994, p.7). 1985 constitutes the first relevant turning point as it marks the year in which ICI definitively retreated from polyethylene production, following a decision made in 1982.[26] The move towards the final segments of chemical production implied a complete transformation of its previous business philosophy. The wide range of products which it used to sell were replaced by relatively few items; the large volumes of production became relatively low-volume batches requiring intermediate products and highly knowledge-based processes. Moreover, the business re-positioning marked the end of the consolidated idea of the financial compensation among businesses: that is, the idea that financial losses in one of the businesses could have been annulled by financial gains in another one. As explained by a manager of the company in an interview:

> ICI had a whole range of businesses starting from heavy petrochemical to chemical to the pharmaceutical end. If you look at the demand for those individual businesses, the corporation as a whole was not generating sufficient profits. At one time that was not actually a problem. At that particular time [during the expansive phase] there were some merits in having this wide business portfolio because if one business was not doing so well then another business could prop it up. That was the strength on Teesside.

It was during the 1990s that the programme launched in the 1980s was accelerated (table 3.5). ICI proceeded to large-scale sell-offs, whose apex was achieved in 1993 with the demerger that created a new company, Zeneca. With this operation, ICI retained the production of industrial chemicals, paints, materials and explosives, whereas Zeneca took over ICI Bioproducts at Billingham.[27] The new ICI started to rely upon relatively few businesses that are expected to ensure the financial viability of the company in the future.

Table 3.5 ICI in transition – The 1990s

YEAR	DEAL- Closures and Sales	DESCRIPTION
07\1990	Closure of the Billingham fertiliser plant	Fertilisers
10\1991	Closure of the Diakon plastics plant	Plastic chips
04\1992	Closure of ADN plant – Wilton	Adn is an ingredient in the manufacture of nylon
06\1992	Announcement of closure of Billingham Phenol Plant	Material used in the motor and construction industries
06\1993	Demerger – ICI and Zeneca	ICI retained industrial chemicals, paints, materials and explosive. Zeneca took over ICI bioproducts at Billingham: pharmaceuticals, agrochemical and seeds
05\1993	Sale of dry ice business – Billingham	Carbon dioxide used by airlines for cooling food to Hydrogas, a subsidiary of a Norwegian firm
11\1993	Sale of Central Engineering Services	Redpath Engineering Services took over the work of ICI's Wilton based engineering support operation
03\1994	Sale of Polypropylene to BASF, announced in 1993	ICI exits from 5% of polypropylene market. BASF becomes Europe's second largest producer
02\1995	Sale of Ethylene Oxide and Derivatives	to Union Carbide (USA) soon to be bought by Dow (USA)
04\1997	Sale of IT, voice and infrastructure services	to IBM Ltd (USA)
12\1997	Sale of the Fertiliser business	to TERRA Industries Inc (USA)
01\1998	Sale of polyester, intermediates and polyester firm	to DuPont (USA)

(cont.)

(table 3.5 cont.)

YEAR	DEAL- Closures and Sales	DESCRIPTION
01\1998	Sale of polyester, intermediates and polyester firm	to DuPont (USA)
11\1998	Closure of the sodium cyanide facility at Billingham	Sodium cyanide
08\1999	Sale of the Wilton cracker (olefin 6)	to Huntsman (USA) – end of joint venture with BP. The purchase also included ICI aromatics at North Tees and Tioxide (now called Huntsman Tioxide)
1999	Sale of the acrylics business	to INEOS, a management buyout French-owned
1999	Sale of infrastructure services	to Etol subsidiary of ENRON
10\1990	Tioxide total acquisition	Producer of titanium dioxide and pigments used in plastics and paints
06\1992	Expansion of the Melinar plant – Wilton	Production of PET (polyethylene terephalate) recyclable plastic
08\1992	Electric supply from Enron	15 year deal for cheap supply of electricity from the Enron gas fired power plant for the Wilton site
01\1993	Announcement of asset swap with BASF	Exchange of the polypropylene plant at Wilton with BASF's acrylics in Germany and Spain
07\1993	DuPont asset swap	ICI takes control of the American company US Acrylics in exchange DuPont receives the Wilton nylon chemical works
03\1993	Rationalisation of ICI Films	Film's commercial division moved from' Welwyn Garden City to Wilton.
04\1993	Opening of Monomer 8 Acrylics Complex	Production of methyl methacrylate used in perspex
1997	Acquisition of Speciality Chemicals	from Unilever
1998	Joint venture with BP	Computerised control system at Wilton

Although entering segments of the market where no clear leadership is delineated and where it wants to gain its dominance, "the key to remaining profitable is internal efficiency" (ICI Annual report, 1985, p.2). This is ensured by the combination of increasing productivity and performances and decreasing costs. In commodity chemical businesses, "profitability depends more on careful management than on substantial new research and capital expenditure" (Arora et al., 1998, p.327).

In 1997, ICI further defined its focus away from commodity chemicals towards speciality chemicals,[28] by acquiring Unilever's speciality chemicals businesses and selling the polyester and titanium dioxide businesses. This shifted ICI "decisively away from cyclical, low-margin commodity chemicals towards higher-value, less capital-intensive, knowledge-centred businesses based on tailoring technology to customers' needs" (ICI annual report, 1997, p.9). ICI's portfolio is now composed of four businesses; in 2000, national starch and paints made up for almost three quarters of the company's turnover (figure 3.8 and table 3.6).

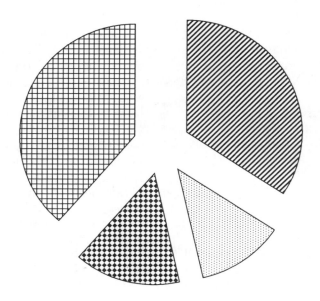

☑ National starch ⊞ Quest ⊞ Performance specialities ⊡ Paints

Figure 3.8: ICI's turnover

Table 3.6 The new ICI

Business area	Business description	Examples of applications
	Decorative paints (interior and exterior paints; varnish, woodstain)	Decorating and protecting
Paints	Refinish paints (vehicle repair paints)	Re-spraying and repairing damaged vehicles
	Packaging coatings (internal and external coatings)	Coating food and beverage cans and flexible packaging
National starch	Adhesives, speciality starches, speciality synthetic polymers and electronic and engineering materials	Adhesives, inks, sealants, baths, worktops, lenses, medical instruments Insulation materials, vehicle components, footwear, construction materials
Performance specialities	Oleochemicals, catalysts, polymers	Natural and synthetic lubricants, personal care ingredients formulation
Quest	Fragrances, fragrance materials, flavours, food ingredients	Prepared food, beverages, dairy products, detergents, fine fragrances

Source: ICI's Annual reports

Operations on Teesside have been heavily penalized by the company's business re-organization. One among the latest initiatives concerned the solid cyanide facility, part of the acrylics business, which was closed in 1998. At the same time, ICI "invested £10 million on a state-of-the-art computerised control system for the Wilton site cracker, a joint venture with BP. ... the new system will, ICI argues, keep the olefins complex at the forefront of the most efficient European producers" (TVJSU, 1999, p.4). The most important investment for ICI on Teesside is represented by Synetix that is believed to be the only ICI base in the area (ibid.). Synetix, known more recently as Katalco, is a science company with about 700 staff working on catalysis, a highly sophisticated element of the industry. In addition to the traditional use of this technology (for fertilisers, methanol and refinery, for various forms of hydrogen and other gas purification but also for the process which takes the sulphur out of the North Sea gas), Synetix is expected to increase company's exports globally, where it is confident that it will assume a leading role in the absence of any dominant player. Collaborative initiatives were undertaken to support this new business.[29] At the end of its business re-positioning, the company – ICI– that once used to identify a place – Teesside – had no significant businesses in the place. The geography of the chemical capital in the area is now more diversified with a large number of foreign-owned players engaged in a plurality of chemical productions (figure 3.9). As verified by Chapman and Edmond in their analysis on the EU chemical industry (2000), the bond between geographical roots and corporate identity is substantially dissolving under the effect of economic integration and the spread of privatization.

To summarize, the ten years between the mid-1980s and the mid-1990s marks the transformation of the chemical industry on Teesside with the main actor of such a change being ICI. The situation of over-capacity afflicting the industry, the low levels of investment and the end of market leadership were the principal factors affecting ICI's performance and forcing it to undertake a business re-organization. Job losses in the company have to be linked to the strategy of concentration and specialization with which it abandoned an array of productions connected with heavy chemicals to enter niche and less volatile markets connected with the light segments of chemicals production. This has also required the reduction of internal costs as the means to maintain adequate profitability levels. Consequently, the cost-cutting policy inaugurated by ICI and centred upon the heavy rationalization of the costs of labour has been consistent with the evolution of the company.

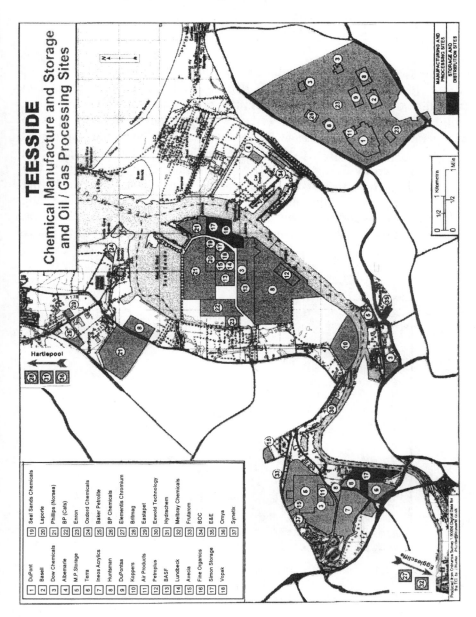

Figure 3.9: Teesside's chemical sites

(Digital data for the TCI. Adapted by permission)

*Changing the Employment Relationship: the Centrality of the Labour
Factor in the New ICI*

The process of restructuring had had a considerable impact on the level of
ICI employment in the UK (figure 3.10). Although it is difficult to ascertain
the full extent of employment decline, given that some workers have
simply changed job or have been deployed elsewhere within ICI, it is no
exaggeration that, on Teesside, in the period 1981-1993, the number of
workers employed directly by ICI has fallen by around 50 per cent
(Cleveland County Council, 1994). At the beginning of the 1980s, ICI in
Cleveland employed around 18,000 workers, equivalent to about 80 per
cent of the total in the oil processing and chemical manufacturing
industries. At the end of the decade it employed 14,500, while the current
employment base of the company is a mere 4,500 workers[30] (refer to figure
3.7).

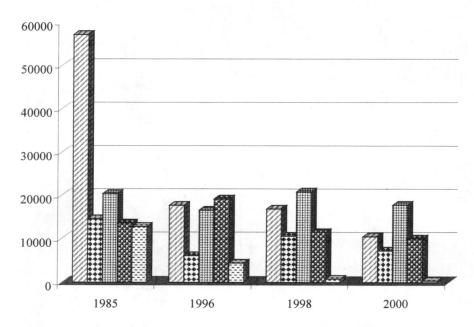

☑ UK ◨ Continent ⊞ The Americas ▧ Australasia & Far East ⊟ Others

Source: ICI's Annual reports

Figure 3.10: ICI's employment trends by geographical areas

What role have labour costs played in the restructuring process? The downsizing of its workforce has not been the only means through which ICI has cut the cost of labour. The company used rationalization to radically alter its model of employment relations. Given ICI's importance in the chemical sector of the area, the whole industry saw the re-definition of employment relations, now characterized by the clear prevalence of company's objectives over workers' interests, and the modification of the previous industrial culture.

There is no doubt that the process of transformation leading to the slow demise of the rooted paternalistic and harmonized system of industrial relations proved painful and hard to accept. For many years, in ICI there has been a tacit denial that the model was at its sunset; this is because the modification of a consolidated industrial culture needed the transformation of the system of symbolic representations crystallized into the initial pact linking the company, the workers and the community and perpetuated during the time by the prevailing organizational culture. ICI's approach to redundancies shows its reluctance in admitting that the old social pact linking the company to the workers and the community was irremediably compromized. During the restructuring phase, and except for specific episodes of plant closure, ICI has never made people compulsorily redundant. Also, during the late 1980s and 1990s when the number of involuntary redundancies generally increased (Deakin and Wilkinson, 1999), the company favoured voluntary terminations of employment[31] and business agreements which ensured that all its operations of selling or acquisition would not involve job loss. "Rather than closing the plants, what we would look for is a good buyer that would see that particular business strategic to their aim and would want to invest in its long-term future" (senior ICI manager in an interview). In practice, ICI's formal commitment towards its workers simply passed the task of industrial redundancies to the companies that replaced it.[32] For many workers the 1980s represented the end of an old working culture.

Re-organization of work and labour prerogatives ICI has implemented large scale use of external flexibility mainly in the form of outsourcing while, internally, it has introduced functional flexibility especially among its most skilled workers.[33] Many of the previously in-house services have been outsourced, notably maintenance, cleaning, catering but also engineering activity, training and consultancy work. From the company's perspective, the use of flexible work arrangements satisfies a twofold objective: it has allowed consistent savings on the cost of labour and it has also decreed the end of traditional work practices such as demarcation and overtime. As stressed by an ICI's manager in an interview:

> we couldn't sustain them [in-house services] anymore. When we provided them internally, we were paying a higher price. ... we make chemicals. Now either you reduce the cost of making it or you reduce the cost of support services. We have tried to do the latter. We want to pay at a market level. For us it was a way to reduce the cost of labour. The over-time was the root of all the problems. On the top of the pay, workers could make more money working extra-hours. If something broke on Saturday or Sunday, we had to wait for the specialists, who were paid a lot. Over-time is now very limited. People have to work 36 hours per week. The company has decided to give benefit time hours: in practice, it will pay an extra 160 hours for each worker. The demarcation, main cause of the problem, has been removed.

Flexibility has involved two aspects. First, the process of business re-organization and outsourcing has clearly produced a cleavage between a core and a peripheral workforce. The much reduced core segment works in the chemical companies, whilst the expanding peripheral workforce is in subcontracting firms. Second, there have been important changes in the terms and conditions, previously rather homogeneous, on which employment in the two segments is offered. Advantageous and stable contracts are typically offered to workers in the first segment of the market, whereas for peripheral workers, wages and working conditions have deteriorated as companies are able to recruit informally and reduce job security. Politically, worker partition is likely to have contributed to eroding the workforce's capacity to express homogeneous interests but also to increasing uneven living standards and patterns of consumption related to the employment status.

The use of outsourcing has numerous implications for the wider labour market. It emerged during the interviews with the representatives from grass roots voluntary organizations and statutory organizations as well as ex-workers that, for ICI and other chemical companies, subcontracting has meant a reduction in the actual price of the subcontracted activity as well as a reduction in labour costs, given that "when you outsource, you've got less people on the book" (interview with an officer of a local economic organization). However, subcontracting also allows companies to cope more easily with demand fluctuations. The cyclical nature of chemical markets does not make it easy to foresee business changes; with the use of service activities only when necessary and for limited periods of time, a company reduces the amount of its fixed costs. In addition, the outsourcing of support activities is deemed to have a direct effect on the provision of services (e.g. quality, costs, time). Finally, the new pattern of productive organization and relations allows the exercise of a heavier and extensive control of chemical companies over subcontracting ones.

Industrial relations The modification of industrial relations at the workplace has been no less profound. It is during the 1980s and, more widely, during the 1990s that the traditional model of consensus between capital and labour entered a crisis. The corporate decision to found the new ICI coupled with a favourable anti-union climate, with new approaches to the management of human resources, exalting teamwork and personal commitment, and with the increasing accountability of companies to the stock market and to shareholders.[34] All the limits connected with the company's traditional industrial culture therefore accentuated. Increasingly, the joint decision-making process and regulation of work practices and employment relations was seen as a constraint on management freedom to adjust work organization according to the company needs and to practise individualized employment relations.

> Those practices were institutionalized and negotiated at the top management level, certainly, local managers did that [accepted those practices] because it gave them a quite easy life. Around the mid-1980s, the top management started to be reluctant to continue to apply them. The culture of the centre was soon passed to the line (focus group with ex-ICI workers).

The recognition of human resources as the most valuable assets and the importance of co-operation and collaboration among capital and labour have not been put under discussion but it is the climate in which they occur that has changed. Collaboration and co-operation are now conceived in a context where company's achievements are prevalent over worker interests and functional to the fulfilment of its business results. With much more limited power, local unionists seem to have accepted the new collaborative culture on Teesside as the only one that can ensure jobs. As the local official for the industry put it in an interview:

> A collaborative culture is growing. Workers have understood that without changes they haven't got any option. They will adapt because they need to.

Industrial Redundancies

The Institutional Construction of the Unemployed People

To polarize the argument, orthodox economic analyses regard people who lose their jobs either as the result of the mismatch between demand and supply of labour (neo-classical view) or as the pool of workers who are functional to the process of capitalist accumulation (Marxist tradition). What it is argued in this section is instead that they are the expression of non-neutral choices made especially by companies but also by unions and individual workers to changing production requirements. In chemicals, the phase of restructuring with the consequent loss of jobs appears to have satisfied the twofold objective of marginalizing undesirable workers, who embodied social and technical values unsuitable for new industrial requirements, and of moulding the remaining workforce around new values. It is important to stress that the process of layoffs has never been impartial. Whilst formally voluntary, redundancy choices have been characterized by heavy management intervention to "encourage" certain types of workers to leave. The underlying aim was to end a culture of work that was considered incompatible with new corporate requirements as well as dangerous for future achievements. As explained by the personnel manager of a medium size chemical company in an interview:

> We had lots of problems with the unions and obviously with the workers. They wouldn't change, they wouldn't acknowledge that they had to change to be more competitive, there was a lack of realism on the shop-floor.

and acknowledged by an ex-worker:

> it was extremely difficult for plant managers to transmit the new values requested by the company to their workers. Especially plant operators, they were extremely resistant to change. They [managers] weren't able to obtain radical change in work culture and in work practices. This is also why there have been business changes. In small businesses management could have intervened better.

Those who were reluctant to abandon traditional work values (job stability, adequate wage levels, good quality of work, collective bargaining) for a new work culture (flexibility and individual responsibility and accountability) became the primary targets. The alignment of "all employees to business aims" and to a system of "360 degree appraisal" which would have characterized "individual performance reward" was deemed necessary.[35] As indicated by a senior manager of a local company:

We looked at the production people. We were able to check who had poor attendance record, sickness record, people who had limited standards in terms of their performance based on competence and skills, and we made a selection, after inviting volunteers. ... Independently from age, skills, etc., the production manager sat down and rated every operator on the books, awarded points for the criteria.

An example of the work practices which local managers considered unacceptable is given below by a personnel manager:

It was time to change [around the mid-1980s]. We had bonus schemes that were put in 30 years before; the machines no longer existed while the bonus schemes were still there. You could walk around the factory at 2 o'clock on any afternoon and people were literally going through the motions. They were not doing anything because they had decided they had done enough for the day, they got the bonus they wanted.

Contrary to what is generally believed, therefore, redundancies allowed companies to move away undesirable members of their workforce and to create a climate whereby the workers left at work accept the new organizational values:

The situation at work is much worse now. People are frightened and unhappy. The family environment has been lost. Now managers expect much more from people, but without training and stuff like that is a bit difficult and it's also dangerous to be flexible in this way. They want people to do more than one thing but people are fed up and stressed about work. Now many more people go on sickness: there is more stress and less commitment (an ICI worker in an interview).

Conclusions

According to the standard view on industrial unemployment, the regulation of the employment relation is the main cause that compromizes a corporation's profitability performance as it leads to the ossification of employment conditions and work practices and to an upward pressure of wages. It has been argued instead that rather than depending on wages, redundancies in the chemical industry on Teesside are the outcome of a process of industrial adjustment initiated by ICI to respond to a changing economic scenario that was jeopardising its market dominance. Unable to maintain technological leadership in a market where the entry of new players soon led to saturation and an industry-wise decrease in profitability, ICI re-organized its business activity and re-configured the model of employment relations that had historically defined the area's capital and labour relationship and enabled the demand-led growth of the industry on Teesside. With regard to its re-organization, until the mid-1980s, ICI was an integrated system, embracing all the phases of the production process from the refinery of raw materials to the downstream activity. The company retained all sorts of support activities in-house. The enhancement of a new way of making business and managing industrial relations has obviously altered the previous production framework. Specifically, the double movement towards progressive specialization on core products and the extended use of outsourcing for non-core activities is leading towards a greater diversification of the sector[36] but also to a growing inter-firm integration whose impact on the quality of labour conditions gives cause for concern (table 3.7). The activity of business selling, of asset swaps and mergers has brought to Teesside the presence of chemical multinationals besides medium and small size companies, which were already settled in the area. At the moment, the area's chemical companies work on different sub-sectors of the chemical market. However, besides a diversified core of chemical producers, there exists an increasing number of companies that surround and support chemical activity. Yet, a further segmentation occurs among subcontracting companies. This label gathers in fact companies specialized in the provision of completely different services. Catering, cleaning, scaffolding or painting companies and, to a certain extent, maintenance companies provide the least specialized and least skilled services; engineering, by contrast, constitutes a highly sophisticated activity. The focus on the relationships between chemical firms and subcontracting ones allows the understanding of the new organization of production in the sector. Chemical companies tend to have privileged and stable relationships only with the group of subcontractors that provide the most specialized services and whose commitment is ensured through good financial compensation. Conversely, the relations with low quality subcontractors are more tenuous, distant and extremely volatile. Two main interconnected reflections can be drawn from the above points. First, there is a dimension concerning power relations to be accounted for. It is clear that local chemical companies exercise a different influence upon their subcontractors in relation to the conditions and the price of their service provision.

Table 3.7 Employment and production change in the chemical sector on Teesside

	Before the mid-1980s	After the mid-1980s
Relations of production	Monofirm. Integrated system of production from the refinery of raw materials to down-stream activity. In-house support services	Inter-firm integration: chemical firms towards specialization; sub-contracting firms: core-peripheral activities
Employment conditions	*Industrial relations:* Co-operative, joint regulation of employment conditions, harmonization of capital and labour interests	Company prevalence, workers acquiescence. Company accountability to stock market and shareholders
	Work practices: Demarcation lines among tasks and occupations; over-time	Segmentation: primary and secondary labour markets
Reproduction of labour	Waged labour according to the pact of stability, security, good work conditions in exchange of continuous growth in productivity	Waged labour according to flexible work arrangements and non-standard contracts. Cost of labour as a non-fixed cost

Therefore, whilst highly specialized companies have a rather wide negotiating power due to their expertise and to the lower level of competition in their market, the same cannot be said for catering or cleaning companies which are subject to harsh competition to obtain and maintain contracts based exclusively on the price of the service. Second, the findings suggest that subcontracting is translating into a new and more intense form of control especially for peripheral companies and workers. This control implies a more or less explicit indication of the conditions with which subcontracting activities have to occur (time, price, qualitative standards, etc.). In general, however, the whole industry is suffering from the ageing of the workforce profile. As for years the industry has not been an active recruiter,[37] it is now experiencing skill shortages which are concerning professionals, managers and chemical engineers, but also the area of plant maintenance (TVJSU, 2000; TCI, 1998).

Redundancies, job insecurity and under-employment in the chemicals industry on Teesside have been the result of the change in the institutions regulating capital and labour relations. It can be argued, in line with the insights of the institutionalist tradition, that the problem of labour has emerged in coincidence with the transformation of the well-established employment pact, founded on the harmonization of capital and labour interests, to a model of industrial relations characterized by the prevalence of capital interests on labour. For decades, waged labour in the chemical industry was understood, produced and reproduced to satisfy a model of capitalist accumulation based essentially on the stability, security and good conditions of waged labour in exchange of continuous growth of productivity, of demand and consumption (refer to table 3.7). The picture changes around the mid-1980s. At that time the convergence of negative business conditions for the companies operating on global markets and the shift in policy values enhanced the view that the flexibilization of employment conditions could have restored company profitability and market rationality. The choice of flexibility and its implementation has had different implications for employers and workers on Teesside. From a company perspective, it has strengthened their capacity to react to market changes; more importantly, it has meant a reduction in the cost of labour associated with the limitation of high work standards to the so-called core manpower. From a labour perspective, there is evidence that flexible work arrangements have generally worsened employment conditions both in the workplace and in the wider labour market. Within workplaces, there is a strong feeling that management control on worker performances has increased the discontent of workers as well as the vulnerability of jobs. For the industrial unemployed, conversely, the chances of getting a new job in the core segment of the market are reduced. For them, flexibility is more likely to mean continuous entry into and exit from the peripheral segment of the labour market and the lack of bargaining capacity. The current model of employment relations is evidently reproducing waged labour but its provision has to occur under particular conditions, namely according to flexible work arrangements and non-standard contracts, allowing a substantial attenuation of worker claims and a wider selection of people for hire. The major drive underlying the re-definition of employment relations and relations of production has been company willingness to return to considering the cost of labour as a non-fixed cost of production. This strategy is therefore ending up transferring a consistent burden of the welfare costs (e.g. national insurance, health, holidays, maternity) from profitable chemicals companies to the subcontracting ones that, regardless of their buoyancy, are called to face the management of complex and expensive work relations.

PART 3 EXPLAINING INDUSTRIAL UNEMPLOYMENT IN THE CLOTHING SECTOR

Introduction

The UK clothing industry is "an old industry, grown out of domestic production of essential consumer goods, rising to national significance in the nineteenth century, to undergo since the Second World War, and especially since the 1960s, a radical shift in location away from industrialized countries of the first world" (Massey, 1995, p.148). Whereas various recessions have hit the industry during the past decades, the distinguishing feature of the current phase lies in the intensity and severity of the restructuring process that, on Teesside, has been characterized by plant closures and redundancies.[38] The significance of the clothing industry in the area has weakened during the second half of the 1990s, and the most recent documents on the economy of the area reserve to it a limited mention:[39] in less than one year, from January to November 1999, approximately 450 jobs were lost in the sector whose estimated employment is of around 2,000 workers.[40] In addition, two years earlier the closure of a plant in Redcar meant the redundancy of 530 workers (table 3.8).

Table 3.8 Details of redundancies in the clothing sector on Teesside

1997	Dannimac	Redcar	530 jobs	Plant closure
1999	Dewhirst	Redcar	404 jobs	Plant closure
1999	M&M Knitwear	Stockton	30 jobs	Downsizing

Source: Press Reports

Clothing on Teesside

Industrial Features

The history of the clothing industry in the area follows two distinct phases (Hardill, 1990). In the late 1930s and, more extensively, in the post-war period, to overcome shortages of female labour, the Board of Trade encouraged the settlement of branch plants away from the traditional clothing heartlands (London, West Yorkshire and Lancashire). As one of the two regions where the industry was under-represented (the other being Wales), the north-east saw the settlement of branch plants in the area (ibid.). The second phase of industrial settlement occurred during the 1960s. A generous regional policy in the form of capital grants and labour subsidies favoured a substantial expansion of the industry during the period in which the traditional heavy industries started their phase of decline. Regional policy actors believed that female-employing activities could contribute to widening the occupational base of the region without undermining its traditional industrial structure.

The clothing industry on Teesside has been characterized by a larger presence of women, almost 90 per cent of the total workforce in the early 1970s, when compared to the 80 per cent of the region and of the country. In addition, at the beginning of the 1970s, 58 per cent of Cleveland's clothing workforce was engaged in men's tailoring compared with 43 per cent for the north as a whole and 27 per cent for the country. As indicated, historically elsewhere men's tailoring concerns tended to employ a greater proportion of men (as cutters) than the industry as a whole (Hardill, 1990). This peculiarity reflected the area's dependence upon ready-to-wear clothes as opposed to made-to-measure clothes. As indicated, in 1972, 58 per cent of clothing workers were employed in men's and boys' tailored outwear, while in 1986, the percentage falls to 25 per cent. Almost 21 per cent of workers worked in weatherproof outwear and work clothing, while almost 15 per cent of workers were employed in women's and girls' tailored outwear (ibid.). Similarly to elsewhere, the industry on Teesside was marked by gender segregation. Cutting, considered as a skilled task, drew a higher pay but was a male preserve, while women were put on the production line as machinists. According to Hardill (1987), however, the automation of the cutting process brought the demise of male employment. Instead, in the sewing process, automation was restricted and this is for two reasons. First, increases in machine efficiency have a relatively minor impact on sewing costs. These account for 15-20 per cent of a machine operative's work as most of the time is spent in loading and unloading fabric. Second, the physical properties of fabrics make it extremely difficult to devise machines that are capable of identifying a single ply. With regard to employment, the first half of the 1970s constituted the period of major expansion and the peak level in Cleveland was achieved in 1975 with 5,207 employees. However, the phase of decline for the industry was imminent and manifested in coincidence with the national economic recession in the late 1970s. No openings occurred in the period 1976-1981, while half of the companies that existed in 1976 had closed by 1981, accounting for a loss of 1,638 jobs (Hardill, 1990). While employment stabilized in the 1980s, during the 1990s there were major job losses. Currently, the industry is dominated by small companies (with less than 10 employees), usually family-based and sometimes of Asian origin. Small firms account for slightly less than 55 per cent of total companies but only a negligible amount of Teesside's clothing workers (almost 4 per cent) (table 3.9). Some are subcontractors to retailers, while others are involved in the production of medium-low quality products channelled through a range of retailers and department stores (TVJSU, 1999).[41] Medium-size companies (11-49 employees) constitute 20 per cent of local firms with 8 per cent of the total employment of the sector. 14.3 per cent of local clothing companies are medium-large size (50-199 employees) and employ almost 25 per cent of the clothing workforce. Finally, the structure of clothing industry on Teesside also presents a few large companies (11.4 per cent of the total) which however employ more than 60 per cent of the local clothing employment. These companies manufacture for the UK's major chain stores (Marks and Spencer -M&S-, Littlewoods, BHS, Next), while some of them exclusively supply M&S.[42]

Table 3.9 Distribution of clothing companies by size and employment

Size	Number	%	Employees	%
1 - 4	13	37.1	37	1.9
5 - 10	6	17.1	38	1.9
11 - 49	7	20.0	158	8.0
50 - 199	5	14.3	494	24.9
+ 200	4	11.4	1,258	63.4
Total	**35**	**100.0**	**1,985**	**100.0**

Source: Teesside TEC

The geographical distribution of local companies shows a concentration of production units in the Stockton and Middlesbrough areas (figure 3.11).

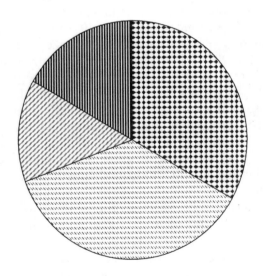

 Middlesbr. Stockton Hartlepool Redcar&Clev.

Source: Teesside TEC

Figure 3.11: Distribution of clothing companies by area

Table 3.10 lists some of the main local companies and their specialization. Three features characterize the industry in the area. First, technological innovation within local firms is low and inextricably connected to company size. Whilst it is true that the nature of the industry confines more than others the introduction of technological processes (Taplin, 1995), the main reason behind such a technological delay lies in the low investment capacity of these firms that often do not find it profitable to undertake new investments when productive, hence profit, returns are not ensured. Second, the tendency towards mergers and take-overs has accentuated in the last few years. Recurrent recessive phases have brought the decline in the number of small activities which have either disappeared or absorbed by bigger units.[43]

Table 3.10 Some clothing companies on Teesside

Name	Production
Baird Menswear Brands	Men's shirts
Bellrise Fashions Ltd	Ladies outerwear, skirts, dresses, suits
Brandtex Manufacturing Ltd	Ladies slacks
Bromley Fashions Ltd	Ladies skirts, dresses, suits
Dewhirst Ltd	Men's shirts
Eurasia Knitwear Ltd	Knitwear
M&M Knitwear Ltd	Knitwear
Meridian	Ladies underwear
Mother Ducks Childrenswear	Childrenwear
Quick a Stitch	Tshirt printing
Radar Clothing	Ladies and men outwear
Scenetex Knitting Company	Knitwear
Steel River Textiles	Sportswear
Supreme Knitwear	Ladies outerwear, boys/girls outerwear
Typhoon International Ltd	Thermal underwear, jackets, outerwear, wet/dry suits

Source: Teesside TEC

Third, since the 1960s, after some decades when clothes were produced for independent shops, the rise of a mass consumption market deeply transformed the nature of the relationship between buyers and suppliers.

Large retailers progressively pushed small ones out of the market while the largest manufacturers increased capacity and automated technologies. Smaller companies turned towards niches of the market. New market trends emerged during the 1980s around relatively high quality/high style products, also in the attempt to respond to competitive pressure from newly industrialized countries trading in cheap standardized products. Teesside's clothing producers have nonetheless continued to rely on major chain stores for their market. Their business relations are hinged upon the so-called "preferred supplier" model.[44] This is when retailers establish a long-term and close relationship with a core of preferred suppliers. The largest clothing producers on Teesside have for long enjoyed the status of preferred suppliers, especially evident among the firms that supplied M&S. In return for stable contracts, M&S required its suppliers to ensure quality, low costs and to respect strict deadlines. At the beginning of the 1990s, for instance, one Claremont branch was able to get newly designed clothes into a warehouse within a week rather than in fifteen days, which was the norm during the mid-1980s. Dewhirst was able to turn over its stock every six weeks (Hardill, 1990). During the last years, this relationship, which allowed suppliers to maintain a reasonable profit, has undergone a transformation that is penalising them. M&S, for instance, returns work or imposes charges when it is not completed on time or to standard specifications. A local manager captures the nature of the new relationships between retailers and producers:

> If they [retailers] decide that they don't want the garments you made, there is nothing you can do. You have to re-work them at your own costs, get them right, if they accept them. If they decide that something you're making is not sellable, they can just decide to pull the plug on that particular line, and you have no work.

Work and Employment Relations in the Industry

Women constitute 90 per cent of the clothing workforce on Teesside[45] and this basic ratio has not varied over time. Similarly to other manufacturing industries where women constitute the majority of the workforce, clothing is characterized by low levels of earning; however, in contrast to them, this industry is distinguished by sweat-shop conditions which confines it at the lowest ranks of the employment ladder (Massey, 1995). Work follows a Taylorist logic. An accentuated fragmentation of tasks[46] makes for repetitive job execution and a rigid sequence of work phases. It is for this reason that, although confined, the introduction of teamwork and the technical improvements of the production process are believed to be leading to a slow modification in the traditional employment practices. First, in local actors' intentions, the adoption of teamwork is expected to improve productivity and work conditions. The following comment by a manager of a local company helps understand the expectations linked to the implementation of functional flexibility:

> With the teamwork, instead of having one skill, people will have two, three four skills, which means that if somebody has got much work and somebody else less work they can move over. That should increase production. It should also make a better work environment, where there is not a huge pressure to produce, produce, produce, it's a much more relaxed way to do it. It's a way of increasing skills, making a better working environment, reducing absenteeism, great problem in the industry, and therefore, increase productivity.

However, several doubts emerge that such experiments, emphasising the flexibility of work, represent a substantial shift towards multi-skilling and new forms of work organization. Also on the basis of previous research (Hudson, 1988; Garrahan and Stewart, 1992; Cumbers, 1996), it would seem that the team work satisfies more the need to ensure task interchangeability and the reduction of production time rather than a real upskilling of workers, which is essential to improve the quality of products and to penetrate the niches of the market. Second, the update of capital assets in some local companies offers the case for divergent readings. Whilst for management, new technology has allowed productivity gains and the reduction of production costs through the substitution of labour with capital, according to the workforce and their representatives, the use of technologies has carried with it, on the one hand, an unquestionable intensification of the pace of production coupled with the de-skilling of workers and, on the other, tighter work control. As indicated in interviews by a local manager and a local unionist:

> There are technologies that allow you to produce an accurate value on how long a job should take, so that you can find out the perfect correspondence between wage and productivity.

But on the other side,

> Technologies are decreasing the skills required to the workers. The people who are speeding the machines do not need too much. Skill is diminishing in the industry in general, in practice people do not do the job.

In addition, there is evidence to suggest that the technical advances implemented by Teesside's clothing companies have been concerned almost exclusively with the production process, whilst no example of technological innovation has occurred to improve products.

Another feature influencing the sociology of work in the industry concerns wages. Low wages were a principal reason for the initial settlement of the industry in the area. Women's earnings supplemented the household's income, dominated by men's wages in heavy industries. During the last two decades, however, this has changed. With the decline of traditional industries on Teesside and the erosion of male employment base, women have increasingly become breadwinners, now as low wage earners.[47] The piecework system has traditionally characterized the industry on Teesside. It includes a basic level of pay to which a firm-based package of benefits and bonuses is attached, calculated on individual output. With the introduction of teamwork in some sections, one of the area's largest companies has also revised the system of pay. Accordingly, previous bonus earnings have consolidated into a higher basic pay (table 4.11); in return, the team agrees to meet a production target. Except for this example, the piecework system continues to be the prevailing system of pay.

Table 3.11 Earning comparison of teamworkers with conventional line operators

Basic or fall back rate   Difference

| Teamworking | £117.43 | 12.8% |
| Conventional | £104.13 | |

Gross earnings (Basic plus bonus)

| Teamworking | £142.71 | 7.7% |
| Conventional | £132.46 | |

Source: Clothing and Textile Conference, 1993

The combination of the circumstances above has generated a problem of recruitment in the industry. The traditional source of workers - young, unmarried women and school leavers- is revealing preferences that cannot be matched by the sector and seeks better employment opportunities in the various branches of the service sector.[48] It is for this reason that, in contrast to the past, employers are showing an interest in women re-entering the labour market. As indicated by the manager of a local company in an interview:

> Usually young people, after sometime spent in the industry, decide that they do not like it. Often you have already provided for their training. That is why there are good chances for older people to be re-absorbed. A good machinist will always find a job. I would rather take in five experienced people than trainees.

Yet, while recognising the specificity of their role, the common discourse justifies women's disaffection to work or their frequent turn over as the outcome of a natural inclination towards domestic work rather than the result of a work environment that does not facilitate their activity. As argued by a manager:

> the sector is women-based and it is well-known that they are not work-oriented, they have got a family load, husband and children.

In contrast to the paternalism of the chemical sector, therefore, the clothing sector on Teesside has a long history of conflicting employment relationships affecting industry performance. As remarked by another local manager:

> The point is that this industry has never been employee friendly. There were dictatorial attitudes and then, the way in which the work is arranged, its inflexibility, favours only absenteeism and turnover. This means that you have to re-train people and the productivity goes down. Undoubtedly, a stable workforce will ensure major productive gains.

The pressure to achieve a consistent daily output, the lack of facilities, such as crèches, and the low levels of wage are the ingredients for the industry to be considered a merely temporary source of earning. High turn over rates have, in turn, the effect of reducing employer investments in training and technology. In line with the institutionalist emphasis, these are the variables that impact the most upon the quality of the production in the sector and, more generally, have great implications for its long-term competitiveness.

Explaining the Current Phase of Redundancies

Responses to New Market Conditions

The most relevant transformation occurring in the Western clothing markets, especially in the last two decades, has been an increase in competition from low labour cost countries (e.g. the Far East first, North-Africa after and Eastern European countries now). These have witnessed both the growth of their domestic industry and the location of branch plants of Western companies, many of which have switched part of their capacity. The 1973 Multi-Fibre Agreement regulated much of the world trade in textile and clothing through the imposition of quotas but also favoured the penetration of Western markets with textile and clothing products from low cost countries. In the first half of the 1990s, when the phenomenon appeared in its relevance, European imports of clothing from Bangladesh increased more than three times; imports from Romania more than twice and from Poland twice. However, China is still the greatest exporter to Europe (15 per cent), followed by Turkey (10.9) and Hong Kong (7.6 per cent) (table 3.12).

Table 3.12   Main EU trading partners for clothing and clothing accessories (million of ECU)

Imports	1990	1996	Diff. 90\96	% on tot.90	% on tot.96
TOTAL	21,290	33,563	57.6		
China	2,286	5,007	119.0	10.7	14.9
Turkey	2,356	3,655	55.1	11.1	10.9
Hong Kong	2,727	2,540	-6.9	12.8	7.6
India	1,193	1,951	63.5	5.6	5.8
Tunisia	974	1,893	94.4	4.6	5.6
Morocco	1,062	1,689	59.0	5.0	5.0
Poland	533	1,633	206.4	2.5	4.9
Romania	344	1,163	238.1	1.6	3.5
Bangladesh	255	1,135	345.1	1.2	3.4
Indonesia	479	1,009	110.6	2.2	3.0
Total	**12,209**	**21,675**	**77.3**	**57.3**	**64.6**

Source: Eurostat, 1996

The latest Eurostat data, elaborated by Istituto per il Commercio Estero (ICE), show that the EU trade deficit for clothing products has increased in recent years: in 2000 it was more than 19,000 million ECU compared to 15,000 million in 1998.

Progressively, global dynamics started to affect clothing industries at the local level. The pressure from international competition centred upon the cost of labour increased the vulnerability of the clothing industry on Teesside and forced its restructuring (table 3.13). The loss of jobs and the closure of plants are the outcome of the process of industrial restructuring undertaken by large-size companies, such as Dewhirst, Baird and Meridian, which have shifted part of their production to developing countries to exploit cheap labour.[49] However, although labour constitutes an important component of production costs,[50] company fall in profitability has not been seriously compromized either by the high level of wages on Teesside or by the high standard of employment conditions.

Table 3.13 Textile wage costs (UK=100)

UK	100
Germany	210
Italy	140
France	140
Portugal	60
Eastern Europe	15-25
Turkey	30
Morocco	20
Far East	7
China	4

Source: Coats Viyella in Financial Times, 16-04-1996

The industry in the area has always suffered from low standards of pay with related implications on employment conditions and relations. The explanation of a company profit squeeze, fuelling the adjustment process and redundancies, lies in the system of distribution which local companies are locked in. As the greatest part of their production is channelled through national retail chains, their role in influencing production and market choices is extremely significant. Buyer demand for quality products at more competitive prices has forced local companies to reduce labour costs by re-locating abroad. It would seem therefore, as suggested by neo-Marxist analyses, that labour-costs savings for larger firms are possible because of their geographical mobility. These companies are unlikely to be trapped into relatively higher costs areas; indeed, they are able to take advantage of cheaper conditions of production elsewhere. As underlined by the manager of a large local company in an interview:

> There are investments but it is very low in the UK. Companies are investing in low-level cost markets, in other countries. ... they [retailers] are making a lot of money on a garment. That's why we have to invest overseas. The best we can do with British factories is to keep them at the size they are and, at the same time, grow the overseas companies. ... We have a big factory in Morocco and we pay 15 pence an hour, in the UK it's £5 an hour.

The negative impact of international dynamics on Teesside's employment levels has been also amplified by the strength of the pound. Employers complain that the strong currency has favoured imports from developing countries. In reality, however, it could be argued that the strong currency has widened margins of profit, since overseas costs of production will be lower. As indicated by a local unionist:

> In the [company's name omitted] case, they [managers] were blaming the strength of the pound, but when I asked them to go back to talk when the interest rates were cut, they answered no. That is because they can source abroad and it's cheaper.

What is interesting from the perspective of the role of wages is that the introduction of the minimum wage does not seem to constitute a major problem. This is partly because many local companies already pay more than the minimum wage (table 3.14).[51]
However, the minimum wage may be used by local companies to intensify productivity. As explained by the manager of a local medium-size company:

> There is a lot of manoeuvring ... Instead of paying them £3.20 an hour and have an hour break over the day, they will pay £3.60 but the breaks won't be paid. So at the end, they will pay the same amount of time.

Table 3.14 Minimum rates and earnings in textile and clothing agreements

Agreement	Increase	Minimum rate or MEL*
Clothing	2.5%	£3.21
Knitting Industries	2.5%	£3.20
Leather Producing	2.8%	£3.40
Textile finishing	3.0%	£4.00

MEL= Minimum earnings level

Source: IDS report, 1998

To conclude, the adjustment taking place in the clothing industry of Teesside reflects the response of local large-size companies to a changing economic scenario that is implying the re-consideration of their role within the international division of labour. Nonetheless, the need to safeguard their relationship with retailer chains rather than the issue of the cost of labour has become the major driver of the process of industrial restructuring.

The Institutionally Constrained Process of Industrial Restructuring

In a neo-classical world, firms adjust quickly and without major problems to their competitors, mainly following a cost-saving strategy based on the intensification of technological innovation and the application of the lowest possible wage. In practice, processes of adjustment occur according to different paths, at a slower pace and with different outcomes. Below it is shown that wage strategies on Teesside are nested in complex institutional arrangements.

Large companies have undertaken a single path of restructuring: the overall reduction of costs through the re-location of production abroad. This has been the outcome of a reactive rather than a pro-active response to a changing external environment. They chose not to upgrade quality or to search for different production and distribution strategies. Only one company is seeking to implement changes in the organization of work.[52] What it is therefore contended here is that, whilst a process of industrial adjustment was inevitable, the choice to cut costs reflects a particular local industrial culture. This is one based on an entrepreneurial class subordinated to retailers and on a workforce trapped into a circuit of marginality, both interacting in a vacuum of proactive industry institutions. This seems to have circumscribed company options for industrial adjustment. The following three subsections develop this claim.

The clothing entrepreneurs Historically uneven power relationships have characterized and still characterize the relations between local large producers and external buyers. The nature of such links and their perpetuation has led over the years to a progressive displacement of the local entrepreneurial class from the decision-making activity. Buyers dictated the conditions at which the relationships could have occurred, although many Teesside's large firms have been privileged suppliers. Therefore, whilst it is undeniable that the relation of dependence stimulated the technological upgrading and the quality of local production, it also reduced company capacity for elaborating autonomous market strategies, for deciding the type of production and the quality of products or their price. In particular, the initially advantageous position of privileged suppliers has turned out to be a constraint, locking local companies into a series of reactive options, when some of these buyers lowered their commitment towards them by ending the so-called "buy British" policy. For instance, as a consequence of the unilateral decision made by M&S to end a 30-year-old relationship of supply, the Baird group will be obliged either to close some plants or to persuade other big M&S suppliers to buy them.[53] A trade unionist stresses the point:

> M&S has always had a dominant position in the market. The relationship with its suppliers is very strict, supplier companies cannot react to their decisions. Now it has taken the political decision to outsource more work from abroad.

Between buyers and suppliers there is also a strict connection concerning their financial performance. M&S's difficulties on the market have an immediate effect upon suppliers' finances. In September 1999, the retail chain issued a profit warning indicating decreasing profits in comparison to the same period the previous year. As a consequence, Dewhirst reported an 8 per cent drop in pre-tax profits.[54] Retailer unwillingness to lose profit has put extreme pressure on domestic suppliers, who are trying to survive either through price cuts or through overseas production. This choice has therefore ended up compromising any type of investment projects on Teesside, as acknowledged by a local manager:

The major pressure behind companies is the retail system. They are squeezing so tight margins that they have to go overseas; we cannot make money and invest in the UK.

On Teesside, the lack of alternative restructuring strategies rather than the mere re-location to low labour cost countries must be, therefore, partly due to the existence of consolidated social relations between local producers and buyers. These relations have affected the culture of innovation as well as wider practices and habits of thought. Indeed, the problem of corporate change is not separated from a company configuration of work practices, of internal relations, of technology, of its market orientation, etc., that is from its culture. In absence of a local leadership able to articulate and implement a business strategy as well as to promote its modification, the transformation path of Teesside clothing companies has been extremely prone to buyer requests.

The workforce Having emerged as a non-competitive industry besides the traditional core sectors of the area, the clothing industry has never achieved a central role in the economy of Teesside. The industry retains a negative connotation in the local labour market because of its low wages and harsh work conditions. The industry attracts peripheral segments of the local workforce who offer their labour at sub-optimal conditions. Two main problems have emerged. First, women's participation appears to be discontinuous: exits from and entries in the workplace are frequent and related to specific phases of their life (marriage, children, income, bread-winner role). Second, because of low wage levels and hard working conditions, cases of absenteeism and disaffection to work are frequent in the industry. It follows that the production process is often prejudiced and its organization is difficult. Partly to solve this problem an important company of the area has undertaken a programme aiming to substitute individual piecework with teamwork. By reducing the pressure on individual workers, this system is supposed to improve worker performance and, in general, the attitudes towards work. As explained by a shop steward in an interview:

With the teamwork, the work is done by a group of 8-10 people. In this way, you avoid the repetitive job ... you get the change. You feel you've got more control on the quality, more input in what it's done. Decision-making, the control of quality, everything is up to the team. Teamwork improves time keeping, people appreciate the different atmosphere.

Workers' negative attitudes towards work reflect the existence of structural problems within the industry. Only few local employers acknowledge these, although evident to workers and people working in local organizations. They refer primarily to the industry's low investment in training provision and, secondarily, to its reluctance to improve work conditions. Thus, according to the regional training officer of the sectoral union:

> Training has never been a serious theme on the agenda of this sector. There is a tradition of not training anybody. You learn your expertise by being at the workplace.

No less relevant in explaining workforce attitudes is the organization of work. As indicated by a local manager:

> An employer needs to understand his workforce necessities. This is a female-based industry. You need to think to work arrangements that facilitate women's problems ... you know, the house and the rest of it. If you offer better conditions, for example the existence of crèches, then it's the company that gains the most, reducing absenteeism and turn over.

Moreover, women in the clothing industry have not had their new role as breadwinners acknowledged. According to a worker:

> The industry is classed as one of those industries that was there as an extra, but now it's not, but nobody has ever recognized this because it's a women industry.

The clothing workforce is trapped in a vicious circle. Its lack of commitment is reproduced by companies that, paradoxically given the labour intensive nature of the industry, have for a long time neglected the centrality of the workforce. Nonetheless, this downward spiral affecting employment relations in the industry is now seriously impacting on the employment level. Increasingly, employer discourses tend to stress how the process of de-localization represents a solution to such problems. Thus, for example:

> When we go abroad, we find grants given by the Government, technical schools, low cost of labour and in general a good atmosphere. Workers are keen to work for Western companies. They don't raise problems as here.

In case of restructuring, a simple rule agreed with the Unions, "last in –

first out", is applied: this implies that the workers most recently employed will be the first to leave the company. From company perspective, this system has a twofold rationale. On the one hand, it provides a good safeguard against industrial disputes as the criterion on which the decision is based is extremely clear. Second, the layoff of the workers most recently employed translates into consistent gains. for the company as the redundancy payment is linked to worker permanence at work. In practice, however, this system does not satisfy the employers. Nor is it appreciated by workers. Both contest the neutrality of the system in relation to the skills of the workforce and its commitment to work. Yet, the contention here is that the process of restructuring in the Teesside's clothing industry has ended up creating a pool of redundant workers who were not necessarily the ones influencing company efficiency/inefficiency. Through the application of an effective procedure for its effects on the wage bill, the industry is moving away some members of its workforce regardless of their skills, experience or their commitment to work. Moreover, the "last in – first out" system is leading to the penalization of specific categories of the workforce, such as young people, women who are re-entering the labour market and, more in general, workers whose employment history has been characterized, for various reasons, by a high turn over. These workers will constitute a fluctuating segment of the workforce in the sense that their entry in and exit from the labour market will be increasingly linked to the expansionary or contraction phases of the industry itself. Therefore, their causalization is going to be reproduced according to a vicious circle.

The formal institutional context In addition to the two dimensions explored above, an important role in explaining the current phase of change is played by the vacuum of sectoral organizations and the more general marginality of the industry within local economic programmes. The clothing sector is an archipelago of productive units detached from each other. To the pressure exercised by the internationalization of clothing trade, not only have the different segments of the industry reacted differently, but the answers provided have reflected the climate of competition existing among similar companies. Medium-size companies have sought to find niches of production or to widen the distributive channels, while many small companies have disappeared because of the lack of adequate financial and managerial capacities. For large-size firms, international competition has had a profound displacement effect as their integration within a particular distributive chain seemed to secure their productive existence from external pressures. Moreover, the business choice made by retail chains to progressively reduce the quantity of production bought from UK manufactures, while exploiting the advantage of overseas production, has opened a competition among local companies which, engaged in maintaining unaltered their level of supply, have excluded any form of horizontal co-operation. As admitted by the personnel manager of a local company in an interview:

> To be honest, I don't know anything about the others. Yes, I don't know who my competitors are. I know that there is another company at the corner of this road, but that's it.

The process of competition among companies is well-described by the local GMB officer:

> Because Dewhirst is going abroad, that will put the pressure on Bairdwear because they are suppliers to the same company. It's a knock-on effect. Once a producer starts doing it, to be competitive with that producer they equally go abroad.

The lack of co-operation among companies has amplified problems that could have been dealt with collectively. The most appropriate example to illustrate this point concerns training. This is a fundamental and expensive phase for every company, regardless of size. Workers to be hired are usually provided with a six-week period of training during which they learn their expertise at the company's expense. It was with the idea to reduce the costs sustained by individual companies[55] (many small and medium companies had progressively reduced their investments on training over the years also because they benefited from the turnover of workers from larger companies) and to improve the quality of new entrants in the industry that an attempt to start a technical school was made roughly four years ago. Disagreements on the funding soon led to the sunset of the initiative. Contrary to the inter-firm initiatives developed by chemical companies to promote and to use to advantage the chemical capital of the area, clothing companies on Teesside have not been able to promote a similar co-operative behaviour. Lack of mutual trust, of management planning, of financial viability, of capacity/willingness to promote activities concerning wider interests than the ones pursued by the single company, have prevailed and have ended up worsening company competitive capacity as they have internalized some costs that initiatives such as the technical school could have externalized.

The analysis of the local institutional context does not offer a more positive picture. The industry is not central to the economy of the area and finds a limited role on the agenda of local authorities, of the local TEC and of local advisory organizations such as the TVJSU. This implies that the economic action occurs within an institutional vacuum: the economic actors (companies and workers) are exposed to any type of external influence. The current phase of economic instability has widely manifested the isolation facing local companies. Moreover, in a situation in which they are constrained by the knowledge of a small amount of information and by the limited awareness of the variety of options of adjustment, changes can neither been anticipated nor turned positively. The only initiative that has been set up, although at regional level, with the precise aim to improve company strategic understanding and their competitiveness, has been implemented by the central Government. According to press reports, a task force headed by the director of the Government's office for the North-East will play a role of supporting companies. Its economic-policy address has already been defined. Given that the local clothing industry will never be able to compete with low cost countries, it is expected that consistent steps will be undertaken to move towards higher quality products and materials.[56]

To conclude, the process of restructuring of the clothing sector on Teesside has suffered from an acceleration during the last three years. Whilst it is not possible to foresee how long this process will last, it will surely result in a substantial downsizing of the industry and in a qualitative change in its productive specialization. It is a common belief among local employers and economic observers that companies are going to specialize in the so-called quick response or turnaround. This implies that the bulk of production will be manufactured in low cost countries,[57] while local plants will supply the market only with specific products or when specific circumstances occur, for instance, when a particular ply, or colour, or model runs out of the market. It has been shown that processes of employment and industrial change are meaningfully shaped by the production relations in which local companies are bound. Company profit squeeze has been determined not so much by the impact of the cost of labour as by the alteration of the buyer-producer relation which has remarkably increased the producers' cost-sensitiveness. The restructuring process has taken the form of re-location to low labour cost countries with job losses on Teesside. The choice concerning the type of industrial adjustment to be undertaken has been also heavily constrained by the institutional framework that has historically forged the economic action in the area. Such an adjustment responds neither to a mechanical process nor to an ensemble of individual preferences. It is rather embedded in the nature of the relationships between local capital and labour, where the former suffers from forms of displacement and the latter embodies the culture of a peripheral workforce. In addition, the absence of formal sectoral organizations has prevented an alternative process of restructuring, based on qualitative upgrading. It can be argued therefore that whereas the current restructuring phase is expected to redefine the industry's profile and to allow a certain recovery in company profits, perplexities remain about the industry's long-term capacity to achieve adequate levels of efficiency. Indeed, the process of adjustment undertaken does not leave room for investment in design technologies and in human resources on Teesside, as it would seem that the implementation of changes in work organization responds precisely to the same logic of cost reduction.

Notes

[1] These terms have been taken from Austrin and Beynon, 1979, quoted by Foord et al., 1985.

[2] Teesside refers to the boroughs of Stockton on Tees, Middlesbrough and Redcar & Cleveland (formerly Langhbaurgh). Hartlepool is a separate entity in labour market terms.

[3] As indicated by Foord et al. (1985, p.10): "British and foreign multinationals took advantage of available subsidies either to invest in new capacity or replace existing, but outdated, technology. For example, ICI replaced its thirty-year old ammonia plants".

[4] See Martin and Rowthorn, 1986, for an outline of three competitive explanations of the process of de-industrialization in the UK. According to the authors, the decline in manufacturing employment could be located within a more general theory of economic development and structural change which sees the expansion of the manufacturing sector during the first phases of economic development and its consequent fall when economies consolidate (the maturity thesis). A second thesis concerns foreign trade; in particular, employment decline in manufacturing is to be connected to the change in a country's/region's economic role within the international division of labour (the trade specialization thesis). Finally, the failure thesis sees manufacturing employment decline as the failure of manufacturing industry to compete at the international scale or to produce an adequate level of output.

[5] As indicated by Armstrong and Taylor, 1993, according to a neo-classical view, three mechanisms are supposed to contribute to adjust labour market temporary imbalances: the fall of wages in an area of high unemployment and their rise in areas of low unemployment; the migration of the workers from low wage to high wage areas; the move of firms from high wage to low wage areas.

[6] Two types of measures had been implemented to encourage industrial settlements in the less favoured regions: RDGs (Regional Development Grants), which were automatic grants, and RSA (Regional Selective Assistance) that instead were decided upon a discretionary basis.

[7] Paradoxically, the most important companies of the area continued to benefit from regional grants to carry out their processes of restructuring and to regain international competitiveness while, contemporarily, axing a great number of jobs; for example, in 1981-

1982, ICI received 65.4 per cent of all the RDG payments in Cleveland county, Foord et al., 1985.

[8] Functional flexibility allows the allocation of labour to a wide range of tasks previously constrained by skill demarcations.

[9] Gallie et al., 1998, provide a detailed study on the transformations of the UK labour market.

[10] The New Deal represents Labour's answer to unemployment. It is a programme comprising four options of work (subsidised jobs, full-time education and training, and voluntary sector work or place on an environmental task force) that unemployed people are obliged to take to avoid reduction in their benefits, Peck, 1998.

[11] Some stances have pointed out the fact that in general the rate could be declining for two other reasons. First, people on training schemes are not counted among the unemployed; second, many old workers may be unwilling to enter one of the schemes provided by local Training and Enterprise Councils (TECs) and decide not to sign for unemployment benefits, Peck, 1998; Webster, 1999.

[12] The negative performance of the service sector and of total employment is explained by considering the re-organization of the local governments' offices. In practice, there have been no huge job losses as figures would suggest; employees in the public sector have simply changed their employer, from the Cleveland County Council to the single boroughs.

[13] Labour is utilized according to changing production needs.

[14] The first modern chemical plant on Teesside was the Eaglescliffe Chemical Company at Urlay Nook producing fertilisers.

[15] The plant applied the method developed by two Germans, Haber and Bosch.

[16] It is a basic element for the production of sulphuric acid.

[17] They were British Nuclear Fuels, Glaxo, Albright and Wilson, British Titan, Procter and Gamble. In 1974, together with ICI, they accounted for 37,000 employees, Northern Region Strategy Team, 1976.

[18] The main products are ammonia, sulphuric acid and fertilisers.

[19] The typical products of heavy organic chemicals are ethylene, benzene and propylene.

[20] Essentially because naphtha was a cheaper feedstock than coal.

[21] Raw materials included, among others, crude oil, natural gas, naphtha, butane, propane; among the intermediate products: ethylene, propylene, ammonia, methanol.

[22] According to Ballace, it is for this reason that the industry became increasingly feedstock oriented rather than capital oriented, quoted in Chapman, 1986, p.41.

[23] Pettigrew, 1985, shows that 50 per cent of sales and 75 per cent of profits originated in the UK.

[24] The term "light chemicals" refers to the products derived from the last phases of the chemical production that provide higher added value. Examples are paints, fragrances adhesives, etc.

[25] Chapman and Edmond, 2000, show how the search for focus on core businesses has been the dominating trait of European chemical companies' strategy during the 1990s in contrast to the trend of the previous decades.

[26] In 1982, ICI and British Petroleum (BP), its major internal competitor in petrochemicals, announced a joint programme, according to which ICI increasingly specialized in the production of polyvinyl chloride (PVC), in which it had a competitive technological edge, and BP in the production of polyethylene. Following this agreement, ICI closed one of its plants in Wilton, with a loss of 700 jobs.

[27] Zeneca's production is articulated on three main divisions: pharmaceuticals, agrochemicals

and seeds and specialities, with key products being Quorn and Biopol, a biodegradable plastic.

[28] In these businesses, firms focus on the quality of products and on customer satisfaction.

[29] Synetix and Kvaerner intend to exploit future demand for methanol as a major source of fuel for cars and buses. A further collaboration has been undertaken with the German group Krupp, focussing on the reduction of ammonia and fertilisers production costs, thanks to the improvement of Synetix catalysts, TVJSU, 1999.

[30] The chemical sector has declined over time and this negative trend has an even greater impact when considered as a proportion of total employment. In more general terms, in fact, manufacturing employment declined at the expense of the service sector, Cleveland County Council, 1994.

[31] This means that many workers left their jobs on the grounds of personal choice.

[32] The most vivid episode occurred in 1994. A year after the business swap with ICI, DuPont announced the closure of five nylon intermediate plants at Wilton, while launching a major expansionary programme in Europe. The intervention of the European Union prevented the loss of 520 jobs.

[33] See e.g. the Staff Agreement of 1991 under which ICI's North Tees site was the first to embark upon flexible working, Cleveland County Council, 1994.

[34] The comparison between two statements contained in two different ICI annual reports (in the first, ICI states its aim as the enhancement of "the wealth and well-being of our shareholders, our employees, our customers and the communities which we serve to operate"; in the second, it is said that "our aim is to maximize value for our shareholders" led John Kay, Professor in Economics, to talk, at the annual conference of the Confederation of British Industry, about a "deformed style of capitalism, based on a mistaken view of the functions of a business organization", *the Journal*, 12 November 1996.

[35] These expressions appear in a confidential document of an ICI senior manager.

[36] The industry produces at least 300 different chemicals, TVJSU, 1999.

[37] The sectoral workforce fell from 30,000 in the 1960s to 12,000 (with 25,000 people indirectly employed) in the late 1990s, TVJSU, 1999.

[38] In this part of the chapter, the term "Teesside" is used in a less restrictive way as it includes Hartlepool where some important companies for the area's economy are located.

[39] See, for instance, the economic audit of the TVJSU, 1999.

[40] Data from Teesside TEC.

[41] Secondary sources on this segment of the industry are practically non-existent and it proved impossible during the fieldwork to gain direct access to the local small companies. Information used derives from the conversations held with local unionists and economic officers which, however, offer only a partial understanding of the dynamics affecting such companies.

[42] For example, this is the case of Dewhirst.

[43] Information from interviews with local trade unionists.

[44] The emergence of this system contributed to the demise of both the "close control" model and the "arms length" model though it has changed substantially neither the retailers oligopoly in the market nor the producers weakness. The "close control" model implies the direct and strict control of retailers over producers in all the stages of the production process, while in the "arms length" model retailers are concerned only about the final product, Crewe and Davenport, 1992.

[45] Calculated on Nomis data, 1997.

[46] For instance, sewing is organized as a batch process with semi-worked fabrics going

through a sequence running from under 5 to over 100 discrete sewing operations, Hardill, 1990, p.108.

[47] From January 1999 and with the re-negotiation of the clothing contract, the average weekly basic pay for a machinist is around £135; it was around £100 in 1987, Hardill, 1987.

[48] Indeed, paradoxically in the clothing sector there are cases of unfilled vacancies.

[49] The Baird group employs 3,000 people in Sri Lanka, *The Guardian*, 23 October 1999. Claremont employs 700 workers in Morocco, while Courtauld Textiles has factories elsewhere in Europe, in the US and Asia-Pacific where it employs roughly 9,000 people, *Financial Times*, 2 December 1998. Dewhirst has plants in Malaysia, Morocco and Indonesia, *Financial Times*, 10 April 1996.

[50] According to Hardill, 1990, it accounts for just over one quarter of the value of sales.

[51] It has been assessed that, in general, the introduction of the minimum wage will increase wage bills by 0.6 per cent. In the clothing sector, wage bills will increase by less than 1 per cent, Low Pay Commission, 1998, p.134.

[52] The adoption of teamwork to substitute the traditional piecework system is expected to improve production capacity and work conditions, both carrying a better balance between costs and profits.

[53] *The Guardian*, 23 October 1999.

[54] *The Guardian*, 23 October 1999, *The Observer*, 13 September 1998.

[55] It is often the case that during or just after the period of training, some of the trainees decide not to accept the job.

[56] *The Northern Echo*, 19 February 1999.

[57] Dewhirst is planning to produce abroad 70 per cent of its production by 2002 from 27 per cent in 1995, *The Northern Echo*, 8 September 1998.

Chapter 4

Brindisi: Between Corporatism and Reciprocity

Introduction

The 1990s were a decade of dramatic transformation for the economy and society of southern Italy. The macro-economic context changed following the modification of State intervention in the economy and the country's participation in the European project of economic and monetary integration. The decade also witnessed the decline of a political class that had linked its existence to the functioning of a macro-economic pact between the north and the south. Such changes have negatively affected the labour market situation and different restructuring paths have followed in different sectors and localities. The chemical and clothing industries in Brindisi have responded to the changing macro-economic context through a variety of restructuring paths; by the same token, they have displayed non-isomorphic employment adjustment strategies.

PART 1 BRINDISI: AN EMBLEM OF SOUTHERN CONTRADICTIONS

Economy and Society in Brindisi from the Post-war Period until the 1960s

The economic features of Brindisi (figure 4.1) in the post-war period were similar to those in many southern Italian areas. It was dominated by agriculture that in 1951 accounted for 70 per cent of the local active population, while industry and services shared almost equally the remaining 30 per cent (Il Tempo, 06-09-1962); income from agriculture represented 55 per cent of the gross output (ibid.).

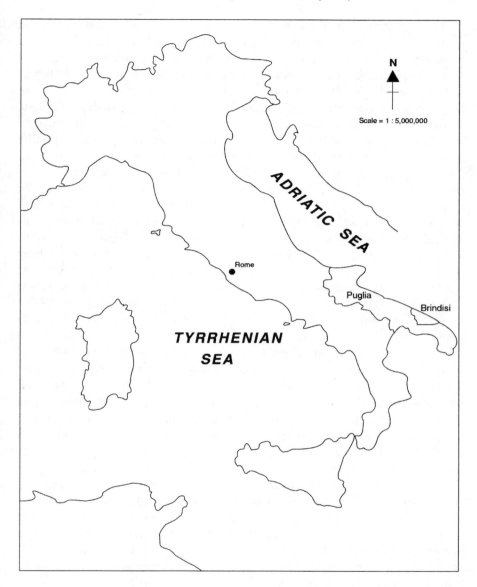

Figure 4.1: Brindisi in Italy

The Agrarian Reform of the 1950s, which should have modernized the primary sector, by expropriating big *latifondi* and distributing land to peasants alleviating the severe rate of unemployment in the area, did not manage to achieve its goals. The consequent fragmentation of ownership as well as the inefficient rationalization of the agrarian space prevented the development of a modern agricultural system in the province.[1] The new owners had limited capital which reduced mechanization and investment; in addition, the absence of a cash crop culture held back capitalist transformation. It is for these reasons that small owners were often obliged to sell their labour as daily workers in bigger properties. Under-employment for men and women was frequent. Brindisi's labour market in this phase was clearly dominated by the traits of an agrarian society and characterized by an overwhelming presence of subordinated workers in agriculture representing 90 per cent of employees (Cecafosso, 1979). Women worked on the family farm while constituting the bulk of the daily workers during the phases of peak production. The feminization of agriculture was a widespread phenomenon, the result of male out-migration and also of men's search for other sources of income (Coppola, 1977). However, women's work was considered secondary, less qualified and, consequently, less well paid.

The industrial activities existing in the area operated in traditional sectors such as food and clothing. Their artisanal nature impinged upon their technological endowment as well as upon their capacity to distribute the output. Development opportunities were therefore deeply constrained (Cecafosso, 1979). From a social perspective, nuclear families constituted the core of Brindisi's society. However, kinship networks constituted a web of support that had an important strategic role for employment opportunities and the share of social responsibilities. Labour was accompanied by wider social commitments: with labour power came the whole worker, with his/her familiar position and his/her web of personal and affective relations. Rules of reciprocity and traditional social codes therefore assumed an important function in the economic system. For instance, the recruitment of workers in the main squares of villages as well as the definition of wages was left to an informal face-to-face bargaining. Similarly, as Sidney Tarrow writes (1979), clientelistic relations existed between local notables and landlords and local families, whereby the former maintained power over the latter given their monopoly over resources (e.g. land) and the provision of subsistence. Local institutional life presented no intermediate institutions or organizations.

Growth Without Development: Brindisi's Industrialization from the 1960s to the mid-1980s

At the beginning of the 1960s, therefore, Brindisi was a peasant-based society. However, a period of great change was underway which would modify its trajectory of development. Like other southern areas, Brindisi became a target of the new phase of State intervention in the south which shifted to an active policy of industrialization through growth poles. This is the period of the "great transformation", of "the capitalist integration" or "modernization" (Martinelli, 1998): the period in which an archaic and agrarian society was transformed into a modern, partially industrialized and mass consumption society (Trigilia, 1992). This was to be achieved through exogenous industrial investment.[2] Between 1950-1973, the Puglia region received 1,257.8 billion Lire of investment with the Taranto province absorbing the largest amount (almost 60 per cent) through its new State-owned steel industry. The Brindisi province received funds for 170.6 billion Lire (almost 14 per cent of the total), 93 per cent of which benefited the chemical sector (Mele, 1975). Steel (mainly in Taranto) and chemicals (mainly in Brindisi) absorbed roughly 4/5 of all resources that went to the region (ibid.). A huge petrochemical complex was built close to Brindisi, which was destined to re-shape the economy and society of the area. The 1971 census gives the full extent of the change: the percentage of the active population involved in the primary sector declined from 64.9 per cent in 1961 to 50.6 per cent in 1971, industry grew from 19.2 per cent to almost 25 per cent (figure 4.2) and came to be dominated by chemical production. In 1971, almost 4,500 workers were employed in this sector, representing more than 24 per cent of the total manufacturing workforce. Other industries, including clothing, were obscured by the impact of these large external investments and were confined to a marginal role in the local economy (Capriati, 1995). The industry remained fairly constant in the following decades, which saw the decline of agriculture in favour of the service sector. No less relevant were the implications of the industrialization process for the local society. The exploitation of large reserves of green labour from agriculture and the construction industry transformed the local society from one centred upon a system of agricultural relations to one in which status was given by the blue overall of industry (Provincia di Brindisi, 1999).

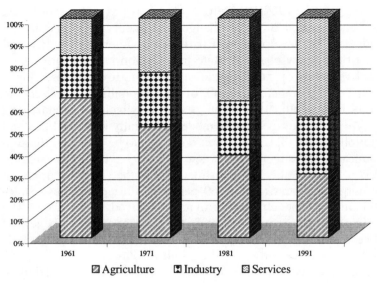

Source: Istat

Figure 4.2: Brindisi's active population by sectors

The power of certain classes such as landowners declined as well as the prestige of some occupations in the public sector while the process of proletarization assumed a positive connotation. The arrival of good work contracts, the stability of employment and its protection through the Cassa Integrazione Guadagni (CIG)[3] were the factors that contributed to raising the status of industrial work. A local sociologist offers a vivid picture of the radical transformation that Brindisi's society was undergoing:

> Workers started to go to work in factories where a rational and coherent organization of work existed, where there was a sequence in which everybody is allocated a task and where it is easy to miss the sense of the whole; it was not as on the land where you saw the blossom of the vineyard and then the harvest. There were people who talked to you using the "Lei",[4] who had completely different styles of life, etc.

It would be misleading however to believe that the settlement of the chemical industry brought a formalization of social relations and of labour market rules. First, the management and implementation of the programme of State intervention soon became a powerful means through which the local political class, especially government Parties,[5] established a clientelistic system of rewards. Financial resources and individual protection, when the crisis hit the industry, went only to individuals and organizations strictly linked to those Parties. The programme of industrialization also allowed the colonization of social life; by assuming a regulative function in social and economic life, they substituted public institutions and their own particular interests for collective ones. In this way, they ended up stifling other forms of collective organization, especially the unions, which became consensus organizations (Donolo et al., 1978). Second, the process of industrialization led to the formation of a partially proletarised working class. It could be argued that the emerging industrial society was based on the complementarity between formal regulation and traditional associative relations (Mingione, 1991; 1993). For example, in addition to working in the petrochemical plant and, therefore, embedded into formal sets of relations and values (primarily technical, e.g. hierarchical relations with supervisors and managers but also membership of trade unions), many workers continued to cultivate their property, which nourished traditional agrarian informal relations (e.g. informal relations with temporary workers, with family helpers but also with local political intermediaries and notables). This became important during the restructuring phase of the mid-1980s when hundreds of workers were made redundant. Without underestimating the trauma of job loss and the reduction of income, the impact was attenuated by the fact that many local workers returned to agriculture to supplement their income and rescue some social recognition.

This peculiar constitution of social relations, hinging upon the co-existence of ascriptive and prescriptive rules, worked its way into the system of employment relations of the newly established Montedison petrochemical plant and, for a long time, blocked the corporatist management of employment relations.[6] As discussed in part two, managers, selected according to their political affiliation, and political leaders became increasingly close in a management of public resources through clientelistic criteria rather than criteria of economic efficiency. Such a management of public companies was bound to have serious implications in the long-term. Yet, although the profits of the State industry companies IRI and ENI[7] were negative at the beginning of the 1970s, the sustainability of the model was questioned only in the first half of the 1980s.

From Dependent Development to Non-Development: Recent Dynamics in Local Society and Economy

At the beginning of the 1980s, Brindisi was hit by the crisis in the chemicals industry. In addition to the negative impact of the oil shock and the slow-down in demand at international level, the main plant also suffered from an unexpected event. The main ethylene cracker blew up in 1977 and marked the start of a restructuring process in which the return to profitability was to be achieved through the modification of corporate culture, with a restoration of healthier corporatist dynamics, and through large-scale dismissals. Shaken by the crisis of the petrochemical plant, the area seemed to suddenly realize that the ambition it had cultivated for long-lasting growth was vanishing. The model of industrialization was flawed. The vertically integrated and capital-intensive plant had produced limited multiplier effects.[8] Whilst it is undeniable that the chemical industry generated hundreds of direct and indirect jobs of good quality, it substantially failed to act as a growth pole (Cerpem, 1990; Ecoter, 1993). The branch plant nature of such a company, vertically integrated with activities located elsewhere in the country, did not favour the development of local firms. Also the initiative launched by Montedison, in coincidence with the restructuring phase of 1978-1983, to favour the start-up of entrepreneurial activities among redundant workers produced scant results. With the redundancy agreement, Montedison committed itself to offer a series of facilities (services, lands, technological and research assistance, etc.) to any redundant workers who were willing to start autonomous business activities. Isomar and Siprosuole were the only two companies that settled within the petrochemical plant, by exploiting the local production of Methl Diphenyl Di-isocyanate (MDI) (Cerpem, 1990). Viesti (1996) reports that 130 new jobs were created and they were not all taken by people on CIG. The lay off of 1700 workers from the petrochemical plant between 1977 and 1983 led to the creation of a pool of middle aged and semi-skilled male workers in the local labour market; many of them, expelled prematurely by the industry, were unable to find a job and ended up enlarging the number of people involved in the local informal economy.

With the end of large-scale State industrial intervention in the south, formally sanctioned under Law 488 in 1992, and of the conception of public companies as the engines of development, the primary objective of State intervention has been the maintenance of personal income and consumption. This has been pursued through public works such as the Brindisi Sud electric power station as well as through income support schemes (Provincia di Brindisi, 1999). In other words, the local fabric has not been able to absorb the shock associated with the crisis of the model of externally-led growth and to promote alternative forms of development. Between 1991 and 1996, the number of employees in the manufacturing sector of the province decreased by 15 per cent, from 17,427 to 14,764 (Istat, 1996). An attempt to slow down these downward trends and activate local resources was made with Brindisi's Territorial Pact, one of the first in Italy. The local social partners (the employers' organization, the three trade unions, the local authorities, the chamber of commerce, some research centres, etc.) have come together to identify the development and employment strategies compatible with local resources and needs. On the basis of the priorities selected, public funds have been requested.[9] Nonetheless, even in this case, the innovative character of the initiative has been dampened by disagreements between the organizations that promoted it and the development agency in charge of selecting the projects destined to benefit from financial support. This again manifests the weakness of the local social context to express economic and social interests untied from political and particularist logic.

At present the unemployment rate is just above 15 per cent (figure 4.3).[10] The recent upward trend is the outcome of two phenomena: first, a growing number of people are looking for a job and, second, forms of under-employment, such as seasonal work, have started to decrease. In relation to the employment dynamics, the data confirm that a declining number of people are involved in the primary sector, whose consistence is substantially reduced (table 4.1). Also, industrial employment has a negative trend compared with Italy as a whole, while employment in the services is constantly rising.

The lasting importance of the primary sector, which has also favoured the emergence of some interesting industrial activities, in the Brindisi economy is however revealed by data on the value of production of the single sectors (table 4.2).

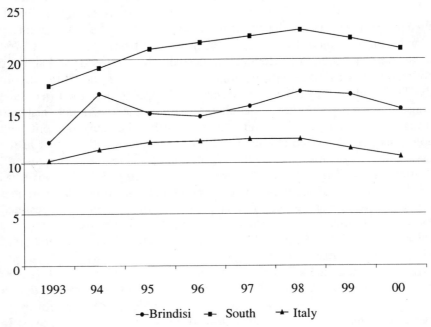

Source: Istat

Figure 4.3: **Unemployment trends by geographical area during the 1990s**

Table 4.1 Employment change in the period 1993-2000 (%)

	Brindisi	**South**	**Italy**
Agriculture	-37.5	-34.7	-3.3
Industry	-3.6	-3.4	0.6
Services	5.3	7.8	9.3
Total	**-6.8**	**-1**	**3**

Source: Istat

The latest available data refer to 1996 and indicate that almost 11 per cent of the value of provincial production is determined by agriculture, at the regional level it is 7.6 per cent. The service sector is the largest, while the manufacturing sector now accounts for 17 per cent of the output compared to almost 22 per cent in the region.

Table 4.2 Composition of the added value by sectors, 1996

	Brindisi	**Puglia**
Agriculture	10.8	7.6
Industry	17.1	21.6
Services	72.1	70.8

Source: Istituto Tagliacarne

Employment in industry revolves around two sectors of external ownership (chemicals and aeronautics, geographically located near the city), and around the food transformation and clothing industries (scattered across the province), both of endogenous ownership (table 4.3).

Table 4.3 Employment in the manufacturing industry, 1996

	Employees	**%**
Food industries	2,029	13.7
Clothing and textile	2,570	17.3
Leather industries	164	1.1
Wood industries and wooden products	563	3.8
Paper, printing and publishing	282	1.9
Coke and petroleum products	51	0.3
Chemicals industries	1,992	13.4
Plastic materials	535	3.6
Mining and quarrying	618	4.2
Metal manufacture	2,571	17.3
Mechanical engineering	734	4.9
Electrical engineering	268	2.5
Transport and communication	1,857	12.5
Other industries	530	3.6
Total	**14,764**	**100**

Source: Provincia di Brindisi, 1999

A recent report by the Province of Brindisi (1999) suggests however that, in connection with the trends indicated above, Brindisi's economy is increasingly characterized by self-employment: the percentage of employees, in fact, decreased from 73.5 per cent in 1993 to 69.4 per cent in 1996. According to this study, the self-employed consist of a minority of "entrepreneurs by choice" and a majority of petty traders who have gone into business because of the absence of other alternatives.

To summarize, although benefiting from massive public investments, the Brindisi area ended up symbolising the flaws and contradictions connected with the regional policy implemented from the 1960s to the 1990s by the Italian State in the south of the country. The process of forced industrialization with the settlement of the chemical industry did not produce a complete displacement effect on the traditional agrarian society of the area: rules of reciprocity were not substituted by neutral and prescriptive market rules but co-determined an institutional configuration whose features influenced the processes of restructuring over the following years.

PART 2 THE ANATOMY OF WORK RE-ORGANIZATION IN THE CHEMICAL INDUSTRY

Industrial Dynamics and Local Corporate Culture, 1960-1980

The Rise and Development of the Industry in the Area

The settlement of the chemical industry in Brindisi originated from the combination of the national political project of the State to attenuate the socio-economic cleavage between the north and the south of the country as well as to expand the nation's chemical industry,[11] and the strategies of the few chemical companies operating nationally during the 1950s. In the industrialization programme of the 1960s, Brindisi was selected as a "growth pole" which cost 130.7 billion Lire between 1962-1968 (Svimez, 1971) and relied upon the chemicals industry. In addition, although formally justified with expectations linked to the expansion of Mediterranean markets, Brindisi, as a location for chemicals, originated from Montecatini's competition with Anic, the two major Italian chemical producers of the time. Montecatini, a chemical and mining conglomerate, entered the petrochemicals business and embarked upon the construction of a huge plant in Brindisi,[12] where it had already had a fertiliser plant since 1929, to respond to Anic's construction of a fertiliser and a petrochemical plant in Ravenna.[13] The plant in Brindisi could refine 1 million tons of oil per annum and the first cracker produced 160,000 tons of ethylene a year. Other products were chlorine, bromine, polymers, PVC and aromatics. At the beginning of its activity in the early 1960s, the plant employed more than 1,000 workers; this number quickly grew to more than 5,000 in 1965. From the very beginning, however, it was clear that Brindisi's sub-optimal production arrangements[14] were having disastrous effects on Montecatini's budgets (Amatori and Brioschi, 1997). To obtain more capital but also to raise capacity for the demand-led boom of petrochemical products, in 1964 Montecatini entered a joint venture with Shell (table 4.4), whose management identified the major limits of the Brindisi plant in its productive arrangements and its excessive workforce. Shell suggested a project of production and work rationalization which was turned down by Montecatini. Two years later, it again became the sole owner of the plant. In the meantime, after the nationalization of electrical energy in 1962, the capital gained by Edison[15] allowed it to invest in petrochemicals production and to become Montecatini's major internal competitor towards which it soon looked for an alliance. The companies merged in 1968. Montedison was born without a precise corporate strategy and from two companies that, because of the excessive diversification of their investments, shared financial and productivity problems (Barca, 1997).

Table 4.4 Business changes in the Brindisi's petrochemical plant

Year	Operation
1929	Montecatini (fertilizers)
1959	Montecatini (petrochemical production)
1964	Monteshell (joint venture Montecatini-Shell)
1966	Shell leaves the company
1968	Montedison (merger Montecatini-Edison)
1987	EniChem-Anic (EniChem-Anic 75%, Montedison 15%, Himont 10%)
1988	EniMont (joint venture ENI-Montedison)
1990	ENI buys the remaining 40% of the company's shares
1990	EniChem (petrochemical production)

Corporate Culture and Internal Labour Market: a Tripartite Pact between Parties, Management and Unions

Although born as a private company, the corporate culture of Montedison was affected by the role it had been given, like other companies, by the Italian State. The public money received to locate in the south of the country to fulfil the role of engine of development, fed a culture of business unaccountability and of political interference influencing the interactions between management and workers, leading to the deterioration of the corporatist model of regulation of employment relations. As argued by Trigilia (1992), the influence of political parties in management undermined efficiency, and companies like Montedison came to symbolize scarce economic efficiency and high political productivity. In Brindisi, the influence of the local political class started with the action of lobbying by the local DC to the national parliament. The management was chosen on the basis of "its capacity to be friendly with politicians so as to obtain more money for the plant", while workers were selected on the basis of their membership of certain trade unions. "There was a time, around the mid-1970s, in which membership of CISL (Confederazione Italiana Sindacati dei Lavoratori)[16] was the decisive element to enter the plant: indeed, I might say that 90 per cent of unionised workers belonged to that union."[17] This DC-led consensus became the mechanism regulating the employment relations. One major effect of this system was the over-manning of the petrochemical plant. Thus, whilst it is true that one of the features of the Fordist model of organization of work was its tendency to generate excessive workforce as demarcation barriers existing between occupations limited worker mobility (see Amin, 1994), the Italian chemical companies accentuated this trait. Indeed, the system of financial incentives to plants in the south under extraordinary intervention, was linked to personnel numbers. In this picture, the unions extended their power both within and outside the workplace, by practising the politics of consensus. They became important actors in decisions concerning which workers should be hired in the plant. As acknowledged by a senior trade unionist:

> Our offices were assaulted by people who wanted to work in the petrochemical plant. It seemed to be a job centre, ... we tried to help as many as we could, those who were close to the union.

Two intertwined dynamics emerged as a consequence. First, although market trends often dictated plant closures or the substitution of some production lines, measures to reduce the workforce were never implemented due to the commitment to safeguarding the existing employment. Second, hiring episodes, which did not respond to any cost evaluation, characterized plant life. An example is given by the immediate hiring, at the beginning of the 1980s, of 700 workers under the so-called Grandi plan before the actual start of the programme that aimed to double plant capacity.[18] In the Brindisi petrochemical plant there were workers who were literally doing nothing all day or reserved marginal maintenance operations. The organization of work reflected the excess workforce. First, as explained by a retired top manager of the company, "there was no scientific approach to define the number of people needed to carry out a task". Indeed:

> there was the so-called K factor [used to hire workers], given by the ratio between the number of working hours in a year and the number of employees. As it was 5 point something, 6 people were deemed indispensable.

Second, the petrochemical plant retained in-house a series of services. Except for the catering and cleaning services, all the others were provided internally. This significantly raised labour costs as those workers were given the same favourable work conditions negotiated under the national chemicals contract, one of the best in terms of wage and employment relations, although their utilization was intermittent.

The Restructuring Phase of the Mid-1980s

The Macro-Economic Picture and the Political Re-organization of the Chemical Sector

The international chemical market, especially for heavy chemical products, suffered a serious backlash during the 1980s. The recession phase was fuelled by the rapid increase in the price of raw materials following the second oil shock in the second half of the 1970s. In addition, during the decade, the competitive advantage of Western companies, based principally on technology, reduced, allowing the proliferation of new producers; these built up their own chemical industry to decrease their dependence on imports. This situation created the conditions for global over-capacity,[19] also exacerbated by a search for economies of scale as a means of reducing unit costs (Ranci and Vacca', 1979). The Italian chemical industry however had already started to experience difficulties by the end of the 1960s. As internal consumption grew more than output, in the five years from 1967 to

1971, the trade deficit rose by ten times (Economia Italiana, 1997). At the beginning of the 1980s, therefore, the competitive position of the main Italian companies was substantially worse than that of their competitors, especially in terms of the burden of debt and the limited amount of research activity (table 4.5). They also lagged behind in terms of business re-organization (figure 4.4). The general economic circumstances and the specific situation of the Italian industry compelled the Italian State to re-organize the sector by delineating its strategic lines. Despite the injection of capital provided by ENI to Montedison at the end of the 1960s, through the acquisition of a consistent number of shares,[20] the management of Montedison was not able to implement the strategic policy it had planned, consisting of the exit from the petrochemical business and the strengthening of its presence in light chemicals.

Table 4.5 Comparisons among the main international chemical groups (1980-1981)

	Income before tax/ turnover	Income after tax/ turnover	Interests and fin. expenses/ gross operating profit	Interests and fin. expenses/ turnover	R&D/ turnover
Montedison	-6.6	-6.3	154.9	11.3	2.2
Anic		-17.2	101.3*	5.1*	1
Rhone-Poulenc	-3.4	-3.8	79.8	5.5	6.1
Atochimie	-8.4	-1	45.6	2.2	1.7
BASF	4.3	1.2	n.a.	n.a.	3.5
Bayer	4.5	1.8	40.6	4.2	8.2
Hoechst	4.2	1.3	29.2	3.2	5.4
ICI	5	1.2	18.3	2	3.6
DuPont	8.9	5.1	9.8	1.6	3.2
Monsanto	6.6	4.3	n.a.	0.8	10.7
Dow Chemical	8.9	6.3	20.6	3.4	3.3

=calculated for 1980
Source: Federchimica, 1991

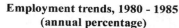

Employment trends, 1980 - 1985
(annual percentage)

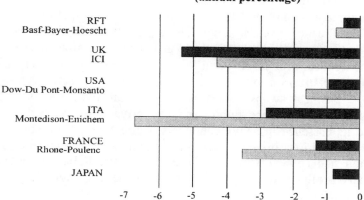

Data for Italian companies 1981 - 1984, for American companies 1982 - 1984

Employment trends, 1985 - 1989
(annual percentage)

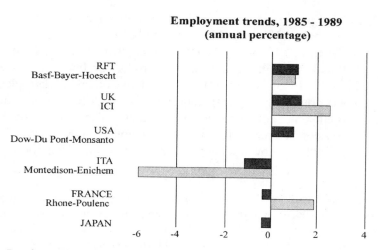

Data for American companies 1986 - 1988

Source: Federchimica, 1991

Figure 4.4: Employment trends in the major chemical companies of six developed countries

Yet, for a long time, private chemical companies (Montedison, Sir, Liquichimica) and EniChem were competing in the same markets with the same products. It was only in 1982 that a concrete attempt to re-organize the sector was made. The National Chemical Plan, put forth by De Michelis[21] and approved by the Italian Parliament, encouraged the two main Italian chemical groups, ENI and Montedison to rationalize. The plan foresaw the specialization of each group in their core activities, also through some business swaps, and aimed at creating two spheres in the Italian chemical industry, one public and one private. Accordingly, ENI consolidated its presence in heavy chemicals, while Montedison sought to concentrate its efforts in light chemicals and pharmaceuticals. The rationalization had some effect: from the mid-1980s, Italian companies started to make profits again even if this was also due to favourable market circumstances (table 4.6).

Industrial Restructuring and Redundancies in Brindisi during the 1980s

Falling demand coupled with rising costs of raw materials and the presence of new producers heavily affected the petrochemical plant in Brindisi, which also had its own technical problems. In 1975, the topping plant, in which crude oil was processed to obtain virgin naphtha and diesel oil, was halted due to technical problems and it started to be supplied directly with virgin naphtha. Then, in 1977, the P2T ethylene cracker blew up. Without the topping plant and the main cracker, the few production lines still active (the Vinyl Chloride Monomer (VCM) plant and the other cracker plant producing 80,000 tons per annum) required the importation of raw materials such as ethylene, polyethylene and butadiene. The viability of the plant was seriously compromized. Reduced production brought a large rise in unit costs. As indicated by a senior manager of Montedison, now in EniChem:

> fixed costs represented 28-32 per cent of the annual turnover, a very high percentage if one considers that they are good when they are below 10 per cent, and we had up to 20 per cent loss for each unit of product. This was because polyethylene for instance was produced for 800 Lire and sold at 750 Lire.

Table 4.6 Net operating income of the main Italian chemical companies during the 1980s (million of dollars)

	1982	1983	1984	1985	1986	1987	1988	1989
Montedison	-717	-315	-26	243	464	527	490	362
Enimont							844	740
EniChem	n.a.	-651	-159	-387	...	131	496	...

The value for Enimont have been calculated pro-forma
Source: Federchimica, 1991

In these circumstances, Montedison decided to close its activity in Brindisi. The company's incapacity to adapt to the new market conditions as well as its intention to pursue the business re-orientation indicated in the National Chemical Plan suggested the dis-investment of the operations in Brindisi as the only viable solution. In 1978 the first 800 workers left the plant. It was the intervention of the State, propelled by massive union-led demonstrations in Rome that forced the company to modify its decision: trade unions and the company were invited to negotiate a process of restructuring without plant closure. They agreed on a restructuring plan through which, using public money, Montedison sought to re-organize production, also through the rebuilding of the ethylene plant (Chemical Week, 23-12-1981), promote new investments in technologies and downsize the workforce. Another 700 workers were made redundant out of a total of roughly 4000 workers in 1983-1984. Wage protection, ensured by CIG, was used extensively, and special laws were approved to allow the termination of employment through incentives such as early retirement schemes. Workers with families and children were given preference when deciding who kept their jobs. The negotiated solution of Brindisi's crisis did not however conclude the history of its problems. During the second half of the 1980s, Montedison's "aggressive policy of growth" (Amatori and Brioschi, 1997, p.141) led the company into other financial difficulties which, once again, ENI was called on to limit. A merger occurred between the two companies, which led to the constitution of Enimont first, and then, with the collapse of Montedison, ENI came to control all Italian petrochemical production (refer to table 4.4).

Regaining Efficiency: Explaining the Redundancies of the 1990s

The 1990s mark the decade in which the process of consolidation of the chemical industry in Brindisi was pursued, with substantial steps taken to regain efficiency. Like its competitors, EniChem rationalized its presence in the chemical market by focussing on core activities (heavy chemical products) and dis-investing from its least profitable businesses (fibres and agricultural businesses). The downward profitability trend of the late 1980s was halted as the process of business consolidation started to be fruitful after 1993 (figure 4.5).[22] Figure 4.6 shows EniChem's most recent financial performance. This strategy has also allowed the company to strengthen its position in the European market, now constituting 90 per cent of its sales (figure 4.7), with some remarkable market shares (table 4.7). In addition, central government's intention to privatize it has led EniChem to pursue a series of joint ventures with foreign companies to exploit company-based competences as well as to reduce competition in certain markets.

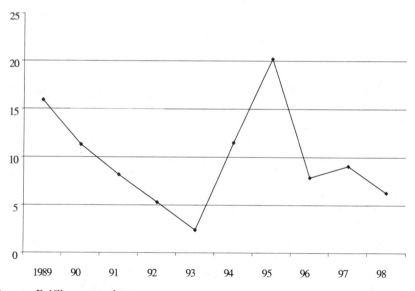

Source: EniChem annual reports

Figure 4.5: EniChem's profits as a percentage of sales during the 1990s

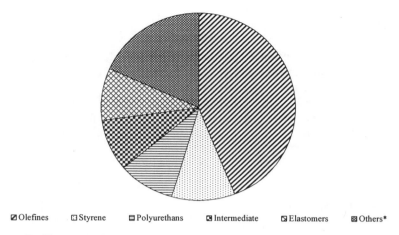

☑ Olefines   ▣ Styrene   ▤ Polyurethans   ◪ Intermediate   ◪ Elastomers   ▨ Others*

Source: EniChem annual reports

Figure 4.6: EniChem's turnover by class of business (million of Euro)

* Others= Products sold by foreign trading companies and services

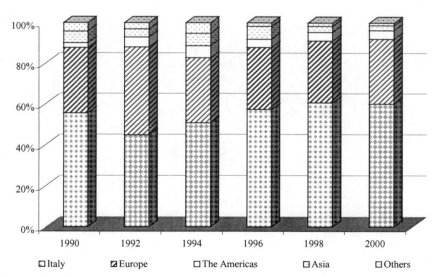

☐ Italy   ☑ Europe   ☐ The Americas   ☐ Asia   ☐ Others

Source: EniChem annual reports

Figure 4.7: EniChem's turnover by geographical areas

Table 4.7 EniChem in the 1990s

Business area	Business description & main products	Examples of application	EniChem position
	Olefins and aromatics (ethylene, propylene, butadiene)	Intermediate products for the plastics industry, solvents, fine chemicals, tyres, antifreeze products	European leader for ethylene, second producer of benzene, third producers of xylene
Petrochemical	Intermediate (phenol)		Second European producer of phenol
	Intermediate for Polyurethanes, Chlorine (MDI, TDI, soda)	Vehicle components, furniture, footwear, construction materials decorating	Third European producer of TDI
Polymers	Styrene	Industrial and food packaging, vehicle components, semi-conductor and micro-electronic packaging	Second European producer of styrene
	Elastomers	Tyres, footwear, adhesives, building products	European leader in SBR and BR tyres

As a consequence, in the 1990s three important companies, one of which has now ceased trading, located in Brindisi. Polimeri Europa was born from a joint venture with Union Carbide for the production of polyethylene and olefins;[23] Montell, a joint venture with Shell, specialized in polypropylene. Finally, European Vinyls Corporation (EVC), which closed in December 1999, was the result of a business agreement with ICI for the production of vinyls. The petrochemicals site is currently the location of EniChem, Polimeri Europa, Montell, ChemGas and Dow Chemical[24] which exploit common infrastructures and facilities. Outside the petrochemicals area, are Exxon-Mobil (formerly Mobil Plastics Europe) and Aventis (formerly Lepetit), historically successful activities in Brindisi, and other locally-owned companies which are consolidating, some of them with funds from the Territorial Pact (table 4.8). The employment trends of some of these companies are indicated in figure 4.8.

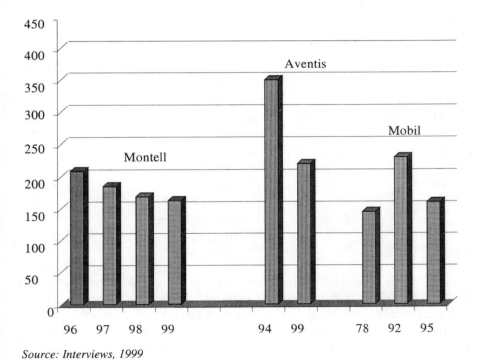

Source: Interviews, 1999

Figure 4.8: Employment trends in some chemical companies in Brindisi (various years)

Table 4.8 Chemical producers in Brindisi

Producers	Business description	Employees
Within the petrochemical plant		
EniChem	Ethylene, butadiene, olefins, aromatics	1,500
Polimeri Europa	Polyethylene and olefins	290
Montell	Polyethylene	163
ChemGas	Gassy substances	n.a.
Dow Chemical	MDI (polyutheranes)	180
Outside the petrochemical plant		
Aventis	Pharmaceutical products	201
Exxon-Mobil	Cling film in polypropylene	160
Europlastic Sud	Plastic materials	n.a.
Europlastica	Plastic materials	n.a.
San Marco Sub	Diving suits	2
Icem	Waterproof products	13
Ri.Be.	Audio and video cassettes	9
Areta	Plastic furniture	27
Camassa	Plastic pipes	20
A.G.Scavi	Plastic materials	12
P.P.E.	Polyethylene containers	19
Polyman	Plastic packing	11
Giano Plastica	Plastic materials	30

EniChem's promotion of the joint ventures mentioned above has also been interpreted as a sign of its complete exit from the chemical sector.[25] The most recent news seems to confirm such an interpretation. EniChem is planning, in fact, to transfer to Polimeri Europa all its value-added activities (such as elastomers, styrene and aromatics), while maintaining businesses to be marginal and, therefore, planned for closure in the near future (e.g. chlorine) (Il Sole-24 Ore, 28-12-2001). In addition, EniChem is defining a joint venture with the Saudi company Sabic which would acquire 51% of Polimeri Europa; by 2005, EniChem will sell its remaining shares. Consequently, the tormented ownership structure in Brindisi is destined again to suffer modifications. As explained by ENI's president, "the heavy chemicals sector is highly competitive on a price basis and highly cyclical on a profit basis. There is zero brand loyalty .... and advantages of product innovation have a short life span" (EIU, 1999, p.15). The return to efficiency is therefore complex and revolves around a variety of strategies, as can be seen below.

Technology-Led Changes

Brindisi's chemical companies have sought to maintain adequate levels of efficiency and market share through the progressive sophistication of their technological apparatus and knowledge. Companies in the area are adopting second generation technologies, namely new catalysts, to obtain enhanced product performance in purity, clarity and variety of uses at lower costs. Technological innovation leading to the intensification of the production process and modification of product is, as theoretically contended by the business cycles approach, generating an almost automatic rationalization of the workforce in Brindisi. As explained by the manager of a local company:

> Technological innovation is the greatest job reducer. Today the companies located in petrochemicals produce two or three times more than when the plant was at its maximum employment peak. I think EniChem now produces 2 million tons of plastic material with 1,500 people. Just before the restructuring phase, with 5,000 people, the production was 700 tons.

The labour-saving impact of technology as an explanatory cause of redundancies is also offered by the officer for the industry of a local union:

> ... the methods of production of ethylene and polyethylene have changed. The replacement of workers coincided with the introduction of new installations. A cracker could once employ 400 people, now there may be 70 or 80.

EniChem's polyethylene production illustrates the effects of technological innovation. In less than a decade from 1993, production, concentrated in one plant rather than three, has doubled reaching 400,000 tons per annum, whilst the number of workers has halved (from 150 to 70) as well as home energy costs (-50 per cent) and maintenance costs (-25 per cent).[26] The process of technological innovation has not created new jobs either; recent productive investments in the area have created no or minimum employment opportunities. For instance, during 1996-1997, Polimeri Europa invested 400 billion Lire in Brindisi, in addition to roughly 800 billion Lire spent between 1992 and 1994. The gas-phase plant uses Unipol PE technology, Union Carbide's most celebrated technology to manufacture polyethylene. The plant combines high-pressure solution and slurry polyethylene technology to obtain maximum effectiveness and versatility of output for different commercial uses, while respecting environmental standards. The new process has improved the quality of output, batch-to-batch consistency is ensured and the production process allows major economic savings. Polimeri is expected to produce 400,000 tons of polyethylene with 300 workers. There were 290 when the company started up (Provincia di Brindisi, 1999).

Changes in Work Organization

The second factor that explains redundancies in the chemical industry is organizational changes, implemented to improve cost-effectiveness. Two processes are underway. First, outsourcing has particularly involved EniChem and a few other companies that had adopted a vertically integrated organization of production. By externalising support activities, they are favouring the rise of autonomous, specialized, companies. EniChem has outsourced maintenance and engineering; it has retained in-house training and logistics while leasing, for instance, security and the fire service to other plants located in the petrochemical area. The choice of outsourcing is dictated by deploying the core workforce to core activities. As the manager of a local chemical company clearly explained:

> Some of the activities that we used to carry out internally with a very low level of efficiency have been given to others who employ the same number of workers or even more. Connected to our company, there are three other little companies that either work our products or give us a service. ... The bigger the companies the more rigidity they develop internally. When in a single system there are highly sophisticated process operations and activities with low professional content, the latter tend to become bottlenecks for the company.

Clearly, in many cases, job losses in the chemicals sector do not correspond to absolute losses but rather to the transfer of jobs to subcontracting companies operating in other industrial sectors, although no data is available on the scale of this phenomenon. The second process consists of organizational changes associated with the adoption of new management models. Therefore, job losses occur as a consequence of internal re-organization brought about by the automation of production processes and the electronic system of control of the production process which has rendered some of the previous workers superfluous. They are also related to the process of multi-skilling involved by new forms of employment policies. Thus, as stressed by a local personnel manager:

> ... our preferred organizational model implies a different way to operate through job enrichment, with more autonomy and qualification. Workers are required to be more flexible, more qualified and responsible ... [for instance] it's worthless putting a supervisor for each three professional workers if the professional who runs the plant is able, because of his/her qualifications and the organization of work, to run it by him/herself.

The EVC Dis-investment: Efficiency and Plant Closure

During 1999, Brindisi's chemical industry witnessed the redundancy of 160 workers in coincidence with the closure of the local EVC plant. This joint venture between EniChem and ICI had become the leader of PVC production in Europe with a series of plants spread across the continent. Job loss in Brindisi can be explained neither by the economic performance of the site nor by inflexibility connected to the presence of trade unions, as we would expect following the orthodox argument. Indeed, as clarified by one of the workers made redundant:

> Brindisi was the only Italian site in which the theoretical capacity [the one allowed by the installations] and real capacity of production [the effective one, accounting for break-downs and maintenance] were the same, that is to say 185 thousand tons of VCM and 140 thousand tons of PVC. And this was obtained with 160 people.

Similarly, a unionist stressed in an interview:

> To render the plant more efficient than the others, we [unions] have swallowed an agreement according to which workers could have been asked to carry out additional tasks to the usual ones. Yet, eight months before the closure, we agreed for the plant to outsource all the services with further savings as fixed costs became variable ones.

The decision to close the plant has been explained by the corporation and local managers as the outcome of a strategy of rationalization aiming to achieve economies of scale in relation to both production and markets, which led to the concentration of production activity in certain sites while closing others. In other words, the Brindisi EVC plant was the victim of an intra-corporate process of rationalization which has no regard for the site's efficiency. This is only partly true. Concretely, a combination of different causes contributed to the plant closure. First, the plant was penalized by market trends. The market for PVC is suffering from saturation and the price of the product is low. For companies like EVC, specialized in just one product, market problems become serious threats to their very existence. Diversification strategies are not possible. Nor are dis-investments. Second, despite having a leading role in the European market, company performance was compromized by competition from countries such as Romania or other Eastern European countries, which are managing to produce PVC at lower costs. This is possible because the quality of the material used is lower and the environmental standards for the production of plastic products are not so stringent as in the European Union. In addition, in these countries, active industrial policies are encouraging the settlement of Western chemical companies through financial incentives and rapid administrative procedures for their localization. Third, the plant has suffered from the slow growth of Mediterranean markets, such as the Turkish or the Egyptian markets, which were supposed to become the major buyers of the Brindisi products. As explained by one of the plant managers:

> The strategy is to cover the local [Italian] market with three sites [Ravenna, Porto Marghera, Porto Torres] rather than with four. Brindisi should have served the Mediterranean market which was thought to be in expansion. This has not happened. Brindisi had started to serve more central markets which, however, are closer to other sites.

The episode concerning EVC confirms that the reading of redundancies and restructuring processes provided by the neo-classical position is mis-placed to the extent to which plant closures are explained exclusively through the argument of profitability. Indeed, the understanding of the corporate motives for shutting down specific plants can, as shown by the EVC case, leave aside profitability evaluations. Such events are more complex and need to be related both to the structure of activities within corporations (MacLachlan, 1992; Townsend and Peck, 1985) and to the wider market situation (e.g. Massey, 1995).

The Quiet Transformation: the Socially-Legitimated Modification of the
Employment Relation and the Corporatist Construction of Industrial
Unemployed

Besides the adjustments above, another process of restructuring is taking place in the local chemical industry. In addition to the strategy of not-replacing retired workers, companies are seeking to achieve greater cost-effectiveness through a unique programme of substitution between fathers and sons. Foreseen by the Law 223/91 among the instruments to be adopted in case of redundancy, the programme allows local chemical companies, with the consensus of trade unions, to invite workers, usually the ones closer to retirement, to leave the company to be replaced by their sons. The convenience of this programme, through which 300 hundred young people entered local companies in the period 1994-1999,[27] is that it allows consistent cost gains. First, new workers cost less than workers who have spent longer in a company, due to career progression. Second, the new, better-qualified workers do not take up extra costs in training. More importantly, the programme is producing the first, positive effects on plant efficiency. An example is provided by a local manager:

> the new workers are able, because they've got the competence, to test the product during the production phase; before, this operation was done by special laboratories, hence the production process used to have some interruptions. In this way, the time for a complete production cycle has been reduced by 15 per cent.

In addition, the programme is an expression of a corporate desire to change the industrial culture, as openly admitted by the same manager:

> The substitution programme between fathers and sons is having beneficial effects: it is making the workforce look younger, workers are more qualified. Obviously there are cost savings but this is not the main reason for us to implement it. The main reason lies in the fact that in this way the company has at its disposal a more flexible and available workforce in relation to its needs.

Younger and more qualified workers, often new entrants in the labour market, are deemed to be culturally more prepared than old workers to accept new labour market rules. Accordingly, with such workers, companies are more likely to start an employment relation on the basis of atypical contracts (part-time, apprenticeship, temporary contracts, etc.)[28]

and implement flexible work practices (job rotation, team work, etc.). It is clear that the use of such instruments is expected to undermine the traditional organization of work within chemical companies as well as the more general conception that a job in the industry is a job for life. It also sanctions the new identity of chemical companies in the community. The market orientation of the industry has amplified the need to abandon any lingering social obligation. As the personnel manager of a local company put it in an interview:

> Companies do not operate for moral or charitable aims, but they are driven by profit and by results, otherwise they do not stand up.

An important aspect of the quiet transformation is that it is legitimized by both workers and unions, fully aware of restricted employment opportunities (in 2000, the unemployment rate in the area was 15.2 per cent) and of national policies on flexible work practices. Motivated by the fact that the new job will benefit the same family, old workers are accepting early retirement. The unions, apart from a few contrasting remarks by some members, have become increasingly attuned to company interests. The comment below by a local union officer confirms the Marxist emphasis on the disciplining function of unemployment:

> For quite a few years now development has been based on geographical competition for funds. Our companies operate in a free market. That's why workers need to understand that things have changed, there have been too many privileges and this is also the unions' fault. Workers must be committed, flexible and learn how to work.

It is in this search to pragmatically adapt to counterpart needs and to look for commonly advantageous conditions that unions have also agreed upon a series of measures enhancing flexibility in the workplace. These are bringing a reduction in costs but, according to expectations, they should also lead to the creation of employment opportunities. With union consensus, Brindisi's chemical companies are in the position of taking advantage of an array of options to implement different flexible work arrangements, including job rotation and team work, longer shifts when there are peaks of production and wage flexibility (thus cutting out overtime).

The corporatist construction of redundant workers It is clear that the process of industrial restructuring, which is leading to the re-composition of the chemical company workforce through the consensual redundancy of some workers and the creation of new employment, has not occurred neutrally. Union consensus, ensuring social peace in a background of State income protection,[29] has allowed local chemical companies to divest themselves of undesirable members of their workforce and to strengthen it around new values. Indeed, after the collective dismissals of the mid-1980s during which social protection criteria were taken into account, company management of the surplus workforce has occurred in a more careful way, increasingly through individual agreements, which have aimed at restoring precisely the conditions of internal efficiency. Therefore, the process of industrial adjustment has combined with specific, contextual, social dynamics, an expression of modified preferences in the labour market. The nature of current redundancies in the chemical sector is understandable not merely by looking at the macro-economic dynamics affecting the industry but also at the way in which contexualized social dynamics shape economic processes and labour market behaviours, defining, for instance, the social groups called to participate in it.

To conclude, the presence of the chemicals industry in Brindisi responded to the national political economy of the 1960s and 1970s pursuing the objectives of the industrial development and modernization of the area. It is with the modification of its original objectives, for the creation of employment opportunities and for the support of incomes, that the industry performance started to be compromized. In particular, the systematic influence of political parties on capital and labour relations, through the twofold co-optation of management and trade unions, altered the traditional regulation of the employment relation. This did not respond to the competitive dynamics between capital and labour but, rather, to political determination. At the beginning of the 1980s, the combination of local, national and international factors created the conditions for the restructuring of Montedison that implied downsizing and redundancies. During the 1990s, job losses have occurred because of company's intensification of the pace of technological innovation and of internal re-organization; in addition, a means to gain cost-effectiveness is consisting of the re-composition of its occupational base through the substitution of older workers with their sons. This is entailing a rise in productivity and the reduction of labour costs. Such a transformation is a quiet one as it is producing no net job losses. Also for this reason, it is taking place with union consensus that reflects worker willingness to maintain job opportunities in the area, although with modified employment prerogatives.

PART 3 INDUSTRIAL UNEMPLOYMENT IN THE CLOTHING INDUSTRY

Production Fragmentation and Non-Competitive Labour Markets

The Current Features of the Industry and Some Historical Indications

The clothing industry is central to the economy of Brindisi; the sector consists of 264 firms and employs slightly more than 2,500 workers, 17.3 per cent of the total manufacturing workforce (Istat, 1996). It is especially crucial if the weight of the informal economy[30] is taken into account.[31] The industry is based on a fabric of small and medium enterprises: craft-based companies of small or very small dimensions constitute the bulk of the local industry. Four different types of production characterize it: jackets and coats, representing the most sophisticated products, shirts, jeans and trousers and, finally, lingerie (table 4.9).

Table 4.9 Clothing production in Brindisi

Product	Company dimension	Segment of the market[32]	Competitive factors
Jackets and coats	Medium/large	Medium/high	Quality, time, specialization
Shirts	Medium/small	Medium/low	Quality/costs
Lingerie	Small	Low	Costs
Jeans and trousers	Small	Low	Costs

The output is only partially sold without the mediation of external buyers, although the province's export of clothing products and furs increased by 13 per cent in 1998 in relation to 1997 (Istat, 1999).[33] Brindisi's clothing companies are embedded in a system of product specialization in which they form one of the links in a more complex production chain (figure 4.9).

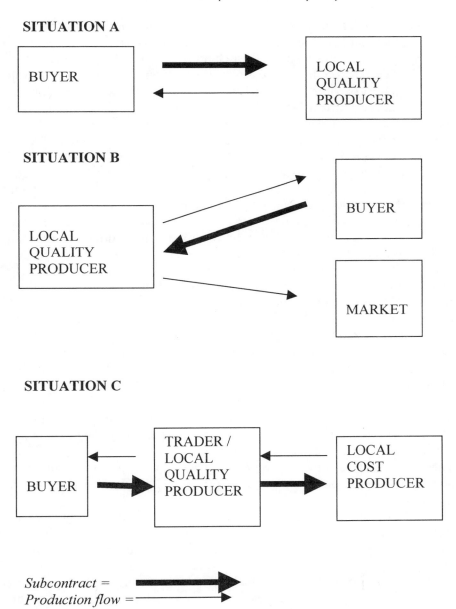

Figure 4.9: Production relations in Brindisi's clothing industry

They are subcontractors of external buyers mainly located in the north of Italy, that can be either big distribution chains or some of the world's most famous fashion designers (Moschino, Biagiotti, Marzotto, Benetton, Dino AR, Perla, etc.). In some cases, part of a firms' production is sold in street markets or little supermarkets. Depending on the quality of the product and on the relationship with the external buyer, local companies can be classified as quality or cost-based producers.[34] Quality producers work directly for the buyers who, usually, supply them with both the fabric and the design to produce the final product. Buyers request limited production batches and operate tight controls on quality. A privileged relationship with buyers is therefore founded upon a combination of the quality of the product, the punctuality of supply and, obviously, the cost of labour which ensures them adequate profit margins. Cost-based producers, mainly smaller and family units, may sometimes have a direct relationship with external buyers. More frequently, though, they sell to a trader or other companies (e.g. more structured companies) which either subcontract to them part of their production or act as a service firm, often supplying them with machines, designs, fabrics, so that producers are attributed the role of assembling the product.[35] In theory, there could be more than one subcontracting step on the hypothetical production ladder. The sequence of steps does however play a determining role in producing a loss of shares in the added value produced and a downward pressure on costs: in this framework, in fact, it is the traders or buyers who, due to their access to the market, decide the price of products. Companies operating in the hidden economy are exclusively cost producers. The vast majority of them are "phase subcontractors": they specialize in carrying out a single operation (such as ironing) rather than in producing the whole ply (Capriati, 1995). Their competitive advantage lies in the capacity to execute labour intensive phases of production at a very low price; this is possible due to tax avoidance.

There is, thus, considerable diversity among local firms. Only some of them are able to meet the qualitative and technical standards required by their buyers. Such companies are financially viable; their focus is on the quality of the product and on efficient time supply. The vast majority of local firms, however, play a marginal role in the clothing production chain. Their only competitive lever lies in price competitiveness, achieved by compressing costs. This segment of the industry works on tight profit margins. Their limited financial viability has a deep impact both on company organization and on its commercial relations with buyers.

The development and consolidation of the industry in Brindisi is related to the restructuring patterns of northern firms. In contrast to the strategies adopted after the mid-1970s by the clothing industry in many industrialized countries (e.g. Germany) to decentralize the most labour-intensive phases of production to developing countries, in Italy the decentralization occurred from north to south.[36] In addition, it focused on quality and product diversification besides cost gains (Fornengo, 1978). It is difficult to quantify the phenomenon in Italy, as data are based on firm-specific case studies. However, as indicated by Viesti (1998), decentralization also occurred during the mid-1980s, as the result of work saturation among northern subcontractors. A survey conducted by Texabb[37] in 1991 showed that almost 54 per cent of a sample of southern companies worked as subcontractors. Specifically, Brindisi's clothing companies displayed a much higher dependence on buyers as more than 81 per cent of local units were subcontractors, with 77 per cent of local employees (table 4.10). In general the differential in the cost of labour for the two areas was 40 per cent (Cerpem, 1991).

Non-Competitive Labour Markets and Local Industrial Cultures

Firms in the sector therefore vary in terms of size and financial viability as well as technological capacity and are split into markets that are not competitive with each other. This structural diversity implies different levels at which wages are offered and accepted, and different social meanings are attributed to wages by different employers and workers. Labour market dynamics in the hidden segment of the local economy[38] have a peripheral nature[39] although, as suggested by several studies, the work in the hidden economy often represents the option of individuals who have limited professional qualifications or who decide to undertake professional paths alternative to the ones connected to the prevailing capitalist mode of production (see review in Chiarello, 1983). Work is the expression of a local economy that does not produce a sufficient number of employment opportunities to satisfy the needs of labour. Wages are low and respond to an underlying culture that claims that a minimal income is better than nothing. Without any legal guarantees, wages become a source of income for irregular workers; entries and exits from paid work are primarily related to the changing needs of a family and to demand fluctuations. These factors allow neither long-term career planning nor the acquisition of technical and professional capacities that are dissipated by the continuous interruptions of the work path (Provincia di Brindisi, 1999).

Table 4.10 A sample of southern clothing and textile companies

Province	Subcontractors		Autonomous		Both		Total	
	L.U.	Empl.	L.U.	Empl.	L.U.	Empl.	L.U.	Empl.
Teramo	75.2	67.6	21.3	28.8	3.5	3.6	100.0	100.0
Chieti	85.4	56.4	9.8	39.7	4.9	3.9	100.0	100.0
Pescara	76.6	51.2	14.1	33.8	9.4	15.0	100.0	100.0
Campo-basso	90.0	88.0	0.0	0.0	10.0	12.0	100.0	100.0
Salerno	40.7	42.3	38.9	31.4	20.4	26.3	100.0	100.0
Potenza	100.0	100.0	0.0	0.0	0.0	0.0	100.0	100.0
Avellino	50.0	27.7	43.8	65.8	6.3	6.5	100.0	100.0
Benevento	85.7	78.4	0.0	0.0	14.3	21.6	100.0	100.0
Bari	31.6	26.5	60.2	64.3	8.3	9.2	100.0	100.0
Taranto	35.7	29.8	50.0	47.4	14.3	22.7	100.0	100.0
Lecce	59.5	52.0	27.8	29.3	12.7	18.7	100.0	100.0
Brindisi	81.5	77.2	11.1	9.1	7.4	13.6	100.0	100.0
Napoli	19.8	18.1	65.8	65.1	14.4	16.8	100.0	100.0
Total	**53.7**	**45.9**	**36.6**	**42.3**	**9.7**	**11.9**	**100.0**	**100.0**

L.U.= Local Units   *Empl= Employees*

Source: Viesti, 2000

This segment also contains entrepreneurs who started their businesses by imitating others, but soon encountered difficulties with the market. As indicated by a local CNA officer, "there has been a lot of improvisation, many have become entrepreneurs but they suffer from a cultural deficit [incapacity to manage a company]". They have not been able to improve their initial status because of the lack of basic managerial instruments and of financial viability and are, therefore, trapped into a short-term vision of the business. Theirs is a busy and endless search for orders, which they manage to meet due to their capacity to compress the cost of labour. Relationships between capital and labour in this segment of the industry are dominated by reciprocity practices. Concretely, workers and employers are bound into situations which may span from complicity (e.g. workers do not pay taxes on their income or do not lose income subsidies, while employers do not pay the indirect costs of labour) to situations of exploitation (these are the cases in which the workers' need to work becomes a source of completely uneven power relations at their expense). In any case, no commitment links employers and workers and this has a great influence on the production process. As activities in this segment of the market are unregulated by the formal institutions of society (Castells, 1989), so too the conditions at which labour is provided have no formal regulation. The definition of working hours, of labour shifts, of job tasks, etc. is left to face-to-face bargaining. Also, the process of wage-setting occurs on the basis of informal negotiations with clear problems of power relations. This concerns exclusively the quantification of a monthly level of earning while excluding all costs existing on top of salary (national insurance, health, pension contributions, etc.). Obviously, the workforce is not unionised and dismissal procedures occur in the absence of orders and according to criteria identified by the employer.

The formal segment of the economy presents cost-based and quality producers in a qualitatively different labour market situation. Employment dynamics in companies competing on cost are similar to those in the hidden economy. Whilst formally respecting collective bargaining, such companies use a series of irregularities to save on the cost of labour; for instance, savings are often achieved through administrative irregularities (companies declare less employees than they actually have) and, especially, through the intensification of work, the elimination of holidays, etc. Mutual distrust renders the work environment tense. The workforce is scarcely unionised and, when this exists, it is not regarded with favour by the employers. The dynamics between labour and capital in the companies indicated as quality producers are rather different. These companies are the outcome of employer commitment to create efficient and profitable economic ventures. Long-term projects inform their action. The propensity to invest in process and product innovation is higher, as is the training of their workforce. At the same time, the workforce consists of qualified and experienced workers who display commitment and loyalty to the company. Turnover is low. A combination of reciprocal and prescriptive rules guide workplace dynamics which tend to be more co-operative and fair. Wages are fixed to national sectoral bargaining.

Pathways to Adjustment and the Specificity of Redundancies

Demand Fluctuations and the Geographical Shift of Production

Companies operating in the hidden segment of the market face competition from low labour cost countries. It is their specialization in standardized products that exposes them to pressure from developing countries; buyers can purchase products of the same quality more cheaply. Competition is taking place in a twofold form: on the one hand, the production of such countries is increasingly attracting the orders of bigger local companies and, on the other, they have stimulated processes of plant de-localization. Redundancies in the hidden segment of the market are therefore related to demand fluctuations: lack of orders produces a shrinking of the workforce. From a theoretical perspective, it is an example of Keynesian unemployment, that is unemployment generated by the demand-side of the economy rather than by its supply-side. In this case, despite the absence of any type of formal regulation of employment relations and the existence of real wage levels which are consistently below nominal ones, companies are unable not only to maintain adequate levels of profit but also to have their existence safeguarded. As stressed by the co-ordinator of the task force for industrial problems for the Puglia region:

> In the clothing industry, in Brindisi, there is a problem of legality. There is a lot of hidden economy and this is the major obstacle for a 'clear labour market'. These companies exist as they exploit the expansive phases of production cycles. And they are also the ones which usually knock down the cost of labour which is the only thing they can govern at company' level.

Other redundancies, roughly 150 jobs in 1999, according to union sources, are occurring in the formal segment of the market. They are the outcome of re-location, by some companies, of part of their production to countries such as Albania or Romania. The logic underlying this choice is clear and responds to well-known trends: the exploitation of the differences in the cost of labour and employment relations. For these companies, plant re-location allows some retention of local production. As indicated by the entrepreneur who first decided to move part of its production abroad, leading to the downsizing of his plant in Francavilla:

> The key point is: is it better to ride the tiger or to let it eat you? We de-localize because it helps us to keep down our costs. With two plants, the average costs will be lowered. It isn't an expedient, a way out but an opportunity to exploit.

Although the shift of the most labour intensive phases of clothing production abroad is based on the cost of labour, managers tend to justify it differently, stressing market entry. As the same manager put it:

> Here in Brindisi we will produce quality products while, there [Albania], we are going to produce products that require less expertise. That way you don't lose orders or clients. The reason for de-localizing isn't just to lower the cost of labour, but also to get into the lowest segments of the clothing market.

By dumping the cost of labour through geographical mobility, the company locating in Albania intends to satisfy the request for standardized products and, at the same time, buyer demands for more quality products. This productive diversification, an all-embracing strategy, combining mass and medium quality productions, is expected to allow them to maintain adequate levels of competitiveness, to safeguard their relationship with traditional buyers and to acquire new ones. Such a process has implied both the downsizing of the production activity in the Brindisi area and job losses.

Forms of Restructuring

The process of restructuring described in the previous section, consisting of plant re-location and involving job losses, concerns a limited number of companies. On the basis of the interviews and of the knowledge of local informants, it can be argued that other restructuring processes have affected a larger number of companies. That is, there have been several different responses to a similar macro-economic scenario, depending on specific micro-economic dynamics. In all these cases, however, the process of transformation has occurred without job losses and the cost of labour has been considered only one of the elements of appraisal. Different forms of restructuring are shown below which, however, are not mutually exclusive.

The search for quality improvements The first example of restructuring is given by a company located in Ceglie which, to avoid competition from low labour cost countries and to strengthen its relationship with its buyers, has rejected the cost-competitiveness choice and decided to rely substantially on improving its production quality. Accordingly:

> We have decided to be in the top segments of the market. Our buyer is looking for quality, it'll never go to Albania. Clearly this requires more efforts on the part of our company, more costs but, in the end, we will reap major benefits.

The achievement of higher product quality implies primarily major and constant investments in technology, improving and speeding up the process of production. In addition, the companies that have chosen this restructuring path are actively engaged in re-training their personnel. In the absence of training schools, this training is carried out internally, often with the aid of expert technicians sent to Brindisi by buyers. As indicated by a local manager:

> We have renewed our technological assets recently. We've got new CAM-CAD machines. These are allowing us to improve the cutting and sewing of the ply. We've also been encouraged by the buyer, whose technicians sometimes come to help us. They've got 30 years of experience in the industry, they were doing these things before us.

Another example is given by a company in Latiano. Besides the attempt to establish an autonomous trademark (see below), the company is seeking to develop an in-house design unit which could provide it with a wider and more diverse range of products than standard shirts. The challenge and the difficulties facing the company are expressed by its manager:

> We're trying to make the quality leap which could launch us. Designing a proper collection and distributing it autonomously, on top of our subcontracting tasks, could free our potentialities and also render us less vulnerable to buyers' whims. However, we're facing totally unknown problems, the efforts are enormous and not only from a financial perspective.

These companies have decided to escape from mass competition and low quality products by focusing on products that will be sold in the higher segments of the market. The buyers in these cases are big retail chains, fashion maisons in the North of the country or specialized outlets. Consequently, a "virtuous circle" is likely to start. Producer quality will attract buyers who will maintain orders and cultivate co-operative relationships which, in turn, will improve the quality of products or processes. The action of these companies is not driven by mere survival in the market. They intend to enter markets where craft-based traditions and technological innovation contribute to creating the right productive and commercial mix. The pursuit of such an objective is not easy in an area characterized by external dis-economies and administrative constraints.

The search for a brand name The logic underlying the restructuring process undertaken by companies seeking to sell products under their own trademark is very different. Such companies are seeking to partially free themselves from retailer-intermediary dependence. Clearly, there is awareness that complete autonomy from the intermediation system is not feasible. However, they wish to achieve a certain visibility in the clothing market, which might eventually enable them to diversify their distribution channels. Thus, one of the entrepreneurs who is involved in such an attempt explains:

> What [the strategy] I'm pursuing, is to remain a subcontractor but, at the same time, try to trade limited batches of production by myself. I'm decentralising the main production in two new companies while this one is destined for my own production.

The effort undertaken by these companies is huge. The limited knowledge of opportunities existing in the market and the often inadequate capacity to seize them constrain action. One example is given by an employer:

> An autonomous trademark is a good idea but by myself it's very difficult to implement, it's very complex. That's why I contacted a northern trader. A new company will be formed with a proper trademark. I'll take care of the production while he'll be responsible for the distribution systems, outlets, markets, etc. This is the weakness of Brindisi's clothing industry.

The search for market visibility explains the initiative of the CNA to set up a consortium of local companies. The fifteen firms which constitute it have prepared a common fashion collection under the brand Confex and have started to take part at some trade exhibitions in the North and abroad. The consortium is also expected to favour the activation of an autonomous distribution channel. At the time of visiting, no meaningful opportunity had arisen for the companies, but this might point more to the novelty of the initiative rather than to its failure.

Product integration Another example of a restructuring path is revealed by a company located in Ceglie Messapica that has broadened the range of services provided to its subcontractor, but also to other companies. In addition to the supply of shirts, this company offers additional services (such as pressing and packing) which are expected to attract further orders. Consequently:

This is the first pressing service for women's clothes in the area. This investment gives us an additional chance. We're offering an additional service to the company we work for but, at the same time, we offer the service to others.

Such diversification is expected to fill a local weakness: buyers complain of the incapacity of Brindisi suppliers to offer other phases connected to the production cycle, such as pressing or washing clothes (Cerpem, 1991).

The restructuring strategies indicated above illustrate the range of responses undertaken by clothing companies to the intensification of competition in the industry. Paradoxically, the challenge of competition has ended up opening new opportunities for the most dynamic firms in the area as they are moving towards higher quality standards that should ensure greater stability in the future.

The Role of the Local Industrial Culture

The above analysis, focusing on the importance of tangible factors on company behaviour, offers only a partial account of the variables that have influenced industrial adjustment choices. The research confirms that a company's internal culture defined, following Schoenberger (1997), as the ensemble of material practices, social relations and ways of thinking, plays a key role in shaping their adjustment path. Restructuring choices are the expression of a company's knowledge and interpretation of the outside world and its position in it; clearly, their internal configuration becomes important during the phases of change and can also constitute an element of vulnerability if traditional and routine behaviour hinders adaptation. Below an analysis of the relations underlying the dynamics between capital and labour is presented, representing a specific aspect of the corporate culture, and of the way in which they have influenced the restructuring processes in Brindisi's clothing companies. First, the experience of cost-based companies, which are the majority in the area, is discussed. The choice to restructure through re-location has occurred in a context in which the relationship between capital and labour is not consolidated but irregular, and where dialogue between employers and workers or/and their representatives is non-existent or problematic. Specifically, relationships within the company are the expression of a pact of temporary convenience, centred exclusively upon the monetary dimension of the exchange, which can break down easily. There is a lack of collective values binding together workers and employers and, consequently, of the strength, continuity and stability that could help during phases of uncertainty. By contrast, when corporate adjustments coincide with quality improvements, companies show greater internal consolidation, with behaviours and work practices that, in some cases, enhance change. Here, the relationship between employers and workers responds to a logic of co-operation. As we would expect, following Akerlof's insights, workers and unions have become active supporters of employers'efforts to make changes which involve a greater attachment to the workforce and to the area. In other words, these companies have a degree of plasticity, which gives them sufficient margins for manoeuvre but, contemporarily, allows them to maintain internal stability (Foray and Garrouste, 1991).

The activities of one of the most important companies in Brindisi province exemplify the first case. The conversation with the company's owner gives a clear idea of the relationships with workers and unions but also of the more general philosophy underlying the business activity:

> Workers have strange ideas. They think that making money is easy. The area lacks credibility in the wider clothing market and it must be said that it is also because of the trade unions. They flex their muscle against poor, local companies and don't understand that the big northern companies, especially in the north-east, have lived for years using irregular work. What is happening here now is the same as what was happening in the north of the country some years ago. Small company here are obliged to do everything according to the rules, anti-fire regulations, anti-this and anti-that, and in the north until a few years ago there were completely irregular companies employing 1,500 workers.

It is clear that workers and union attitudes are both believed to hinder company interests. Yet, when the decision to move part of the production abroad was taken, the company in question "laid off 100 workers who have not been given their last pay check and the trade unions were prevented from entering the company" (il Quotidiano, 6-5-1999). The difficulty inherent in governing internal dynamics has a clear influence on the way in which these companies interpret and think about themselves in the external environment. In general, the ensemble of local institutions is perceived as hostile, always an obstacle, to economic action. In addition, although initially adhering to the commitment of the CNA towards local industry through promotional initiatives, the company de-localising in Albania later deemed this commitment to be unsustainable. Such initiatives are believed in fact not to help competition. Relations are now difficult: local formal institutions' alleged lack of understanding of a company's concerns translates into a lack of support for local collective initiatives.

> Local authorities don't pay too much attention to the sector. Even from the local employers' association all we've had is criticism. The fact is that they don't know the difficulties of being in the market. It's easy to talk in theory, but in practice we're the ones involved in an everyday struggle.

In the same local context, however, other firms have embraced completely different paths of adjustment based on a different industrial culture. Employment relationships founded on the mutual respect between employers and workers/unions have helped to improve internal quality and efficiency. According to a local employer:

> Employers need to understand workers. They are not objects that you move around according to your whim. They want to feel important and responsible for what they do. We had problems at the beginning because of absenteeism: we talked about the sense of responsibility and of the possibility to negotiate family leave when necessary. The problem has practically disappeared in our company.

On the other side, the commitment towards the organization to which they belong is clearly expressed by some workers:

> I have no doubts about the solidity of this company. Here there is a very good relationship between employers and workers. They have got great experience and our trust in them is total. We have no fear, together [management and workers] we can overcome this moment which is a bit problematic, and carry on along the path of quality and specialization. Albania [production de-localization] doesn't worry us.

Here is a choice of restructuring which implies neither plant downsizing nor job losses. In addition, such employers are aware of the social role they carry out:

> It was a clear-cut. We don't want to penalize our workforce and we won't. We really believe that they are highly qualified and this is a great advantage, we can't afford to waste these opportunities.

The industrial culture symbolized by these companies goes with an awareness of the marginal attention paid by local authorities to company needs. A recurring story among enlightened managers is one of an everyday struggle against a heavy, often blind, bureaucratic apparatus, unable to provide the area with basic infrastructure or even to enhance investment projects that could favour the expansion of production and employment. Certainly, their privileged relations with quality buyers help them to overcome many of these problems. Some recognition is however given to efforts by the CNA to promote initiatives expected to improve intangible assets, such as the feeling of trust and co-operation, in a sector dominated by competition, mutual distrust and, in general, by a producer isolation.

Prospects at the End of the Period of Restructuring

The current period of restructuring affecting the clothing industry in Brindisi will not leave the profile of the sector in the area unchanged. First, Brindisi and other Western clothing areas are expected to be further penalized by the implementation of policy agreements towards the elimination of trade barriers for imported products (Il Sole-24 ore, 10-07-1999) (table 4.11).[40]

Table 4.11 Markets whose accessibility is increased by the full application of the Uruguay Round Agreement

Textile and knitted goods	Textile products	Clothing
EU	EU	EU
South Africa	South Africa	Canada
Australia	Canada	Japan
Canada	New Zealand	New Zealand
Japan	USA	Bolivia
New Zealand	Bolivia	Colombia
USA	Colombia	Peru
Bolivia	Peru	Uruguay
Colombia	Uruguay	Malaysia
Peru	Philippines	Philippines
Uruguay	Thailand	Thailand
Malaysia	Egypt	Egypt
Philippines	Tunisia	Tunisia
Thailand		
Egypt		

Source: NOMISMA 1995, adapted from De Rubertis, 1998

Subcontracting companies are likely to suffer the most. According to a survey conducted by the CNA, "35 per cent of subcontracting companies are at risk [nationally]", as they are the last link in the production chain. In order to reduce their fixed costs, certain buyers are expected to re-internalize some of the previously-subcontracted production phases (Il Sole-24 ore, 14-05-1999). Second, a slow down in orders for southern companies will also occur because one of their major competitive advantages, the low cost of labour, is progressively reducing (Provincia di Brindisi, 1999). This is the outcome of a controversial agreement signed in 1994 between the then Italian budget Secretary, Pagliarini, and the then European Commissioner for Competition, Van Miert. By removing the system of financial discounts (in the form of lower indirect costs of labour) benefiting companies located in southern Italy, the agreement is leading to a sharp rise in costs of labour in the presence of unchanging locational and economic disadvantages.[41] Paradoxically, employers and many local economic observers believe that the set of circumstances that are challenging local economic stability might turn out to be positive for the industry. They will sweep away the area's more inefficient and unprofitable companies while consolidating the most reliable economic units. It is expected that many local cost producers, whose competitive lever lies in the cost of production, will not be able to face the competitive pressure from low labour cost countries. They will be penalized both by the relatively higher costs of labour locally and by the de-localization move that more structured companies have started to make in an attempt to enter the least sophisticated segments of the clothing production. Squeezed by this double trend, these companies are likely to end up in the hidden segment of the local economy where their existence will be subject to an inconstant and marginal demand. A different trend is likely to affect more consolidated companies; for them the current restructuring phase will certainly imply the definition/re-definition/consolidation of their product and market strategies. One aspect of this process concerns the type of production. The qualitative increase in gross production to be offered to buyers or to be put directly on the market is the widely-recognized strategy for escaping from the cut-throat competition involved in mass production. In doing this, therefore, local companies are entering niche segments of the clothing market which, whilst lowering competitive pressure, could also lead to a certain autonomy from external buyers.

Another dimension which is likely to suffer from a re-configuration as a consequence of the on-going transformation is the organization of production. To reduce the fixed costs connected to the management of stocks in warehouses, buyers and traders are not buying great batches of goods, twice or three times per year as before, but they are purchasing small batches of product which may differ from time to time (Provincia di Brindisi, 1999). Consequently, orders are becoming more frequent and irregular, requiring a greater elasticity of the production processes and a quicker supply. This transformation of the sector has generated many positive expectations. Obviously, many problems remain unsolved and many weaknesses (e.g. the lack of a production filière or a greater inter-firm co-operation) slow down the opportunities of a sector that, according to the local CNA officer, "could do more and doesn't". Nonetheless, after all, the industry in Brindisi is believed to benefit from two major advantages when compared to many developing areas. First, the quality of the local workforce is incomparably superior to that existing in central Europe or North Africa, although the gap is narrowing as a consequence of the training, which the latter are receiving from Western companies. Second, despite low capital investment, a shift in production implies high access costs (Viesti, 1998) and is undoubtedly a sub-optimal solution for buyers or traders who need small batches of production in a short time. "Remote de-localization" and "outwarding processing" seem therefore to play in favour of the local industry.[42] Moreover, Brindisi's companies are benefiting from a legislative instrument that, although pursuing a diverse objective, is having a counterbalancing impact on the cost of labour. This is a specific, territorial-based, agreement, implemented to favour the emergence of irregular companies into the official market. The "graduality contract", signed the first time in 1991 by the CNA, the local trade unions and the association of employers, is intended to favour the progressive up-grading of employment standards and wage levels in the local clothing companies operating either irregularly or in the hidden economy, to those defined by the national sectoral contract. The latter was suspended in all the provincial territory for a period of four years. At the beginning of the period, companies that adhered to the re-alignment contract paid 75 per cent of the salary nationally established wage. The full amount was going to be gradually reached over a period of four years. All the previous irregularities for these companies were cleared. The agreement was suspended in 1994[43] and re-negotiated in 1996 (table 4.12) and again in 1998 with the definition of 2002 as the final date for achieving full correspondence of local wage level with the national one. Although attuned to the economic, to the social and production conditions of the area, to date the contract has been signed by less than half of local clothing companies.

Table 4.12 Percentages re-alignment of Brindisi's clothing companies to national collective contract levels

1\07\1996	65%
1\07\1997	70%
1\01\1998	75%
1\07\1998	80%
1\01\1999	85%
1\07\2000	100%

To summarize, driven by heightened international competitive pressures, the adjustment process in Brindisi's clothing industry has assumed a variety of forms in which the cost of labour assumes diverse importance. In addition, only some of these restructuring processes have impacted on firm employment levels, leading to a reduction in the workforce base. Redundancies are the outcome of two different dynamics. In the hidden segment of the local economy, job losses are generated by demand-side fluctuations. In the formal segment of the economy, job losses have resulted from the de-location of a very few companies towards developing countries in an attempt to reduce the costs of labour. It has been argued, however, that such trends concern a marginal number of production units. The vast majority of local firms have undertaken adjustment paths based on longer-term prospects. Restructuring choices are influenced by the set of social relations and ways of thinking, constituting a company's culture. By analysing a specific aspect of the local industrial culture, that is the relations between capital and labour, it has been shown that in the absence of sedimented values binding employers and workers or in the presence of conflicting internal dynamics, companies are unable to mobilize those intangible resources enhancing more demanding adjustment processes other than mere cost-cutting strategies. Conversely, the organizations displaying both formal and reciprocal forms of interaction between employers and workers seem to be more able to undertake longer-term growth strategies.

Notes

[1] As indicated by Cecafosso, 1979, two-thirds of them had an average dimension below one hectare.

[2] Martinelli, 1998, identifies two sub-periods in the industrialization phase of the 1960s and early 1970s. In the first decade, it was mostly State-controlled industrial groups that used the incentives and invested in the south. Private northern companies implemented a second wave of investments in the area. In both cases, companies benefited from the extraordinary funds managed by the Cassa per il Mezzogiorno, a special State agency for the development of the south.

[3] CIG (Short-Time Earnings Compensation) supplements the wage of workers temporarily laid off or working less than full hours. It has represented the most important means of income protection foreseen by the Italian legislation for restructuring crises.

[4] In the Italian language this is the most formal way to address a person.

[5] The presence of the chemical industry in Brindisi is widely recognized to be due to the political action of Italo Giulio Caiati. He was an important member of the Democrazia Cristiana (DC-Christian Democrat Party) belonging to the political group led by Andreotti, who aimed to establish a web of political consensus around him.

[6] Corporatism is "an institutional arrangement for linking the associationally organized interests of civil society with the decisional structures of the State", Schmitter 1979 quoted in Perrucci, 1994, p.491.

[7] Istituto per la Ricostruzione Industriale (IRI) and Ente Nazionale Idrocarburi (ENI) controlled and managed, with public money, numerous companies that entered the system of "Partecipazioni Statali" (PP.SS.) (State holdings). The story of PP.SS. ends at the beginning of the 1990s due to the process of privatization.

[8] The disappointment has been greater also because the multiplier effect of such investments were supposed to be spontaneous and unproblematic events.

[9] This approach reverses the logic underlying the previous regional policy, in the sense that it deals with a "bottom-up" approach, favouring the activation of local resources. In Brindisi, three areas of intervention were identified by the pact: initiatives to promote business activities, interventions to improve and support such initiatives and interventions to improve human resources.

[10] The modification of the Istat classification of labour forces makes it difficult to compare data prior to 1993.

[11] As indicated by *Chemical Week*, 02 -12-1981, p.31, "for a decade, the Italian government ... has subsidized many of its [chemical industry] projects. World-scale plants were built, but they lacked the necessary worldwide sales and distribution systems. The result has been rampant over-capacity and a constant flow of red ink".

[12] The site had a surface of $5km^2$, four times the extension of the city. 45km of roads and 20km of railway were built internally to the plant area to allow the movement and transport of raw and final materials. A dock pier allowed the docking of medium-size ships.

[13] At the time, Enrico Mattei guided the company.

[14] As indicated by a local informant, for example, three plants rather than one produced the yearly quantity of ethylene.

[15] Edison was the biggest Italian electric company.

[16] This is the trade union close to the former DC.

[17] Comments respectively by a senior petrochemical manager and senior trade unionist.

[18] Alberto Grandi was the then ENI chairman.

[19] Some European countries such as Portugal, Yugoslavia and Turkey entered the

petrochemical production at the end of the 1970s along with some Middle Eastern countries such as Iran, Iraq and Saudi Arabia, Ranci and Vacca', 1979.

[20] In practice, ENI became the main shareholder of Montedison but it used only half of its shares to avoid the alteration of share allocation, Barca, 1997.

[21] Gianni De Michelis was the then Minister for PP.SS.

[22] The 1994 and 1995 values reflect a particularly favourable economic conjuncture for the company: the rise in exports above all towards China, the rise in the products prices and the devaluation of the Italian currency, *EniChem annual report*, 1995.

[23] In 2001, EniChem concluded a business swap with Dow Chemical to which it gave the poliuterans business in exchange for 50% of Polimeri Europa which belonged to Union Carbide Corporation (company controlled by Dow Chemical). Polimeri Europa is now completely controlled by EniChem.

[24] Production was suspended in December 2001 due to a difficult economic situation at international level and has not re-started yet.

[25] Moreover, as pointed out by some managers in Brindisi, single product corporations are by their very nature extremely fragile on the market.

[26] Data from an interview with a senior manager of the plant.

[27] Data from union sources.

[28] The use of non-standard contracts has been enormously encouraged by national legislation over the last decade.

[29] It is worth stressing that the law foresees the modification of the redundancy criteria it fixes in case of agreement between unions-employers. These can consequently identify other methods of dismissal or categories of workers subjected to it.

[30] Companies operating in the hidden economy are referred to as those that during their activity systematically violate fiscal (e.g. the lack of registration at the chamber of commerce or the declaration of less turnover implying less tax burden) and contribution (e.g. use of workers not formally hired or paid less than foreseen by sectoral bargaining) laws.

[31] Trade unions and Confederazione Nazionale Artigiani (CNA) estimate that official figures concerning companies and employees should be doubled to show the actual dimension of the sector.

[32] This refers both to the standards of quality of goods produced by a company and to the market outlets to which the product will be eventually sold.

[33] This could also be the effect of the purchase of local production from buyers located abroad. Nonetheless, there is no evidence of such a phenomenon.

[34] Capriati uses this taxonomy with reference to the clothing firms in southern Italy, Capriati, 1995.

[35] It is not unusual that fabrics are already cut to ensure the perfect correspondence between the quantity of fabric and the quantity of final product, Provincia di Brindisi, 1999. This is also done to avoid valuable fabric being retained by the local company and used to outsource products that will end on street markets.

[36] At the national scale, the growth of the industry coincided with an increase in exports rather than in foreign direct investments, Fornengo, 1978.

[37] Texabb is a service society for the national association of textile and clothing companies.

[38] This account comes from secondary sources and from the direct experience of local unionists.

[39] However, one must consider, as suggested by Thomas and Thomas, 1994, p.486, that "the informal sector relates to the remainder of the economy very differently in different places, reflecting socio-economic and, crucially, national and local political circumstances".

[40] In 1998, Europe promoted the liberalization of trade barriers with the former Soviet satellite countries, while an even greater impact is expected from the Uruguay Round Agreement that foresees the dismantling of all trade barriers by 2005, Ministero dell'Industria, 1997.

[41] Refer to the recently published report by the Provincia di Brindisi, 1999, for a general picture of the economic and industrial conditions of the area.

[42] Remote de-localization usually refers to the shift of production in non-European countries, such as Mauritius, Sri Lanka, etc. The outward processing implies that a part(s) of the production is (are) made in low cost countries but assembled in Italy so as to assume the "Made in Italy" denomination.

[43] Those who signed it acknowledged that a series of negative conditions had consistently worsened local companies convenience to subscribe to it. It has been reckoned that from 1996 the cost of labour has increased by 34 per cent, Provincia di Brindisi, 1999.

Chapter 5

The Regions Compared and Theoretical Reflections

Introduction

The examination of the complex restructuring processes involving the chemical and clothing industries of Teesside and Brindisi as well as their main productive and employment implications (see table 5.1 for a summary) leads to focus specifically on the explanatory variables behind redundancies and restructuring (part 1) and their linkage with the theoretical framework outlined in Chapter Two (part 2). Looking across the two sectors in the two regions, four factors have emerged as the main causes leading to redundancies and industrial restructuring (table 5.2 summarizes the analysis). In contrast to much of the current literature on the theme, which emphasizes the primary role of economic factors, the evidence shows how institutionally embedded relations are important co-explanatory variables of the processes of change: symbolic relations and institutional set-ups affect company knowledge as well as adjustment options. Moreover, employment and industrial change is solicited by factors of different origin that overlap, so no linear relation of cause and effect can clearly be indicated.

Table 5.1   Summary of the processes of restructuring on Teesside and Brindisi

TEESSIDE

	Chemical sector	**Clothing sector**
Forms of restructuring	Business re-positioning: from heavy to light chemicals; Change in the employment relation	De-localisation
Management of redundancies	No compulsory redundancies; re-deployment; sell-offs; subcontracting	Last in - First out
New productive and labour relations	Inter-firms integration; vertical disintegration of production	Quick response
	Core/periphery workforce: stability v vulnerability	Example of teamwork

BRINDISI

	Chemical sector	**Clothing sector**
Forms of restructuring	Technological innovation; work reorganisation; dis-investment; change in occupational mix	De-localisation; niche production; product integration; trademarks
Management of redundancies	Corporatist; income support through CIG; defensive solidarity; substitution programme	National sectoral contracts; informal rules
New productive and labour relations	Multinational companies; locally-owned companies; subcontracting	Qualitative improvements; consolidation; inter-firms co-operation

Table 5.2 Causes of redundancies and restructuring in the chemical and clothing industries of Teesside and Brindisi

CHEMICAL INDUSTRY

	Teesside	Brindisi
Productive decentralisation	Subcontracting: core v peripheral companies	Integrated processes of production; subcontracting
International competition	Business re-organisation with plant closures, sell-offs, business swaps	Technological innovation; work re-organisation; dis-investment; costs reduction
Capital and labour relations (corporate culture)	Paternalism; wage and benefits linked to profitability; unions and workers' consent	Corporatism; defensive measures; income support measures
Institutional configuration	Centrality in the local economy; TCI activity; ICI's role	Centrality in the local economy; corporatist

CLOTHING INDUSTRY

	Teesside	Brindisi
Productive decentralisation	Buyers-producers relation: re-location	Buyers-producers relation: re-location
International competition	Mediated by buyers	Mediated by buyers
Capital and labour relations (corporate culture)	Conflicting; displaced employers v marginal workforce	Pacts of temporary convenience (mutual benefits); conflicting Consolidated: mutual commitment
Institutional configuration	Marginality in the local economy; no inter-firm cooperation; no common services	Defensive measures; graduality contract; CNA activity

PART 1 SECTORALLY-RELATED AND PLACE-SPECIFIC CAUSES OF REDUNDANCIES

Productive Decentralization

The Clothing Industry

Both the clothing industry of Teesside and especially of Brindisi are part of a flux of productive decentralization. Thus, whilst subcontracting is allowing clothing to exist in the two areas, the nature of productive relations concerning local companies and external buyers has emerged as a principal factor in determining job loss in the clothing industry of Teesside and, to a lesser extent, of Brindisi. This is for a series of reasons. Local industry is relegated to the most labour intensive phases of the production process; the highest value-added phases, usually connected to the commercialization of products, are reserved to buyers. This means that local industry lacks the capacities to widen productive horizons to other spheres of clothing production, especially to important phases that are upstream and downstream the productive process itself, such as design or commercialization. From a financial perspective, such production relations prevent local producers from seizing opportunities along the value chain. Additionally, it is the buyer and not the producer who defines the price of both intermediate and final products. Yet, the subcontracting nature of the industry does not affect the economic dimensions alone. It impinges directly on both the material and social practices that come to define the culture of a specific company. Buyers are important agents in influencing decisions about investments and the links that local producers entertain with them represent a primary source of embeddedness: it is the network of relations with other firms more than the one with local institutions that shapes productive activity. It follows therefore that the level of profitability is highly dependent on the relationships with buyers: clothing producer sensitivity to the cost of labour, in fact, reflects buyer strategies. For instance, the preference of fashion houses to quality products usually reduces the sensitiveness to price.

What has emerged on Teesside and Brindisi is that the form and speed of restructuring undertaken by local companies have been mediated and widely shaped by the production relations in which they are involved. The investigation of the nature of the relationships between buyers and producers provides therefore a robust explanation of corporate action (e.g.

adjustment strategies) and culture (e.g. the values underlying economic action). Furthermore, it is the modification of the previous buyer-producer relationship under the effect of the competitive pressure brought about by low labour cost countries that has urged the process of restructuring of local industries. Specifically, redundancies on Teesside and in Brindisi have resulted from a reactive strategy by certain local companies to shift production abroad to answer buyer requests for good quality products at competitive prices. The type of productive relation in which companies are locked gives buyers the power to decide the price of products and, indirectly, the cost of production. In turn, buyer strategy has been influenced by the growing trend towards the internationalization of production to take advantage of the spatial differences in the cost of the factors of production. However, comparing the scale of restructuring and job losses in the two areas, it can be suggested that uniform trends affecting the sector internationally are being mediated by distinctive place-specific economic arrangements. On Teesside, the profit squeeze suffered by local companies, leading to large scale redundancies, has been amplified by the existence of an oligopoly of retailers who control the market where a plurality of producers compete to supply them. Teesside's main clothing producers have limited margins of manoeuvre as they are totally subject to retailer whims. Secondly, the rise in the quality of clothing products from the newly industrialized countries, at competitive prices, has swept away Teesside's competitive advantage. In Brindisi, although exposed to the same cost-based competition, employment in clothing has suffered much less. First, the sector is differentiated. Accordingly, only cost-based producers appear to be much more exposed to cost-cutting strategies. Second, the quality of the production is of medium level; therefore, the vast majority of local productive units have maintained their appeal for buyers.

The Chemical Industry

The diverse nature of the production cycle in the chemical industry, an integrated process, makes the relevance of inter-firm relations less important in explaining redundancies in Teesside and Brindisi. However, whilst not a direct factor leading to job losses, the account of the relations of production which emerged after ICI's product restructuring is relevant for understanding the transformation of employment conditions in the sector. The choice made by the company to concentrate on core businesses has led, on the one hand, to a greater diversification of chemicals production on Teesside, given the arrival of an array of new producers, and, on the other, to an expansion in the number of subcontracting companies, due to the outsourcing of almost the totality of services. The current division of labour in the area is centred on a core of chemical companies, surrounded by quality subcontractors with which they entertain privileged relationships as they provide them with specialized services such as engineering or training. Relationships with the circle of lower quality subcontractors, involving maintenance, cleaning and catering activities, are instead characterized by volatility. The most visible effects of such a re-organization of product relations have been the reduction of the cost of labour and the widening of chemical companies' control over subcontracting ones. ICI's restructuring has profoundly impinged upon the employment conditions of the sector which, in contrast to the past, are now dominated by flexible and temporary work arrangements. Progressive concentration on core activities undertaken by local chemical companies has paved the way for the substantial segmentation of the labour market into a core and peripheral segment. Accordingly, advantageous and stable employment contracts are being offered to a shrinking number of workers, whilst the employment conditions of the workers engaged in subcontracting activities have worsened. The harsh competition among subcontracting companies to obtain and protect contracts from the chemical companies has led to a compression of the costs at which services are provided. To meet competition which is increasingly being based on prices and delivery time, subcontracting companies have made growing use of non-standard contracts and flexible work arrangements which are allowing them to consider the cost of labour as a non fixed-cost. This has brought about deterioration both in wage levels, as companies are often able to recruit informally, and in employment conditions, as flexibility often means intensification and job vulnerability. In summary, whilst it is true that the process of outsourcing has preserved a large amount of jobs once held in-house, this has been achieved through a meaningful attenuation of labour prerogatives. On a substantially smaller scale, in Brindisi too there is evidence of subcontracting aiming to reduce the fixed nature of the cost of labour. Even in this case, outsourcing has entailed the reduction of worker prerogatives. The impact of such a process is however limited. It has involved only EniChem and a few other companies that, at the beginning of their activity, had adopted a vertically integrated system of production, and it concerns only a relatively small number of service activities. The younger companies had already adopted organizational systems satisfying more cost-effective solutions.

International Competition

The Clothing Industry

As widely stressed, the clothing industries of Teesside and Brindisi are being exposed to international competitive pressures. However, the analysis of the implications of international competition on employment dynamics in the two areas requires a distinction between the macro-level and the micro-level. At the aggregate level, it is undoubted that the clothing industry has suffered from a radical re-configuration. The pressure from low labour cost countries, which have flooded the market with cheap products whose quality is constantly improving, has led to the internationalization of production. The impact of these dynamics on local companies has however depended on the system of relations in which they are embedded. This explains the variety of restructuring processes undertaken as well as their diverse effects on employment. In certain cases, qualitative adjustments have been implemented to enter niche productions and have often preserved the employment base; in others, companies have preferred cost-cutting strategies or the shift of production to more convenient locations from a cost perspective, and, therefore, leading to job losses locally.

The Chemical Industry

Restructuring processes and associated job losses in the chemical industry of Teesside and Brindisi are closely influenced by changing international markets. It is widely acknowledged that the industry, especially heavy segments of the production, is cyclically affected by profitability crises, determining periods of restructuring and downsizing. These follow the phases of expansion and accumulation of the industry which however lead to the semi-permanent problem of over-capacity (Chapman, 1991; Financial Times, 18-11-1997). Specialized in heavy chemicals, both Teesside and Brindisi suffered from the backlash of the crisis that hit the industry already after the mid-1970s. The two oil shocks and the entry of new producers, eroding the technological edge of many European chemical companies, compromized the performance of chemical companies in the two areas. Their responses to a common problem however have been diverse. On Teesside, redundancies derive from the modification of the business specialization of the area's major company. In Brindisi, they are mainly related to the labour saving effects of technological innovation and organizational changes. Teesside has substantially modified its productive profile following ICI's decision to move away from heavy chemical production towards commodity and, then, speciality chemicals where the technological edge constitutes an important obstacle to extensive competition. This is consistent with ICI's new strategy to reduce business vulnerability and to ensure more adequate levels of profitability. The business re-orientation has implied the closure of some plants, the sell-off of marginal businesses, and business swaps to acquire new activities and market shares. This process of restructuring has been synonymous with layoffs and with a series of other measures that have coincided with the termination of employment in ICI. In Brindisi, the response to international pressure has centred upon the intensification of technological innovation. The major local companies have engaged in plant renewal as well as in the adoption of new methods of production through joint ventures with foreign companies, also in order to reduce competition in certain markets. Both strategies have increased plant capacity and the overall improvement of quality. Other local companies have implemented organizational changes leading to redundancies. The second major step taken to maintain competitive edges on international markets has been the overall reduction of costs which has been achieved essentially through an increase in labour productivity. In Brindisi, redundancies have been managed through early retirements and a progressive substitution of older workers with younger and more qualified personnel, whose greater general knowledge has been deemed to positively impinge on productivity performances.

Capital and Labour Relations and Corporate Culture

As it is apparent in the case study chapters, the strategies of the chemical and clothing companies of Teesside and Brindisi to recover profitability have not responded to universalistic patterns but have appeared to be rather heterogeneous. Similarly, it has been maintained that employment change, specifically job losses, are only one of the possible consequences of industrial transformation. An important explanation of the variability of industrial restructuring and employment change lies in corporate culture, which creates the situated knowledge defining the company itself, framing the definition of its economic objectives and the way in which they are pursued, and, specifically, in the relations between capital and labour.

The Clothing Industry

The salience of company practices, as spatially and historically rooted social constructions, has been extremely relevant for the clothing sector in Brindisi. The industry in the area offers a clear example of polarized economic behaviour among companies responding to the same macro-economic scenario. Company culture, defining primarily the relations between capital and labour, constitutes a major variable in driving restructuring processes and job losses. Accordingly, redundancies are occurring in those companies where the relationship between employers and workers is conflicting or problematic, the expression of a pact of temporary convenience. On one side, there are employers who, by choice or because they lack adequate professional and financial resources, are engaged in cost-cutting strategies which prevent them from investing in long-term business prospects as well as in human resources. On the other side, there are workers who accept the low wage level offered in absence of any alternative opportunity in the local labour market. Because of the instability of the internal relationship, these companies lack collective values, or a culture of work that would enable them to respond to change. By contrast, qualitative and jobless adjustments have occurred in local companies that have managed to consolidate internal behaviours and work practices. These companies are characterized by a stable business activity that also ensures the stability of workers' employment. Both elements contribute to sediment practices and relations of work that have a great influence on company strategies as well as on their change.

On Teesside, the reactive nature of the restructuring path undertaken by the major local producers, consisting of a partial shift to low labour cost countries, reflects a prevailing corporate culture that has circumscribed company options for change. Accordingly, the subordination of the local entrepreneurial class to external buyers has affected both the decision-making process concerning their business activity and the appropriation of consistent shares of surplus. Decisions concerning the quality of products, their price but also technical innovations and other investments in the company reside externally. Indeed, they coincide with buyer production and market strategies. With the modification of buyer strategies and especially, their decreasing commitment to local companies, the latter have found themselves confronted with a series of new problems which could not be faced. At the same time, because of the hard conditions of work and low wage levels, the women who have traditionally worked in the clothing no longer wish to do so. This is compromising the low-cost option. The industry is trapped in a vicious circle: the lack of workforce commitment is mirrored in a company neglect of the centrality of labour despite the labour intensive nature of the industry.

The Chemical Industry

The case of the chemical industry on Teesside clearly illustrates how the employment relation, hinging upon a unique construction of the relationship between capital and labour, became a key variable in ensuring economic success in a specific period, but also how it shaped the downsizing of the employment base and the modification of work practices when the economic scenario changed. The genesis of the industry in the hands of ICI created the conditions for particular capital and labour relations to be established. Indeed, Teesside's chemicals culture was the reflection of ICI's paternalistic model of industrial relations, characterized by harmonization and joint regulation of employment relations and of those beyond the workplace. In particular, formal and tacit agreements established a system of employment practices tying wage and benefit increases to the profitability of the company itself. The modification of the macro-economic picture during the 1970s and 1980s had a major impact on ICI's configuration of employment relations. The end of the period of intense accumulation compromised the company's micro-economic equilibrium; its profitability started to decrease and ceased to be ensured by a wide business portfolio. The business strategy implemented to recover from profitability loss, centred upon the specialization of production, revealed the incompatibility of employment practices connected to the previous organization of production. It can be argued therefore that the type of restructuring process implemented and the impact of employment change find in such practices a major explanatory factor. The existence of place-specific employment relations, the legacy of sedimented social practices, explains the management of dismissals as well as union and worker attitudes during the process of industrial adjustment. Compulsory redundancies were limited in numbers, while the company encouraged voluntary retirements. It also sold many of the businesses that were becoming marginal to its new business strategy. Both the effective demise of the ICI presence on Teesside and the modification of the employment relation went uncontested. This is because the traditional fit between worker well-being and company profit had led, on the one hand, to the reinforcement of ICI's power in the decision-making process and, on the other, to the weakening of the labour movement as the climate of consent was never compromised by possible confrontation. The pattern of restructuring of the chemical industry in Brindisi has been characterized by company implementation of a combination of adjustment strategies whereby profitability has been achieved, for instance, by coupling the intensification of the pace of technological innovation and the adoption of new organizational models. The impact of these processes of restructuring on the employment base of the industry has been much softer. Local companies have been engaged in gradual employment adjustment strategies aiming to minimize labour disruption. Reduction of overtime work and bonuses, functional and time flexibility, as well as voluntary retirements and a programme of sons replacing fathers, have all been means to search for an internal solution to redundant personnel and to avoid the termination of the employment relation. The search for an alternative to axing jobs finds an explanation in the corporatist model of governance characterising industrial relations in the industry. Decision-making involved negotiation between capital and labour, with the mediation of public institutions. The level of independence of chemical companies in Brindisi, with regard to redundancy decisions and management, has been diluted by the bargaining with trade unions and other local, sectoral, organizations.

Institutional Configuration

The investigation of restructuring on Teesside and Brindisi has also provided evidence of the role of institutional configuration on strategies of adjustment. As sets of interrelated instrumental (e.g. laws, system of education, training, company governance structure, etc.) and symbolic practices (cultural rules, routines, etc.) or organising principles available for organizations, institutions frame company choices. They influence, on the one hand, economic rationality (in this case, the interpretation of the cost of labour) and, on the other, the restructuring options that are conceived sustainable in the context in which they take place.

The Clothing Industry

The process of harsh restructuring in the clothing industry on Teesside illustrates how the set of instrumental practices available to local companies and local policy makers contribute to explaining their decisions regarding adjustment. The sector lacks not only a basic system of inter-firm relationships but also the ensemble of common services that enhance a local industrial system, such as training schools, design units, etc. The climate of competition that characterizes relationships between companies therefore adds further costs. Second, the sector is embedded in a wider institutional context which has traditionally seen the clothing industry as a marginal one in the economy. The recession that has recently hit the industry has unfolded in a climate of disinterest, impotency and resignation: indeed, the institutional vacuum present on Teesside has substantially constrained company choices. Finally, the drive towards the re-location of production, that has become the prevailing adjustment process undertaken in the area, has been partially favoured by national economic policy: the strong pound has encouraged re-location.

In Brindisi, the institutional set up has been different. Clothing companies have showed different trajectories of restructuring and the reduction in jobs has been limited. First, companies have benefited from national employment legislation to face temporary crises. Measures allow the shortening of working hours or the reduction of the working week before proceeding to the dismissal of workers; more importantly, companies and workers are protected by the special measures provided by the legislation on productive crises (ordinary or extraordinary CIG[1]): redundancies are avoided as workers are entitled to receive income protection from the State. In addition, the contract of graduality, signed by local trade unions and employers associations, has been important in helping some local companies to respond to change by keeping the cost of labour lower than the national level. Then, thanks to the work of the CNA, some examples of inter-firm co-operation have emerged to partially limit its reliance on the subcontracting.

The Chemical Industry

The chemical industries too show that the presence of formal institutions and the existence of more subjective and symbolic aspects connected to the spatiality of economic activity play a salient role in explaining company options regarding restructuring processes. Although the number of jobs axed by ICI has been remarkably high during the phase of its restructuring, it is commonly acknowledged on Teesside that the impact of employment change could have been much greater if ICI had not pursued a careful policy of business re-positioning in recognition of its historical role on Teesside and if the action of sectoral organizations such as the Teesside Chemical Initiative (TCI) had not been incisive. There is little doubt that ICI's restructuring process has been profoundly shaped by the formal links as well as by the tacit conventions that the company established. Sell-offs and swaps were favoured, while initiatives to attract other chemicals multinationals to Teesside were implemented so as to preserve the production capacity of the area. In addition, although subcontracting virtually all its service activities, ICI ensured the new companies the maintenance of orders for at least one year.

In Brindisi, the corporatist nature of the local institutional set-up, where unions and other local institutions intervene in company decision-making processes, constitutes the framework in which the chemical industry has restructured. Moreover, the national legislation protects employment through a variety of alternative measures. Indeed, local companies have terminated employment contracts with their workers only in a limited number of cases, while they have used alternative measures to seek the least disruptive steps to cut costs. As a consequence, one has witnessed the reduction of overtime work and bonuses and, especially, the encouragement of voluntary retirements. All this responds to a logic whereby employment change is addressed, managed and sustained by an institutional configuration which, in general terms, discourages large-scale layoffs.

PART 2 CONCEPTUALIZING FROM BELOW

The Complexity of a Socio-Economic Phenomenon

How can industrial unemployment be theorized from the evidence above? There is no doubt that, under conditions of perfect competition, efficiency is the result of an economic use of resources and that the most efficient firm is the one that earns the highest revenue per unit of output. In reality, however, firms need to respond to diverse influences, so the goal of profit maximization is not always the primary one. As showed, profitability is a relative measure rather than an absolute one. It does not diverge simply between sectors. Companies pursue different forms of efficiency in response to different sets of possibilities and external constraints. The market in which they operate and their strategies in it represent, for instance, a primary source of profit making or squeezing. In the chemical sector, companies engaged in the heavy segments of the production are more exposed financially and economically to the cyclical trends determined by international competition than the ones that operate at the light end of production. In the clothing industry, niche production is ensuring wider margins of profit than mass production. Also macro-economic circumstances heavily affect profitability levels. Second, company change may revolve around a variety of variables. Profitability pursued through a reduction in the cost of production factors and/or a rise in products prices goes with different forms of efficiency. Decisions on whether to intervene on the cost of labour may imply evaluations on expected future returns. Companies may decide, as some of Brindisi's clothing companies have, to sustain heavier costs of labour today in order to achieve better results in the future. ICI's case serves to clearly point out that the link between profitability and wage levels is a historically contingent argument; profitability varies in relation to space and time. The economic history of the company demonstrates that a cost-effectiveness level is not incompatible with good employment relations. The phase of intensive demand-led growth, benefiting company accumulation process, was based on a system of social and employment relations that coupled the possibility to maintain an intensive pace of growth with the existence of high standards of employment conditions and wages. Third, companies may choose to return to profitability by acting on non-economic variables. The modification of the institutions underlying company internal dynamics, especially, the relations between capital and labour, concretely affects performance. A plurality of examples emerge from the fieldwork whereby companies have modified the cultural values that were regulating their internal dynamics or influenced workers or other group preferences. Emblematic is ICI's re-definition of its model of employment relation or the application of the substitution programme in Brindisi.

The various aspects highlighted above lead to an interpretation of redundancies and restructuring as complex phenomena in which sector-specific and place-specific dynamics exercise a combined influence on companies' decision concerning restructuring processes. In the light of the reflections developed above, the reading of processes of industrial change and redundancies provided by some among the most credited strands of the neo-classical literature and the solutions proposed appear extremely partial. By maintaining that markets provide a spontaneous and natural order in which companies operate according to the most efficient solutions, such stances make a-priori assumptions about the nature and the existence of prevailing forms of economic rationality. The evidence presented above draws a different picture of processes of employment and industrial change. First, stimuli to corporate response are diverse and arise from the variety of possibilities and constraints connected to the organization of production and the transformations taking place in the wider market; the mono-causal nature of the processes of adjustment is therefore denied. Second, companies adapt creatively to changes in their micro- and macro-economic conditions. Accordingly, restructuring forms do not assume homogeneous traits and cannot be defined according to a-priory taxonomies, whilst their impact on employment levels do not represent a necessary outcome of deterministic economic imperatives but constitutes a dimension in which companies retain wide margins of manoeuvre.

How can industrial redundancies be theorized more positively? Some of the findings lend support to some of the alternative macro-economic perspectives reviewed in chapter two as well as to some efficiency wage models whose conceptualizations help to further deepen their analysis. As indicated, international demand is an important factor in explaining job losses in the chemical industry of Teesside and Brindisi. The insights provided by the Schumpeterian approach help to illustrate the way in which the cyclical nature of the business cycle affects employment levels. The cyclical character of the chemical industry implies that it is characterized by phases of investment in productive capacity, followed by periods of over-capacity. Layoffs may occur in a down swing as companies close plants or restructure or during an upswing when technological innovation, implemented either to respond to a rise in demand or to maintain a competitive edge on other companies, produces labour saving effects. The Marxian tradition instead provides a convincing account of job losses involving the clothing industry. Driven by the vertical integration of economic relations between producers and buyers, employment change in the two areas has resulted from processes of adjustment centred upon the spatial division of production and labour. The determination of sectoral employment and unemployment dynamics and their characteristics are therefore the result of the way in which clothing companies are re-organising production over space to exploit competitive advantages connected with the costs of labour. From a different perspective which, however, complements the above macro-analyses, the efficiency wage models that emphasize the social nature of preferences help to highlight the institutional arrangements affecting wage determination. The ICI case clearly illustrates that the type of business adjustment undertaken to regain profitability has also responded to a modification in the wage relation. This, by allowing among other things to offer better employment conditions than those set in the local labour market, satisfied the company's need to contain internal conflicts, in line with the Bowles model, as well as to generate feelings of trust and solidarity with its workers as in Akerlof's view. In certain clothing companies in Brindisi too, worker behaviour, deriving from sentiments of trust towards their companies, explains the form of adjustment undertaken, leading to a preservation of employment levels. Some findings confirm the emphasis attributed by institutionalist perspectives on the institutions of labour in explaining industrial and economic dynamics. Accordingly, job losses in the chemicals sector on Teesside have to be seen as the outcome of the transformation of the traditional employment relation regulating employment dynamics in the industry. Similarly, it is the conflicting nature of capital and labour relations in certain clothing companies in Brindisi and on Teesside and the lack of any regulation of their employment relations which compromize the implementation of longer-term adaptive strategies.

Each of the interpretations above provides a partially convincing account of the dynamics of industrial and employment change. First, by interpreting restructuring paths and job losses as the ultimate outcome of crises involving the economic and social systems, this literature fails to account for the role of individuals and collective agencies. The same limit, but for opposite reasons, relates to the efficiency wage models as they fail to account for the complexity of the phenomena under investigation which respond to mutual influences involving structures and agency. Second, each of these approaches has offered a partial interpretation of the phenomenon. This deficit is to be seen as a direct consequence of the partiality of the angle of investigation. The focus on specific aspects has produced fragmented analyses that, while contributing to an understanding of the phenomenon in relation to their departing point, have failed to recognize and highlight the interdependent nature of each of the dimensions identified.

The Role of Agency: Companies and Other Socio-Economic Actors

The findings necessitate a finer approach to the role of agency. The focus on companies suggests their twofold theoretical status. On the one hand, and as conceived within orthodox economic literature, they are individual agents whose action represents the most important determinant of phenomena of industrial and employment change. On the other hand, in this study, they have emerged as collective agents, epitomising complex economic and social dynamics shaped by the process of interaction between management, workers and unions, and expressed in the wage relation. The latter conceptualization echoes with the old institutionalist tradition, which considers companies as the locus in which capital and labour relations occur. However, the analysis here suggests that company material and social practices are also affected by the interests expressed by other collective organizations such as trade unions, organizations representing sectoral interests, as well as by worker individual preferences. In other words, the capital and labour dichotomy does not exhaust the multiplicity of collective and individual subjects and the inter-related nature of their constraints and opportunities that impinge upon both the way in which profitability is pursued through restructuring dynamics and the employment trends in and out of the workplace. Some examples from the research illustrate this point. The heterogeneity of restructuring paths undertaken by clothing companies in Brindisi have to be related primarily to the type of internal relations which draw a distinction among local companies. Differences in the mutual commitment between workers and employers have become a discriminating factor in explaining the choices concerning how to read and react to economic change. Then, the action of sectoral trade unions, mobilized to encourage companies to subscribe to the graduality contract, and the CNA's promotional initiatives have widened company adaptive opportunities. Also the dynamics of the chemical industry in Brindisi clearly show how actor specific interests have been influential. The corporatist model regulating the employment relations has ensured least disruptive solutions for employment, seconded by both workers and trade unions. The enhancement of redundancies, producing no net job losses, has been accepted by workers in a local economic context that, unable to create an adequate number of employment opportunities, constrains their choices. On Teesside, the role of TCI, which has been active in promoting local resources and infrastructures, has been important in influencing employment prospects. Furthermore, ICI's ability to honour the social pact with the community and to avoid the enforcement of a limited number of compulsory redundancies has been possible as other chemicals companies, wishing to exploit locational advantages, settled in the area. Therefore, company behaviour responds neither to a unique rationality, nor can it be determined a-priori. This is precisely the consequence of the non-standardized and non-universal framework of institutions and relations a company expresses. Paths of restructuring are characterized by variety and their impact on employment dynamics is neither inevitable nor necessarily negative. It follows that redundancies and restructuring processes become institutionally shaped themselves. They are constructed by individuals and collective actors whose preferences and constraints deeply influence the character of restructuring, the type of employment change, as well as the impact and management of job losses.

By contrast, both in the mainstream neo-classical conception and in the Marxist one, the firm as an institution is annihilated. For the former, companies are merely as production functions, "automatic transformer[s] of inputs into outputs" driven by profit maximization (Pitelis and Wahl, 1998, p.252), while for Marxism companies are the sites where the capitalist organization of the means of production is articulated. In the neo-classical approach, processes of restructuring are explained in terms of economic inefficiencies that only market mechanisms can reverse, while redundancies are seen as unproblematic events. Within the Marxist view, company profitability crises are mechanically ascribed to the working of the capitalist accumulation process and redundancies conceived as the necessary outcome of such a dynamic. The common element of these two dominant positions is that top-down explanations are privileged; also the role of individual and collective agency is reduced. Similarly, although the Schumpeterian approach acknowledges firms as active actors in search of innovation, companies tend to be trapped into the phases of business cycles which become the parameters confining entrepreneurial action. In this conceptual framework too, company restructuring processes are determined by their reaction to external economic dynamics.

Despite their acknowledgement of the reciprocal interactions between individuals and the institutional environment in which they operate, the dynamics described by the efficiency wage models that stress the social nature of preferences concern exclusively the relations between capital and labour. These models do not account for the asymmetries and divergent interests which exist within capital and labour. The explanation of industrial unemployment comes to be ascribed ultimately to company definitions of efficiency and profitability.

The Geographical Specificity of Redundancies

The research has revealed the significance of geographical context. Capital and labour are differentiated across space and the institutional endowment of a company too is spatially specific. Concretely, the process of wage determination is the outcome of interactive processes in a specific spatial context, involving companies, workers and other organizations. The strategies of these actors are, in turn, the expression of conveniences, pursuits, and limits, shaped by a plurality of external stimuli and of cultural conditions that have a contextual origin and respond also to sedimented practices. Economic dynamics and processes of change therefore find an explanation in the local institutional framework, defining individual and collective action. In addition, this interaction is shaped by legacies that are historical, institutional and related to the local labour market.

The corporate culture established by ICI on Teesside provides a good explanation of the way in which institutions and space are inseparably interwoven. ICI's re-positioning, through plant closures, business swaps and sell-offs, and a complex policy concerning worker dismissal, can be read as the willingness to honour the paternalistic pact linking the company to the community. Accordingly, ICI avoided compulsory redundancies, offered good retirement deals and sought to sell its marginal businesses together with their workforce. Similarly, the uncontested nature of its process of change reflects the historical weakness of the labour movement in the area unable to distinguish its action from that of the company. Restructuring processes and employment change thus are not events that happen to people; they rather reflect individual and collective strategies shaped in place.

The evidence of the spatial specificity of institutional interaction and its influence in accounting for processes of restructuring and job losses challenges the geographical a-specificity characterising conventional economistic analyses, both neo-classical and structural. In these conceptualizations, economic events are seen to impact on local contexts but places are treated as spatial containers of economic activities. They attribute no significance to the way in which company preferences are influenced by local relations and by the institutional context in which they operate. Geographical specificity and context are simply secondary factors in explaining redundancies. Similarly, preference models, whilst acknowledging the social nature of preferences and, therefore, creating the theoretical potentials to account for the geographical specificity of institutions expressing them, are unsatisfactory because they fail to articulate and investigate such preferences. The same fault can be found in the old institutionalist tradition that has rarely appreciated the territorial dimension of institutions and regulation. And yet, the acknowledgement of the institutional nature of redundancies leads to the appreciation that such phenomena are open to the asymmetric and power relations of place. Companies, workers, other social groups, such as unions but also the State, are not neutral agents; by expressing preferences, they are able to influence and address choices and outcomes in the labour market. Therefore, rather than being driven by them, they actively modify them. Following the institutionalist insights, it can be held that the understanding of employment dynamics is necessarily connected to the understanding of the nature of market and non-market relations. Specifically, the regulation of non-market relations is believed to express the achievement of a relative order on the repartition of duties and benefits among social groups. There is no spontaneous generation of social order springing from the unconscious co-operation ensured by price. Instead, institutional order is a compromize based on social relations characterized by conflicts. But in contrast to Marxist analysis, in which capitalist social relations revolve around class antagonism, an institutionalist perspective retains a more pluralistic vision of social and economic relations, assuming that the definition of employment relations is multiple, including collaboration and negotiation. For example, the awareness of sectoral dynamics guided the action of trade unions in the chemicals sector in Brindisi. They accepted technological innovation with its labour saving effects and company attempts to contain costs; in return, they sought minimal employment adjustments and favourable redundancy payments. The example also shows how union bargaining power is shaped by national laws as well as by the constraints imposed by a local economic context characterised by fear of unemployment and scarce employment opportunities.

In summary, rather than being seen as mere economic events, employment and industrial changes come to be interpreted as complex socio-economic processes shaped by the interplay of individuals and groups' actions which are influenced by sectoral trends and institutional influences, that are spatially and historically specific. Decisions about industrial and employment restructuring respond to rational decision-making processes but also to symbolic relations that are sedimented in time and spatially-specific. It is precisely the unique alchemy of relations crystallized by companies and expressed in the definition of the employment relation that explains the specific manner through which efficiency and profitability are pursued.

Note

[1] In the Brindisi's province, 26,888 hours were agreed to local companies in 1994. In 1999, they became 105,189 hours (Istituto Nazionale di Previdenza Sociale, INPS, 2000).

Chapter 6

The Social Value of Labour and Economic Performance

The Contribution of an Institutionalist Perspective on Industrial Unemployment

In the last decade or so economic geography and, specifically industrial geography, has witnessed a move towards explanatory accounts that emphasize social and cultural context. As indicated by Barnes (1999, p.17), these accounts "have come in various shapes and sizes" and centre on a plurality of categories of analysis such as social power, cultural identity, institutional situatedness, etc. The study of institutions and their role in shaping industrial activity represents one of the fields in which the intersection of industrial geography and institutionalism is expected to produce important theoretical and empirical contributions, even though there has always been an interest in this topic (refer to the work of Danson on segmented labour market and Hayter and Watts on enterprises). The institutionalist perspective adopted in this work to study industrial unemployment represents an attempt in this direction. It has been claimed and shown on the basis of the evidence that such processes cannot be understood and explained solely as the outcome of firm profit maximising behaviours aiming to restore their profitability compromized by the rigidity of the cost of labour. They are rather understandable by considering that corporate action is embedded into a set of formal and informal institutions that affect the process of wage determination and, through it, the definition and the pursuit of profitability and efficiency. In other words, whilst highlighting the ways in which the forces of capitalist economic development such as accumulation, competition, technology, etc., generate spatially differentiated outcomes in terms of employment, it is held that those forces shape and are shaped by a complex matrix of institutions. The specific contribution of an institutionalist perspective to industrial redundancies lies therefore in understanding the extent and manner in which processes of restructuring and redundancies are shaped and mediated by specific institutions and the processes through which they take place. Such an understanding needs the abandonment of the mainstream methodological approach to economic action, with its conception of rational maximising actors and perfectly competitive markets, and the adoption of an institutionally oriented conception of human action. It is institutions, formed through the prevalence and permanence of certain individual habits and developing autonomous properties that become the basis of economic action.

This theoretical and methodological approach paves the way for a perspective on industrial unemployment emphasising precisely those dimensions that conventional economic analyses do not explain. First, the focus on the informal and formal institutions that enter the process of wage determination and on the way in which they are arranged in the regulation of the employment relationship makes it possible to disclose the processes and motivations of different nature that influence processes of employment and industrial change and explain why they occur in the way they do. It has been contended that such institutions affect corporation definition of economic rationality and mediate their employment strategies that tend to respond to a plurality of criteria (e.g. social sustainability). Second, through the identification of the institutions shaping restructuring processes and redundancies and the way in which they do so, such a perspective makes it possible to highlight some specific dimensions affecting them. One refers to the economic landscape. By their very nature institutions tend to evolve incrementally and in a self-reproducing way. They are therefore important bearers of industrial histories that, on the one hand, affect the way in which economic and industrial dynamics impact on corporations and, on the other, explain their responses through adjustment strategies. In addition, it claims the inherently socio-cultural nature of technological change that is deemed to be dependent on the cultural setting within which it takes place rather than as a process disembodied from society. Ideas of "path dependency" and "lock in" suggest that particular trajectories of industrial development as well as of industrial restructuring connected to technology have a significant institutional matrix. An institutional perspective on redundancies also encompasses consideration of the cultural foundation of the space economy. Processes of industrial and unemployment change are affected by individual identities, lifestyles, patterns of consumption through the formation of conventions and norms both inside and outside the workplace. At the same time, as cultural processes represent the main means through which knowledge, attitudes and cultural values are transmitted, they assume a key role in determining a specific outcome of industrial and employment change. Third, the adoption of an institutionalist approach to industrial redundancies also makes it possible to highlight the inherently spatial nature of institutional interaction and the consequent spatial specificity of processes of employment and industrial change. The work has focused mainly on the local aspects of the regulation of the employment relationship. It has extended to the local scale the framework that institutionalists and regulationists apply for national economic configurations, by looking at the way in which local capital and labour, local social networks, work cultures in and out of the workplaces, locally and regionally specific institutions and organizations, provide stability to local industrial activity but also shape the processes of change. The analytical privilege reserved to the local dimension through the study of two local case studies does not imply that an institutionalist perspective is specifically best equipped to deal with the local dimension. Thus, whilst it maintains that national as well as supra-national mechanisms of regulation have local varied impact and that regulation has a local foundation, reflecting the variety of local institutions entering the definition of the wage relation, it suggests that what is important is to focus not only on the scale at which industrial phenomena occur but especially on the relations between geographical and regulatory scales.

Some Theoretical and Policy Implications

The concept of regulation is a consistent theme running throughout current academic and policy debates concerning the labour market. The institutional regulation of labour market dynamics has come to be generally seen as the major obstacle to the free working of market forces and the institutions of labour as the source of the rigidity that prevents economic and industrial development. The best solution indicated to solve the problem of labour is the flexibilization of the employment relation; only complete freedom for companies to adjust their factors of production according to market conditions constitutes the guarantee for their economic performance which, in turn, benefits labour. In much of the literature, the source of the problem of industrial unemployment is therefore taken for granted: external intervention in market dynamics undermines the action of companies as profit-maximising agents; their activity in various sectors and places may be changing, but the fundamental origin of their problem remains the same. Industrial unemployment is the outcome of homogeneous restructuring processes, driven by mono-causal dynamics.

As argued in this book, redundancies cannot be reduced to mere economic phenomena, the inevitable outcome of industrial restructuring processes. Corporate patterns of adjustment are neither uniform, definable a-priori, nor the result of profit maximising behaviour. They are instead continuously subject to the actions and strategies of individuals and groups that influence the process of wage determination and, through it, the definition and the pursuit of profitability and efficiency. Restructuring and redundancies are not events in which people have no role except one of reaction or perhaps of support. Restructuring and redundancies are shaped institutionally and dialectically – they are processes. The interpretation of industrial unemployment that has been advanced is different from the readings offered by dominant stances as it has put the wage relation and institutions that regulate it at the centre of the analysis. The underlying assumption has been that such institutions constitute the major source of the heterogeneity in the restructuring paths undertaken by corporations as well as of their differentiated impact on employment. Prevailing institutional arrangements relating to the employment relation also explain variations in employment performance at the aggregate level under the same recessive conditions. This is because, in contrast to the neo-classical conceptualization and in accordance with institutionalist insights, it has been assumed that the quality of labour and its contribution to production are not reducible to the labour contract and, therefore, cannot be subjected exclusively to monetary exchange. Indeed, the bilateral arrangement between employer and worker is incomplete because neither the content of work nor the future conditions under which it will take place can be anticipated. Consequently, there is not a simple relationship between pay and productivity (Cartier, 1994). It follows that the formal and informal institutions of labour, a reflection of wider societal arrangements, that regulate the relationship between capital and labour, constitute the critical factor for explaining corporate performance and change. In this perspective, therefore, the study of industrial unemployment and restructuring has been approached through the processes of institutionalization and regulation. Accordingly, they have been held as institutionally constructed processes and as such geographically situated.

The empirical investigation at the heart of this work has reinforced this theoretical standpoint. As illustrated in the two case study chapters on Teesside and Brindisi and in the comparative one, the nature of the causes leading to job losses from the chemical and clothing industries is varied and cannot be reduced merely to the cost of labour and to its binding (and, therefore, rigid) regulatory outcomes. As shown, different definitions of profitability emerge in the two sectors and among companies in the same sector; this is because companies pursue different forms of efficiency in response to different sets of possibilities and external constraints and, in most cases, the goal of cost minimization is not always the primary one. By the same token, it has been argued that corporate practices of adjustment do not necessarily lead to the reduction of employment. The perspective on industrial unemployment proposed here constitutes a clear alternative to mainstream interpretations which, in their efforts to produce models offering refined and general accounts of the phenomenon, have ended up reducing and simplifying its complexity. Beyond abstract models and conventional analyses, a more concrete understanding of the problem of industrial unemployment has been deemed possible and indeed has been put forward. By looking at the plurality of institutions that shape the definition of the wage relation and regulate the way in which profitability and efficiency are pursued, three aspects – complexity, agency and geography – contribute to refine the interpretation of industrial unemployment. Complexity refers to the plurality and interrelated nature of both economic and social variables that may trigger profitability crises and the strategies that companies may decide to undertake to maintain and restore profitability. Agency allows us to highlight the subjective processes, expressing individuals' and groups' choices, which dialectically define the rationality and viability of economic processes. Geography consists of both the spatial specificity assumed by economic phenomena and the cultural endowment of an area that shapes economic processes, according to the societal values in which they are embedded. Decisions made and actions implemented by corporations respond to motives of economic rationality but also to routines, customs, and internal norms that are temporally contingent and spatially-specific.

The specific focus of the work on industrial unemployment and restructuring seems, at first sight, to hark back to the debate on themes that, whilst at the forefront of the theoretical and empirical interest during the decade from the mid-1980s to the mid-1990s, have since then acquired a certain marginality (see amongst others, Danson, 1986; Martin and Rowthorn, 1986; Massey and Meegan, 1985). Indeed, after the period of heavy industrial restructuring involving both private and public corporations and massive job losses, which particularly affected the areas revolving around traditional manufacturing industries, it has become apparent that the subject has lost its appeal especially among academics.[1] The modification of the industrial structure of many industrial countries, with the reduction of the weight of heavy manufacturing industries, the expansion of services and the increasing percentage of self-employment, suggested that the problem of industrial unemployment had disappeared from the economic and labour market scene. In reality, the neglect of the area of investigation in question, I believe, is not justified. This is for two main reasons. First, 'traditional' forms of industrial unemployment, deriving from the downsizing and closure of plants are still common and often produce spatially concentrated problems of labour. Second, new forms of industrial unemployment are emerging brought about by the processes of continuous restructuring that represent the novel feature of corporate adjustment to market conditions, by vertical disintegration of productive processes, by processes of subcontracting and re-location. In other words, on the one hand, there are still cases of radical restructuring leading, for instance, to plant closures and massive job losses in old and new sectors of the economy and, on the other, there is continuous restructuring that, whilst not producing a major impact on the employment levels in terms of job destruction is nonetheless changing the employment relations. As a consequence, new forms of under-employment are emerging as well as new forms of economic and labour weakness. Therefore, the fact that industrial unemployment does not manifest itself in the 'traditional' manner does not mean that it does not exist at all. The need to account for a phenomenon that is assuming complex features, primarily because of the modification of productive relations, and that is affecting traditional and new categories of workers, explains the choice of the theoretical and analytical apparatuses underlying this work. The conceptualization of industrial and unemployment change according to an institutionalist perspective constitutes a potential breakthrough in economic geography. Besides the causes of different nature that lead to restructuring and redundancies, such an approach allows us to account for the institutional framework that governs the relationships between capital and labour and, therefore, the evolution of economic processes in the contemporary phase of capitalist development. That is, it does not simply acknowledge the salience of the formal and informal institutional configuration on restructuring and redundancies but, more importantly, seeks to explain such economic processes in the light of societal values that guide economic action.

Two strictly related implications can be drawn out from the analysis. First, the institutionalist perspective adopted here allows us to transcend the debate that, in the last two decades, has monopolized much of the academic literature and policy making activity because of the support it gained in political discourses of diverse traditions (Boyer, 1988; OECD, 1994;

Industrial Redundancies

CEPR, 1995). This has revolved around the dichotomy "rigidity versus flexibility", "institutional regulation versus market forces", or "regulation versus de-regulation". The emphasis of this debate is misplaced and concretely misleading. It is misplaced because the key issue for industrial unemployment and restructuring relates to the type of regulatory solutions that allow certain economic and labour performances to be consistent with the values that a society considers economically legitimate. It is misleading because discourses praising the spontaneous and beneficial effects of de-regulation of the employment relation have in reality become the means to re-define individual and collective responsibility within the productive process and labour market. De-regulation does not necessarily enhance the free working of productive and market forces, but moves the problem of industrial unemployment (the problem of labour) from a collective to an individual level. On the one hand, the manifestation and persistence of unemployment are attributed to individual deficits (lack of adequate training, skills, values appropriate for the organization in which they work, etc.); on the other, the conditions to safeguard jobs or to re-enter the industry (labour market) depend in first instance on the workers and unemployed themselves (Peck, 1998). In this theoretical frame, collective institutions are supposed to retreat from any type of involvement in labour market dynamics. Companies and the State no longer have responsibility to intervene to correct labour market failures for the same reasons that they do not exist as such: failures are individual and not determined by occurrences in the economic or social realms. Consequently, the legitimacy of the systems of production and of State is by no means threatened. The progressive retreat of institutions from direct or indirect intervention may be likely to amplify the problem of industrial unemployment rather than alleviate it. By creating the conditions for the emergence of sharp differences within and between spaces of production, restructuring strategies are deeply influenced. At a local or company level, the flexibilization of employment practices is leading to the dichotomy between core and peripheral productive activities and core and peripheral workers; the latter are trapped into a vicious situation according to which their individual deficits are the causes that lead them to be outside the core of the production process. This is, in turn, the main obstacle to obtain future better working conditions. At the same time, trajectories to re-enter the workplace are designed to satisfy the technical and social practices of the organization. At a systemic level, the deregulation and individualization of the employment relation, with the aim of responding to the novel demands of production and of allowing swift adjustments of wages and labour contracts to market conditions, are prone to contradictions (Brunetta and Dell'Aringa, 1990). For one, international competition is only partly conducted on the base of costs. When, more frequently, adequate performance is connected to quality, innovative capacity, research and development, etc., the link between individual effort, productivity, employment practices and wider economic performances returns to the fore in the debate. Second, and related to the preceding discussion, the study of industrial unemployment through an institutionalist perspective allows a theme that political rhetoric seems to have darkened to be openly put back into both the theoretical and political debate, that is the social value attributed to labour. The thrust towards reforms aiming to lighten the burden of the indirect costs of labour sustained by employers and to reduce State intervention for reasons of fiscal efficiency, without any parallel reform in the basic relations of production, raise questions about the reproduction of labour (Burawoy, 1985; Boyer, 1993).[2] Yet, pursuit of the myth of the wage as the mechanism regulating the sphere of production and the parallel rolling back of the welfare state is widening the role of social economy and/or third sector as well as of the sphere of social reproduction (domestic work). Regulatory dilemmas emerge and relate primarily to how to co-ordinate social reproduction effectively and whether alternative routes to mainstream economies may serve to the scope or whether they become only a means to relieve the task of the State and of mainstream economy. Studying industrial unemployment through the institutions regulating labour has emphasized precisely how the problem of the efficiency of labour and, consequently, of corporate performance, cannot be dealt with unless the social costs of labour are taken into consideration. Such a problem does not reside so much in the dilemma between efficiency and equity, but rather between individual and collective efficiency, that is between efficiency in a classical sense and efficiency at the level of community (industrial efficiency and social cohesion) (Bazzoli, 1994). In other words, the nub of the problem revolves around the definition of the aim of production and the conditions of workers' involvement in it rather than the mere regulation of the exchange of labour. Open recognition of the problem of the social cost of labour, of the need to secure its reproduction and to ensure the protection of the intangible property of workers constitute themes of rupture with the current theoretical and policy debates and a source of further investigation. Rather than supporting the progressive retreat of employers from any type of commitment towards their workforce, following only labour cost consideration, there is the need to explore the way in which the mode of production may be transformed and the way in which the institutions of labour within industrial production may ensure its economic viability – as sources of economic efficiency - and institutional viability – capacity for social cohesion. Yet, this implies the need to tackle primarily the transformation of industrial organization and the revision of the logic concerning the costs of economic and industrial action.

The study of industrial unemployment through an institutionalist perspective paves the way for a re-thinking of policy measures to tackle the problem. An institutionalist agenda distances itself from the dominant policy in three ways. First, it recognizes a role for demand-side policies, besides the necessary labour market reforms. A plurality of interventions could stimulate demand as a source of employment opportunities. There are few chances to create economic and employment opportunities without policy programmes aiming to improve productive conditions, through infrastructures and services, and to ensure an adequate level of investments avoiding inflationary outcomes. Second, an institutionalist policy is sensitive to promoting the role of a variety of individual and collective actors at the local level in the definition of economic and labour market priorities. Without degenerating into parochialism, such an approach would enhance the connectivity of local contexts that, for many observers, is the critical factor for economic success rather than the mere presence of local relations among institutions (Hudson, 1999). This type of relationship could enhance companies' ability to anticipate and respond to changing external circumstances rather than oblige them to adopt purely reactive strategies. Third, the institutionalist approach put forward here considers as a critical factor the democratization of collective negotiation within firms and at national level. Specifically, the re-definition of enterprises as institutions in which workers and trade unions become actors implies the re-definition of new employment conditions, of a new articulation of the spheres of production and allocation and of the organization of social time. Public action should become more flexible in the resolution of conflicts and problems and should refer to the more general political economy. These suggestions go beyond dominant assumptions according to which the intrinsic supply-side qualities of the workforce and of the context are sufficient to create employment and economic development opportunities. Concretely, the blind faith in the beneficial implications of de-regulation and supply-side policies on employment creation and industrial development is likely to produce limited results, especially in the areas of old industrialization. Indeed, these are areas characterized by the domination of externally owned or controlled companies. By creating their own internal labour markets through in-house and task-dedicated training, often for a limited range of occupations, these companies have in most cases prevented skills diversification in the wider local labour market and, especially, the formation of an entrepreneurial and institutional culture equipped to tackle the challenges of the changing economic environment and able to overcome the burden of past institutional legacies, locking in their development paths.

From the preceding discussion, some final remarks can be drawn. What emerges is the centrality of the employment relationship not simply for understanding industrial unemployment but especially for understanding the aims of economic action and the processes underlying it. In other words, the regulation of capital and labour relations, through the institutions of labour at different levels (company, local, regional, national) becomes the critical factor in accounting for current industrial and employment processes of change. In contrast to the dominant attack on labour prerogatives and individualization of the employment relation in order to improve the dynamic of productive forces and for a better allocation of resources, following a perspective of individual maximization (Sengenberger and Campbell, 1994), the institutionalist perspective suggests that the key condition for this to happen lies in a new compromise between capital and labour. A new and more coherent definition of the institutions regulating the exchange and the use of labour would provide the basis for a more collective and, therefore, more democratic as well as viable way of solving labour problems.

Notes

[1] The only recent literature focuses specifically on plant closures (e.g. Pike, 1998; MacLachlan, 1992; Watts and Stafford, 1986).
[2] This involves a wide range of processes that are connected to the company, but also to the household, to the community and to the State (from biological procreation to education, from training to caring, etc.).

Appendix

Research Methodology

An Institutionalist Epistemology

The methodology employed to carry out the comparative study of Teesside and Brindisi, consistently with the theoretical framework advanced in Chapter Two, rests upon four assumptions. First, it assumes that the market, the major expression of the economic logic of capitalism, is an institution itself. This implies that exchanges are organized and founded upon economic and non-economic (e.g. social, ethic, legal, etc.) institutions and rules. It follows, consequently, that, besides relations of exchange, the market is also characterized by relations of production and re-allocation of resources. The main implication for an investigation on industrial unemployment is that the analysis cannot focus merely on the moment of the exchange of labour (or its end); also, the wage (price of labour) cannot be the only parameter of investigation. Accordingly, as it is maintained that the wage relation represents more than the contract between employers and workers (labour in exchange for corresponding pay) and, specifically, that it embodies the institutions that regulate capital and labour relations (definition of profit, content and coherence of labour provision, etc.), such institutions become the main object of investigation. Second, the study of institutions has the scope of providing an understanding of the ensemble of rules, habits and other social forms that frame the actions and strategies of individuals and groups and influence both the process of wage determination and the wider wage relation. Redundancies and restructuring are not something that happen to people, but they are processes in which people are both affected and participate. By bringing institutions to the centre of the analysis, this methodology allows the disclosure of the processes and motivations of diverse nature that determine processes of employment and industrial change and explain why they occur in the way they do. The idea of the rational man driven by maximization behaviour is therefore dismissed as individuals are deemed to act following sedimented ways of thought or action, generating habits. Third, by assuming habits rather than rational choices to be the basis of human action, an institutionalist methodology of industrial unemployment claims the primacy of collective action over the individual one. Formal and informal institutions, formed as durable and integrated complexes of shared habits, become the dimensions that mediate both actor actions and outcomes. Preferences are endogenized in individual behaviour and interests are acknowledged as autonomous but not independent. Following this perspective, redundancies are not seen as the result of the action of independent actors (firms and individuals), but rather as the outcome of inter-relations between individual and collective actors. In particular, the enterprise is attributed a salient role. It represents the institution at the heart of the capitalist imperative and of the social relations underlying it. In contrast to neo-classical and structuralist analyses, it is investigated as an institution crystallising a complex web of social relationships which determine a specific corporate culture[1] and drive economic decisions. Finally, by accounting for actor action and the processes that influence it, the institutionalist methodology proposed here acknowledges that industrial unemployment is an open process, determined also by power relations. In other words, it considers the salience of the aims of the economic action (not only of its means) as well as of the processes underlying it (not simply its results).[2] In addition, it maintains that the outcome of both these processes is historically contingent and geographically differentiated, not only in terms of institutional forms but also in terms of their socio-economic effects. By claiming that labour market phenomena come to be regulated in geographically distinctive ways, this approach maintains that labour market processes are spatially varied both in their causal origin and the manner of their operation.

The epistemology indicated raises a central question about the role of method within social sciences. Following Commons (1934), the primary objective of an institutionalist investigation, which is shared here, is to disclose patterns of explanation. They allow the understanding of human behaviour by placing it within its cultural context and by building categories of investigation starting from the identification of similarities-differences and of relations between parts and whole. An institutionalist investigation is holistic in two ways. First, one cannot separate the logic and the empirical nature of reality and, second, human systems are interconnected and, therefore, not logically separable (Bazzoli, 1994). Underlying this is a conceptualization of science which accounts for social phenomena and their evolution as the expression of the historically-determined behaviour of individuals, groups and institutions that shape them and are shaped by them. In contrast, the neo-classical tradition is based on a hypothetical and deductive method of analysis. Deduction rests on hypotheses that limit the explanative variables (exogenous to the analysis) and the variables to be explained (which are endogenous). Thus, what is explained is the logical consequence of premises set a-priori: these are laws that allow connections among abstract categories. By indicating a logic link between explanation and prediction, this method leads to the formation of general laws able to explain trans-historical and trans-cultural realities; science assumes a predictive aim. Individuals are deemed to be driven by the logic of rational choices which becomes the most efficient mechanism of economic co-cordination. In this picture, institutions as well as technology and preferences are assumed as given and do not intervene in the representation of the market.

Implementing the Analytical Framework

Two aims underlie the empirical work. It first seeks to investigate the main causes of redundancies and industrial restructuring in the chemical and clothing industries of Teesside and Brindisi. Second, it attempts to identify and study the institutions that affect the wage relationship and shape processes of change in the two sectors of the two areas. The questions have not been tackled exclusively through the analysis of aggregate indicators, as contemplated by the most credited analyses on industrial unemployment (table A.1), but rather through the focus on the processes fuelling industrial and employment change as well as on the agents involved in it.

That is, whilst considering, for instance, profitability trends, sector output growth, employment trends or process innovation, the analysis has sought to highlight the complex nature of the processes object of investigation, where institutional, economic and spatial aspects intertwine, and reflect on the overlapping interactions among them (Silverman, 1993; Flowerdew and Martin, 1996). The focus is on corporate strategies, on the strategies of other formal institutions (e.g. trade unions, local authorities, local sectoral organizations, voluntary organizations working with unemployed workers) as well as to consider individual preferences.

Table A.1 Theoretical positions and main methodological variables

Theoretical positions	Key methodological variables
Wage rigidity argument	Profitability, cost of labour, labour productivity, union density, labour market corporatism, laws regulating employment relations
Keynesian interpretation	Manufacturing investments, interest rates, manufacturing output, GDP growth
Marxism	Profitability, (excess) productive capacity, accumulation rate, labour productivity, investment rate, consumption levels, union density, industrial disputes
Neo-Marxists	Capital ownership, structure of activities within corporations, investment rate, productive capacity, work organisation, labour productivity, industrial relations, industrial policies, job and social characteristics
Schumpeterian theory	GDP growth, sectors output growth, investment rates, patents, product and process innovations, R&D
Preference models:	
Based on methodological individualism	Shirking model: organisation and practices of work, labour productivity, control systems, trade union presence Fairness model: unemployed behaviour
Based on the social nature of preferences	Shirking model: company internal disputes, organisation of work, control systems, worker participation, trade union presence Fairness model: employers-workers relations (e.g. organisation of work)
Based on competitive group strategies	Participation model: firm governance structure (wage system, capital/labour partnership) Insiders/outsiders model: hiring costs, cost of training, level of productivity, trade union presence

(cont.)

(table A.1 cont.)

Theoretical positions	Key methodological variables
Old institutionalism	At company level: profit strategies, system of production, organisation of work, working conditions, trade union presence, quality circles, workers' participation At collective level: bargaining system, labour legislation, education system, structure and dynamics of the welfare system, industrial policies
Regulation theory	System of production and accumulation, system of bargaining, macro-economic policy orientation, consumption patterns, welfare system
Theory of conventions	Work routines, interpersonal relations, customs, traditions, shared expectations, learning processes, transmission of skills, use of equipment and tools

Much of the analysis has revolved around the chemical and clothing companies of Teesside and Brindisi. This has been consistent with the theoretical and methodological centrality attributed to companies as primary source of processes of employment and industrial change; they have been seen as agents reflecting the specific interests of capital, but also as institutions representing the definition of capital and labour relationships -through the regulation with workers and unions- and the wider social relations they reflect. The diverse strategies undertaken to restore or maintain profitability, as well as the variety of possible employment adjustments, represent the outcome of a unique decision-making process in response to external or internal pressures of diverse nature. Their choices should be deemed as the most adequate solutions considered their internal culture, their material (e.g. technical resources) and social (e.g. human resources, organization of work) endowment as well as the symbolic representations and perception of their role in a particular community, result of spatially and historically specific relations or sedimented practices. Second, the centrality of company role in shaping employment change has been assessed in connection to the management of redundancies. The analysis has focused on the decision-making process leading to redundancies and on the criteria followed in order to implement them. In the first case, the investigation on the actors involved in the decision, on the process through which the decision was taken and the climate of such a process, has accounted inter alia for the existence and the nature of industrial relations in local companies, for the perception of their responsibility towards the community in which they are located as well as for their wider productive strategies. The combination of these elements shapes businesses action as institutional and cultural systems affect not only the definition of what is rational economic behaviour, but also whether this behaviour is compatible with the wider social environment in which it manifests. The criteria used to select particular sections of the workforce to make redundant are other means through which companies shape employment change. In contrast to what is generally portrayed in economic analyses, corporate restructuring processes do not end up simply enlarging the pool of unemployed people from a purely quantitative perspective. Restructuring paths involving job losses offer companies the opportunity to actively intervene in the selection of professional profiles that are more suitable to the requirements of the organization of production and work that they intend to achieve and pursue after the phase of adjustment. Finally, the role of companies on processes of industrial and employment change has been considered by looking at the impact of their restructuring choices on the local productive fabric and employment relations. Large scale restructuring processes, involving a plurality of companies, but also the action of a single company, may have deep effects on the productive profile of a whole sector. Besides quantitative changes, a sector is likely to suffer from qualitative transformations attaining, for instance, its productive specialization or the level of technological endowment. Also inter-firms relations may undergo a modification towards a closer integration in the productive cycle or, on the contrary, towards a greater segmentation of activities. By the same token, restructuring strategies may lead to the re-definition of the prevalent model of employment relations. This includes primarily firms internal labour markets (e.g. the upgrading of the technological apparatus leads to a modification of the organization of work) but also the modification of the demand for labour with its effects on the features of the supply side.

Together with companies, trade unions have been considered the other active agents of industrial and employment change. Trade unions have been conceived as institutions rather than as organizations. They are not merely bearers of worker interests in contrast to those represented by business, but they have also a wider collective role. Within the capitalist system, they promote the compromise between conflicting interests and the need for industrial development. In this framework, therefore, they become a source of regulation and control of capitalist tendencies. The employment relation is the institution in which conflicts and common interests find a mediation, where the productive role of workers and employers, as complementary to each other, is recognized, and where conflicts may become a source of change. The presence of trade unions at the workplace and their co-ordination as well as the climate of industrial relations, reflecting distinctive industrial cultures, represent important variables to influence corporate decisions of change, to affect the quantitative impact of job losses and the categories of workers most affected. This research has analysed the role of unions in two ways. First, the investigation has considered their responses during a phase of industrial restructuring. At firm level, agreements concerning the modification of the organization and practices of work, through for instance the implementation of forms of internal flexibility, and, in general, the search for negotiated and gradual employment adjustment measures, widen the firms' menu of options for restructuring and avoid the exclusive reduction of the employment level. These are also the means to reduce the number of redundancies actually enforced. Unions' influence on industrial and employment change occurs also at a wider level. By affecting labour demand (e.g. through agreements on changes concerning labour processes), unions' choices shape the features of the supply-side of the labour market. Second, unions affect employment dynamics also through their involvement in the decision-making and management of redundancies. This occurs both at the workplace, where the dismissal of certain workers or categories of workers produces a re-configuration of the workforce around different technical and cultural values, and at the level of the wider labour market, which sees the creation of pools of unemployed workers characterized by specific features. It is somewhat counter-intuitive that trade unions' specific strategies reflect constraints and opportunities, spatially and culturally specific, that inevitably lead to solutions favouring, for instance, certain workers rather than others or favouring employed workers rather than the unemployed ones.

Industrial and employment change is also affected by the action of local institutions (e.g. local authorities) and sectoral organizations (e.g. Chamber of Commerce, employers' associations). By providing infrastructures – from the areas destined to industrial settlements to childcare – but also training and social services or by adopting active industrial policies or job creation initiatives, local authorities play a key role in facilitating and supporting industrial activity. The presence and the activism of local sectoral organizations have been deemed to enhance productive activity and to have a positive role when periods of change are underway. As shown in the case study chapters, by developing promotional activities, these organizations have favoured inter-firm co-operation and agreements towards the reduction of external diseconomies and a common reaction to economic change. The analysis has also considered voluntary organizations engaged in activities for unemployed workers. By providing training and other services between welfare and the labour market, they act as intermediaries through which some unemployed acquire new social and professional skills to participate again in the labour market. Processes of industrial and employment change have been explored also through the investigation of workers' experience of being made redundant. In addition, the focus on their current strategies to re-enter the labour market accounts for the modified production and work requirements.

An institutionalist investigation of processes of redundancies and industrial restructuring recognizes the power of context. In this specific case, this has implied a consideration of two sectors and two areas. The focus on the two sectors has allowed the investigation of the two explanatory levels that are considered salient for industrial and geographical phenomena (Sayer and Morgan, 1985). The first consists of the sectoral analysis in which companies operate; this provides an explanation of local sectoral performances whose changing trends impinge upon companies' decisions; the second concerns the dynamics of individual companies to find out about what happens in themselves. As indicated by Sayer and Morgan (ibid. 149), "what happens on the ground also depends on how resources are organized in the factory and on the kinds of responses to the conditions at both levels, both of which can vary considerably". Company performance, therefore, cannot be detached from the knowledge of sectoral trends or from the knowledge of the wider local institutional conditions that affect both the nature of company internal resources and the way in which they are used. Such knowledge has been acquired through analyses of other subjects; as indicated, these include workers and redundant workers, trade unionists, public officers and members of voluntary organizations. By holding different sensitiveness and perceptions of the problems and by representing diverse economic and social interests, they have contributed to provide a realistic picture of the complexity of reality. This methodology has also virtually effaced the problems connected with the "view from above", derived from conducting interviews only with managers (Forthergill and Gudgin, 1985).

Methods of Analysis

Interviews and Focus Groups

Semi-structured interviews[3] and focus groups[4] have been the main instruments used to grasp the qualitative aspects connected to the processes of industrial restructuring in the two industries and their impact upon the employment/unemployment dynamics. The interviews were conducted with four different groups of interviewees (employers-plant/personnel managers, workers, socio-economic organizations – local institutions, and voluntary organizations working with unemployed) (table A.2), using four slightly different checklists (table A.3).

Table A.2 Organizations and individuals interviewed

BRINDISI

CHEMICAL SECTOR   CLOTHING SECTOR

Personnel or plant managers   Employers
Workers   Workers
Sectoral trade unions   Sectoral trade unions
Associazione Sviluppo Industriale   CNA
Federmoda

Trade unions
AssIndustria Brindisi
Puglia Region – Task Force on Employment
Voluntary organizations working with unemployed
Private consultants
Experts on local economy
Cultural centre

(cont.)

(table A.2 cont.)

TEESSIDE

CHEMICAL SECTOR

Personnel or plant managers
Workers
Trade unions
Teesside Chemical Initiative
Training Centre

CLOTHING SECTOR

Personnel or plant managers
Workers
Sectoral trade unions

Chamber of Commerce
CBI – Regional Office
Local TEC
Local Economic Agency
Local Authority – Industry division
Private Development Organizations
Voluntary organizations working with unemployed

All the interviews were transcribed and coded. Connections among such codes constituted the basis for a code map which, in turn, facilitated the interpretation of the fieldwork material, the link between its analysis and the theory, and the identification of elements of novelty. Although the research has adopted an intensive methodology and, therefore, relies heavily upon primary sources, it has however been complemented and strengthened by the use of secondary material. Quantitative data (national and international statistics) has been used in particular to update existing employment-unemployment trends and to provide novel insights into the main dynamics affecting the labour market and industrial structure of the two areas examined. Further background information was traced through back-copies of newspapers and magazines as well market surveys. In the case of the chemical sectors, an important source of data was found in the annual reports of the major chemical corporations, obtained directly from the companies. These have been particularly useful in reconstructing the trend of their main financial and economic indicators as well as their employment over the years.

Table A.3 Main themes of investigation during the interviews

Pattern of employment change in the company/industry

Employment trends in the company/industry
Phases of redundancies
Number of job losses
Categories of workers most affected

Causes of redundancies/restructuring

Economic (e.g. demand, cost of labour, tech. innovation, etc.)
Non-economic (e.g. laws, organization strategies, etc.)
Attitudes and behaviour of the workforce (e.g. inflexibility, reservation wage, etc.)

Management of redundancies

Categories of workers made redundant
Criteria adopted
Decision-making process

Employers' responsibility

Workers' behaviour in the labour market

Development and employment prospects

Productive implications for the company
Productive implications for the area
Employment prospects in the company
Employment prospects in the area

Such data were the source of important preliminary information to the actual interview with chemical managers which, according to Schoenberger (1991), is essential for making the most of the limited amount of time which executives are often willing to concede to researchers.

The Two Sectors

The chemical and clothing industries have been selected because they display a different use of the factors of production. While the most important phases of clothing production require a large input of labour, technological characteristics assume a primary relevance in determining performance in the chemical industry, affected by capital assets and technological innovation. This distinction serves as a means of examining how the cost of labour affects restructuring processes. In addition, it should influence choices concerning the quantity and the quality of the workforce. Yet, the production process in the two industries – e.g. the integration of the cycle of chemical production as opposed to the fragmentation of the clothing industry – should affect differently the organization of work and, consequently, the character of industrial relations in terms of workers/unions' strength in influencing the process of wage determination and their capacity to express unitary interests.

The choice of the chemical and clothing industries is also related to their role within the industrial structure of Teesside and Brindisi and within the local industrial culture, both influencing the construction of the wage relation. The chemical industry is a key industry in the economy of both areas in terms of output and employment. Historically central in local policies and party programmes, the sector has also assumed a specific cultural connotation as the source of wealth and employment on stable bases. By contrast, the clothing sector has been reserved a marginal role in both localities. In Brindisi, the industry existed prior to the settlement of the chemicals, but has ended up being shadowed by it. On Teesside, the clothing industry emerged as a buffer sector to heavy industries, absorbing the large reserve of female workers. It has always maintained a marginal image even if, with the collapse of base industries and the rise of male unemployment, women's earnings have become, in many cases, the only source of income. However, an important difference distinguishes the clothing industries of Brindisi and Teesside. In Brindisi, the dimension of the sector in terms of productive units is much larger than on Teesside; moreover, together with metal manufacture, it employs the highest percentage of employees in the province (17.3%).

The Regional Case Studies

According to the literature on research methodology, the case study method is appropriate "when investigators desire to a) define topics broadly and not narrowly b) cover contextual conditions and not just the phenomenon of study and c) rely on multiple and not singular sources of evidence" (Yin, 1993, p.XI). The preference for this approach is because the research has sought to analyse employment and industrial change in the context in which they are occurring. This is consistent with the consideration that the context, embodying the interplay of socio-economic aspects determined by formal and informal rules shared by people over time, influences the dynamics of industrial unemployment. Two similar localities have been selected as case studies. Teesside, in the North-East of England and Brindisi, in the South-East of Italy, are both industrial areas. Although each one industrialized in a diverse period (Teesside at the end of the nineteenth century – Brindisi in the late 1950s) and from completely different initial conditions (the existence of natural resources on Teesside; State-led identification of a growth pole area in Brindisi), their prosperity has been connected to the presence of a few dominant industries (chemicals, steel and iron and shipbuilding on Teesside; chemical and energy in Brindisi). After the mid-1970s, both suffered de-industrialization, with particularly dramatic effects on the areas' industrial structures and labour markets. High levels of unemployment and industrial job loss have led, on the one hand, to the redefinition of the previous models of industrial relations, deemed incompatible with any future process of development and, on the other, to the modification of strategies of participation in the labour market.

Teesside and Brindisi however display their own institutional contexts that are important in understanding their industrial dynamics. Company decisions concerning restructuring and employment adjustments are influenced, in fact, by laws, business relationships, local and national policies, but also by local cultural rules and symbols. Organizational behaviour is therefore subject to pressures of both the instrumental and symbolic institutional environment (Usui and Colignon, 1996). On Teesside, industrial development was achieved through the pervasive and paternalistic influence of large companies that generated a socialised culture of compliance and co-operation among employers and trade unions. Brindisi, instead, presents the traits of a latecomer economy. The decline of traditional agrarian society, brought about by the process of partial industrialization, led neither to the formation of an industrial working class nor a complete process of industrialization. It follows that self-employment is pervasive as well as the presence of informal economic activities. In other words, the micro-regulation of employment relations and practices, hinging upon rules of reciprocity, sides the formal regulation deriving from the application of national laws.

Notes

[1] Refer, among others, to Saxenian (1994) and Schoenberger (1997). Schoenberger defines corporate culture as the ensemble of material practices, social relations and ways of thinking. Material practices include, inter alia, technology and the organization of production, the division of labour and tasks. Work can be seen as a material and social activity. Through it, skills and meaning of what is done are developed as well as understandings and expectations about the social practices involved in the economic activity.

[2] It is evident that underlying the institutionalist methodology lies an ethical representation of capitalism. In contrast to the efficiency and neutrality heralded by the neo-classical paradigm, institutionalism assumes that the problem of labour is primarily an issue concerning its social costs and economic power.

[3] Semi-structured interviews are interviews developed through inputs, by leaving the interviewee the widest opportunity to answer. With this method, the risk of going beyond the topic is counterbalanced by the opportunity to collect a deeper and richer set of information.

[4] The focus group is a group interview in which it is the interaction among individuals that produces a considerable amount of data about the topic discussed. The limited number of participants and the complex internal dynamics are the main limits of this method (Morgan, 1997, 1998).

References

Aglietta, M. (1978), 'Panorama sur les theories de l'emploi', *Revue Economique*, pp. 81-119.

Aglietta, M. (1979), *A Theory of Capitalist Regulation*, Calmann-Levy, London.

Akerlof, G. (1982), 'Labour Contracts as Partial Gift Exchange', *Quarterly Journal of Economics*, Vol. 97(4), pp. 543-69.

Akerlof, G. (1984), 'Gift Exchange and Efficiency-Wage Theory: Four Views', *American Economic Review*, Papers and Proceedings, pp. 79-83.

Akerlof, G. and Yellen, J. (eds.) (1986), *Efficiency Wage Models of the Labour Market*, Cambridge University Press, Cambridge.

Allum, P. A. (1974), 'Il Mezzogiorno e la politica nazionale dal 1945 al 1950' in S. J. Woolf (ed.), *Italia 1943-1950. La ricostruzione*, Laterza, Bari.

Amatori, F. and Brioschi, F. (1997), 'Le grandi imprese private: famiglie e coalizioni' in F. Barca (a cura di), *Storia del capitalismo italiano*, Donzelli Editore, Roma.

Amin, A. (ed.) (1994), *Post-Fordism: a Reader*, Basil Blackwell, Oxford.

Amin. A. et al. (1998), *Welfare to Work or Welfare as Work? Combating Social Exclusion in the UK*, Paper presented to the Annual Conference of the RGS\IBG.

Aoki, M. (ed.) (1984), *The Economic Analysis of the Japanese Firm*, Elsevier Science Publishers, Amsterdam.

Aoki, M. et al. (1990), *The Firm as a Nexus of Treaties*, Sage Publications, London.

Arestis, P. (1992), *The Post-Keynesian Approach to Economics*, Edward Elgar, London.

Arestis, P. (1996), 'Post-Keynesian Economics: Towards Coherence', *Cambridge Journal of Economics*, Vol. 20, pp. 111-35.

Armstrong, H. and Taylor, J. (1993), *Regional Economics and Policy*, Harvester Wheatsheaf, London.

Arora, A. et al. (1998), *Chemicals and Long-Term Economic Growth*, John Wiley, New York.

Arrow, K. (1963), *Social Choice and Individual Values*, John Wiley and Sons, London.

Arrow, K. (1974), *The Limits of Organisation*, WWNorton and Company, London.

Artis, M.J. (1998), The Unemployment Problem, *Oxford Review of Economic Policy*, Vol. 14(3), pp.98-109.

Ashenfelter, O. and Layard, R. (1986), *Handbook of Labor Economics*, Vol. II, Elsevier Science Publishers, Amsterdam.

Ashton, D. (1986), *Unemployment under Capitalism*, Harvester Press, Brighton.

Bagnasco, A. (1988), *La costruzione sociale del mercato*, Il Mulino, Bologna.

Baker, P. (1993), 'Production Restructuring in the Textiles and Clothing Industries', *New Technology, Work and Employment*, Vol. 8(1), pp. 43-55.

Baran, P. and Sweezy, P. (1966), *Monopoly Capital*, Monthly Review Press, USA.

Barbash, J. (1989), 'J.R. Commons: Pioneer of Labour Economics', *Monthly Labour Review*, Vol. 112(5), pp. 44-9.

Barbash, J. (1994), 'Americanizing the Labor Problem: The Wisconsin School' in C. Kerr and P. Staudohar (eds.), *Labor Economics and Industrial Relations*, Harvard University Press, Massachusetts.

Barca, F. (a cura di)(1997), *Storia del capitalismo italiano*, Donzelli Editore, Roma.

Barnes, T. (1999), 'Industrial Geography, Institutional Economics and Innis' in T. Barnes and M. Gertler (eds.), *The New Industrial Geography*, Routledge, London.

Barrel, R. et al. (1994), 'Prospects for European Unemployment' in J. Michie and J. Grieve Smith (eds), *Unemployment in Europe*, London Academic Press, London.

Bazzoli, L. (1994), *Action collective, travail, dynamique du capitalisme: fondements et actualité de l'économie institutionnaliste de J.R. Commons*, Doctoral Thesis in Economic Sciences, Lyon.

Bean, C. (1994), 'European Unemployment: a Survey', *Journal of Economic Literature*, Vol. 32, pp. 573-619.

Becattini, G. (1990), 'The Marshallian Industrial District as a Socio-economic Notion' in F. Pyke et al. (eds.), *Industrial Districts and Inter-Form Cooperation in Italy*, ILO, Geneva.

Bellandi, M. (1996), 'Innovation and Change in the Marshallian Industrial District', *European Planning Studies*, pp. 357-68.

Best, M. (1990), *The New Competition*, Harvard University Press, Cambridge.

Beynon, H. et al. (1986), *The Growth and Internationalisation of Teesside's Chemicals Industry*, Middlesbrough Locality Study, Working Paper n. 3, University of Durham, Department of Geography.

Beynon, H. et al. (1994), *A Place Called Teesside*, Edinburgh University Press, Edinburgh.

Blanchflower, D. and Oswald, O. (1994), *The Wage Curve*, The MIT Press, Cambridge, Mass.

Bluestone, B. and Harrison, B. (1982), *The Deindustrialisation of America*, Basic Books, New York.

Boltanski, L. and Thevenot, L. (1987), 'Les économies de la grandeur', *Cahiers du CEE*, n. 31.

Bottomore, T. (ed.) (1984), *A Dictionary of Marxist Thought*, Blackwell, Oxford.

Bowles, S. (1985), 'The Production Process in a Competitive Economy: Walrasian, Neo-Hobbesian, and Marxian Models', *American Economic Review*, Vol. 75(1), pp. 16-36.

Bowles, S. et al. (1989), 'Business Ascendancy and Economic Impasse: A Structural Retrospective on Conservative Economics, 1979-87', *Journal of Economic Perspectives*, Vol. 3(1), pp. 107-34.

Boyer, R. (ed.) (1988), *The Search for Labour Market Flexibility*, Clarendon Press, Oxford.

Boyer, R. (1993), 'Labour Institutions and Economic Growth: a Survey and a "Regulationist" Approach', *Labour*, Vol. 7, pp. 25-72.

Boyer, R. and Hollingsworh, J. R. (1997), *Contemporary Capitalism*, Cambridge University Press, Cambridge.

Braverman, H. (1974), *Labour and Monopoly Capital: The Degradation of Work in the Twentieth Century*, Monthly Review Press, London.

Brunetta, R. and Dell'Aringa, C. (1990), *Labour Relations and Economic Performance*, MacMillan, London.

Bruno, M. and Sachs, J. D. (1985), *Economics of Worldwide Stagflation*, Harvard University Press, Cambridge.

Burawoy, M. (1985), *The Politics of Production: Factory Regimes under Capitalism and Socialism*, Verso, London.

Byrne, C. and Rigby, D. (1999), *The Industrial and Social Impact of New Technology in the Clothing Industry into the 2000s*, Paper produced for the International Labour Organisation, Geneva.

Cahuc, P. and Kempf, H. (1993), 'Le taux naturel de chomage: fortunes and infortunes d'un concept' in M. Lavoie and M. Seccareccia, *Milton Friedman et son oeuvre*, Presses Universitaires, Montreal.

Caire, G. (1996), 'Institutionnalistes, regulationnistes, conventionnalistes: n'est pas heterodoxe qui veut', *Economies et Sociétés*, Vol. XXX(9), pp. 225-32.

Calmfors, L. (1995), 'Labour Market Policy and Unemployment', *European Economic Review*, Vol.39, pp. 13-61.

Calmfors, L. and Driffil, J. (1988), 'Bargaining Structure, Corporatism and Macroeconomic Performance', *Economic Policy*, pp.14-61.

Capriati, M. (1995), *Il settore tessile-abbigliamento nel Mezzogiorno*, Report for Artigianform, Roma.

Capriati, M. (1996), *Economia aperta e sviluppo locale*, Clua, Ancona.

Carabelli, U. and Tronti, L. (eds.)(1999), 'Managing Labour Redundancies in Europe: Instruments and Prospects', *Labour*, Vol. 13(1), pp. 3-39. Special Issue.

Carter, E. et al. (eds.)(1993), *Space and Place*, Lawrence&Wishart, London.

Cartier, K. (1994), 'The Transaction Costs and Benefits of the Incomplete Contract of Employment', *Cambridge Journal of Economics*, n. 18, pp.181-96.

Castells, A. et al. (1989), *The Informal Economy*, John Hopkins University Press, Baltimore, London.

Castro, A. et al. (eds.) (1992), *International Integration and Labour Market Organisation*, Academic Press, London.

Cecafosso, N. (a cura di) (1979), 'Situazione socio-economica della provincia di Brindisi', *Quaderno della Rivista di Previdenza Sociale*, Grafischena, Fasano.

CEPR (1995), *Unemployment: Choices for Europe*, Cepr, London.

Cerpem (1990), *Dall'emergenza allo sviluppo*, Report for Associazione degli Industriali della provincia di Brindisi, Bari.

Cerpem (1991), *Il filo dell'abbigliamento. Il decentramento produttivo nel tessile-abbigliamento dal nord al sud Italia*, Bari.

Chandler, A. (1984), 'The Emergence of Managerial Capitalism', *Business History Review*, Vol. 58, pp. 473-503.

Chandler, A. (1990), *Scale and Scope: The Dynamics of Industrial Capitalism*, Harvard University Press, Cambridge, Mass.

Chapman, K. (1986), *Chemicals and the Cleveland Economy*, Department of Geography, University of Aberdeen.

Chapman, K. (1991), *The International Petrochemical Industry*, Blackwell, Oxford.

Chapman, K. and Edmond, H. (2000), 'Mergers/Acquisition and Restructuring in the EU Chemical Industry: Patterns and Implications', *Regional Studies*, Vol. 34(8), pp.753-67.

Chiarello, F. (1983), 'Economia informale, famiglia e reticoli sociali', *Rassegna Italiana di Sociologia*, n. 2, pp. 211-52.

Christopherson, S. (1998), 'Why do National Labour Market Practices Continue to Diverge in a Global Economy?', *Institute for European Studies*, WP 98.6.

Clark, J. M. (1923), *Studies in the Economics of Overhead Costs*, University of Chicago Press, Chicago.

Cleveland County Council (1994), *Changes in the Chemical Industry and the Impact on Cleveland in the 1990s*, Cleveland.

Commons, J. (1924), *Legal Foundation of Capitalism*, MacMillan, New York.

Commons, J. (1934), *Institutional Economics. Its Place in Political Economy*, MacMillan, New York.

Coppola, P. (1977), *Geografia e Mezzogiorno*, La Nuova Italia Editrice, Firenze.

COREI, (1995), *L'Economie Institutionnaliste. Les Fondateurs*, Economica, Paris.

Costabile, L. (1995), 'Institutions, Social Custom and Efficiency Wage Models: Alternative Approaches', *Cambridge Journal of Economics*, Vol. 19, pp. 605-23.

Cox, K. R. and Mair, A. (1988), 'Locality and Community in the Politics of Local Economic Development', *Annals of the Association of American Geographers*, Vol. 78, pp. 307-25.

Crewe, L. and Davenport, E. (1992), 'The Puppet Show: Changing Buyer-Supplier Relationships within Clothing Retailing', *Transaction Institute of British Geographers*, Vol. 17, pp. 183-97.

Crouch, C. (1985), 'Conditions for Trade Unions Wage Restraint' in L. Lindbeck and C. S. Maier (eds.), *The Politics of Inflation and Economic Stagnation*, Brookings Institution, Washington.

Crouch, C. (1993), *Industrial Relations and European State Traditions*, Clarendon Press, Oxford.

Cumbers, A. (1996), 'Continuity or Change in Employment Relations? Evidence from the UK's Old Industrial Regions', *Capital and Class*, n. 58, pp. 33-57.

Danson, M. (ed.)(1986), *Redundancy and Recession*, Geo Books, Norwich.

D'Aponte, T. (1972), 'Montedison: geografia di una ristrutturazione', *Nord e Sud*, n. 215.

D'Ercole, M. (1993), *Innovation in a Mature Industry: Evidence from Textile-Clothing*, MA Thesis, Maastricht.

Deakin, S. (1992), 'Labour Law and Industrial relations' in J. Michie (ed.), *The Economic Legacy*, Academic Press, London.

Deakin, S. and Wilkinson, F. (1999), 'The Management of Redundancies in Europe: The Case of Great Britain', *Labour*, Special Issue, Vol. 13(1), pp. 41-89.

De Rubertis, S. (1998), 'Cambiamenti globali nel tessile-abbigliamento', *Bollettino della Societa' Geografica Italiana*, n. 2, pp. 255-73.

Dei Ottati, G. (1995), *Tra mercato e comunita': aspetti concettuali e ricerche empiriche sul distretto industriale*, F. Angeli, Milano.

Dicken, P. and Thrift, N. (1992), 'The Organisation of Production and the Production of Organisation: Why Business Enterprises Matter in the Study of Geographical Industrialisation', *Transactions of the Institute of British Geographers*, Vol. 17, pp. 279-91.

DiMaggio, P. (1990), 'Cultural Aspects of Economic Action and Organisation' in R. Friedland and A. F. Robertson (eds.), *Beyond the Marketplace. Rethinking Economy and Society*, Aldine de Gruyter, New York.

Doeringer, P. and Piore, M. (1971), '*Internal Labour Market and Manpower Analysis*', Lexington Books, Mass.

Donolo, C. et al. (1978), *Classi sociali e politica nel Mezzogiorno*, Rosenberg and Sellier, Torino.

Dosi, G. (1982), 'Technological Paradigms and Technological Trajectories', *Research Policy*, Vol. 11, pp. 147-62.

Dugger, W. and Sherman, H. (1994), 'Comparison of Marxism and Institutionalism', *Journal of Economic Issues*, Vol. XXVIII(1), pp. 101-27.

Dumenil, G. and Levy, D. (1996), 'Une hétérodoxie critique, constructiviste et marxiste', *Economies et Sociétés*, n.9, pp. 183-92.

Durkheim, E. (1984), *The Division of Labour in Society*, MacMillan, London.

Economia Italiana, (1997), *L'industria chimica e farmaceutica*, n. 3.

ECOTEC (1989), *Cleveland Clothing Training Initiative*, Final report.

Ecoter (1993), *Pacchetto localizzativo Brindisi*, Rapporto finale, Roma.

Edwards, R. (1979), *Contested Terrain*, Heinmann, London.

Edwards, R. (1993), *Rights at Work*, The Twentieth Century Fund Inc, Washington.

Eggertsson, T. (1990), *Economic Behaviour and Institutions*, Cambridge University Press, Cambridge.

EIU (1999), *Sustaining Profitable Growth*, Chapter 3, London.

EniChem *Various Annual Reports*.

Farkas, G. and England, P. (1988), *Industries, Firms and Jobs*, Plenum Press, London.

Federchimica (1991), *Struttura, risultati e problemi dell'industria chimica in Italia*, CeRich-Federchimica, Milano.

Finch, J. (1998), *A Grounded Theory Paper for Economics*, Paper presented at European Association for Evolutionary and Political Economy Summer School, 14-24 July, Kenmare, Ireland.

Florio, M. (ed.) (1991), *Grande impresa e sviluppo locale*, Clua, Ancona.

Flowerdew, R. and Martin, D., (1996), *Methods in Human Geography*, Harlow, Longman.

Foord, J. et al. (1985), *The Quiet Revolution*, Special Report for BBC North East.

Foray, D. and Garrouste, P. (1991), 'The Pertinent Level of Analysis in Industrial Dynamics' in G. Hodgson and E. Screpanti (eds), *Rethinking Economics*, Edward Elgar, Hants.

Fornengo, G. (1978), *L'industria italiana dell'abbigliamento*, Il Mulino, Bologna.

Fothergill, S. and Gudgin, G. (1985), 'Ideology and Methods in Industrial Location Research' in D. Massey and R. Meegan, *Politics and Method*, Methuen, London.

Fothergill, S. and Guy, N. (1990), *Retreat from the Regions: Corporate Change and the Closure of Factories*, Jessica Kingsley and RSA, London.

Freeman, C. et al. (1982), *Unemployment and Technical Innovation*, Frances Pinter, London.

Freeman, C. and Soete, L. (1994), *Work for All or Mass Unemployment*, Pinter Publishing, London.

Friedland, R. and Robertson, A. F. (eds.) (1990) *Beyond the Marketplace. Rethinking Economy and Society*, Aldine de Gruyter, New York.

Friedman, M. (1951), 'Some Comments on the Significance of Labor Unions for Economic Policy' in D. McCord Wright (ed.), *The impact of the Union*, Kelley&Millman, New York.

Friedman, M. (1968), 'The Role of Monetary Policy', *American Economic Review*, Vol. 58, pp. 1-17.

Friedman, M. and Friedman, R. (1979), *Free to Choose*, Harcourt Brace, New York.

Gallie, D. (ed.)(1988), *Employment in Britain*, Blackwell, Oxford.

Gallie, D. et al. (eds.)(1994), *Social Change and the Experience of Unemployment*, Oxford University Press, Oxford.

Gallie, D. et al. (1998), *Restructuring the Employment Relationship*, Clarendon Press, Oxford.

Gamble, A. (1988), *The Free Economy and the Strong State: the Politics of Thatcherism*, MacMillan, Basingstoke.

Garrahan, P. and Stewart, P. (1992), 'Management Control and a new Regime of Subordination: Post-Fordism and the Local Economy' in N. Gilbert et al., *Fordism and Flexibility: Divisions and Change*, MacMillan, London.

Gimble, D. (1991), 'Institutionalist Labour Market Theory and Veblenian Dichotomy', *Journal of Economic Issues*, Vol. XXV(3), pp. 625-48.

Glynn, S. and Booth, A. (1987), *The Road to Full Employment*, Allen & Unwin, London.

Goodwin, R. (1991), 'Socio-political Disruption and Economic Development' in G. Hodgson and E. Screpanti. (eds.), *Rethinking Economics*, Edward Elgar, Hants.

Gordon, D. et alt. (1982), *Segmented Work, Divided Workers: the Historical Transformation of Labour in the United States*, Cambridge University Press, Cambridge.

Gorz, A. (1982), *Addio al proletariato*, Edizioni Lavoro, Roma.

Gorz, A. (1999), *Reclaiming Work*, Polity Press, Oxford.

Granovetter, M. (1973), 'The Strength of the Weak Ties', *American Journal of Sociology*, Vol. 78, pp. 1360-80.

Granovetter, M. (1985), 'Economic Action and Social Structure: The Problem of Embeddedness', *American Journal of Sociology*, Vol. 91(3), pp. 481-510.

Granovetter, M. (1990), 'The Old and the New Economic Sociology: a History and an Agenda' in R. Friedland and A. F. Robertson (eds.) *Beyond the Marketplace. Rethinking Economy and Society*, Aldine de Gruyter, New York.

Gregory, D. and Urry, J. (eds.) (1985), *Social Relations and Spatial Structures*, MacMillan, London.

Gribaudi, G. (1980), *Mediatori. Antropologia del potere democristiano nel Mezzogiorno*, Rosenberg&Sellier, Torino.

Grossman, S. and Hart, O. (1981), 'Implicit Contracts, Moral Hazard, and Unemployment', *American Economic Review*, Vol. 71(2), pp. 301-7.

Hampden-Turner, C. (1990), *Corporate Culture*, Hutchinson, London.

Hardill, I. (1983-1987), 'Is There a Future for the Rag Trade in the North', *Northern Economic Review*, Vol. 8(14), pp. 32-41.

Hardill, I. (1987), *Cleveland Clothing Industry*, Background Report, Cleveland County Council.

Hardill, I. (1990), 'Restructuring in the Cleveland clothing industry' in P. Stewart and P. Garrahan (eds.) *Restructuring for Economic Flexibility*, Aldershot, Hants.

Hart, P. (ed.)(1986), *Unemployment and Labour Policies*, Gower, Aldershot.

Harvey, D. (1969), *Explanation in Geography*, Edward Arnold, London.

Harvey, D. (1989), *The Condition of Postmodernity*, Blackwell, Oxford.

Hayek, F. (1946), *Individualism: True and False*, Blackwell, Oxford.

Herod, A. (1991), 'Local Political Practice in Response to a Manufacturing Plant Closure: How Geography Complicates Class Analysis', *Antipode*, Vol.23 (4), pp. 385-402.

Hicks, J. (1973), *Capital and Time*, Oxford University Press, Oxford.

Hoang-Ngoc, L. (1996), 'Le classicisme des nouvelles théories keynésiennes du chômage d'équilibre: ses fondements, ses implications normatives', *Economies et Societes*, n. 19, pp. 5-45.

Hobson, J. A. (1922), *The Economics of Unemployment*, Allen&Unwin, London.

Hodgson, G. (1988), *Economics and Insitutions*, Polity Press, Cambridge.

Hodgson, G. (1992), 'The Reconstruction of Economics: Is There Still a Place for Neoclassical Theory', *Journal of Economic Issues*, Vol. 26(3), pp. 749-67.

Hodgson, G. (1993), *Economics and Evolution*, Polity Press, Cambridge.

Hodgson, G. (1998), 'The Approach of Institutional Economics', *Journal of Economic Literature*, Vol. 36(1), pp. 166-92.

Hodgson, G. and Screpanti, E. (eds.)(1991), *Rethinking Economics*, Edward Elgar, Hants.

Holmlund, B. and Lofgren, K-G. (1990), *Unemployment and Wage Determination in Europe*, Basil Blackwell, Oxford.

Hudson, R. (1983), 'Capital Accumulation and Chemicals Production in Western Europe in the Postwar Period', *Environment and Planning A*, Vol. 15, pp. 105-22.

Hudson, R. (1986), 'Producing an Industrial Wasteland: Capital, Labour and the State in North-East England' in R. Martin and B. Rowthorn (eds.), *The Geography of De-industrialisation*, MacMillan, London.

Hudson, R. (1988), 'Labour Market Changes and New Forms of Work in 'Old' Industrial Regions' in D. Massey and J. Allen, *Uneven Re-Development: Cities and Regions in Transition*, Hodder and Stoughton, London.

Hudson, R. (1989), *Wrecking a Region*, Pion, London.

Hudson, R. (1994), 'Institutional Change, Cultural Transformation and Economic Generation: Myths and Realities from Europe's Old Industrial Areas' in A. Amin and N. Thrift, *Globalisation, Institutions and Regional Development in Europe*, Oxford University Press, Oxford.

Hudson, R. (1999), 'The Learning Economy, the Learning Firm and the Learning Region: a Sympathetic Critique to the Limits to Learning', *European Urban and Regional Studies*, n.6, pp. 59-72.

Hughes, J. and Perlman, R. (1984), *The Economics of Unemployment*, Harvester Press, Brighton.

Humphries, J. (1976), 'Women: Scapegoats and Safety Valves in the Great Depression', *Review of Radical Political Economics*, n. 8, pp. 98-121.

Humphries, J. and Rubery, J. (1984), 'The Reconstruction of the Supply Side of the Labour Market', *Cambridge Journal of Economics*, n. 8, pp. 331-46.

ICE (2001), 'L'Italia nell'economia internazionale', *Rapporto ICE 2000-2001*, ICE, Roma.

ICI   *Various Annual Reports.*

IDS (1998), *Pay in Textile, Clothing and Footwear in 1997*, Report 752.

ILO (1980), *The Employment Effects in the Clothing Industry of Changes in International Trade*, ILO, Geneva.

Institute of British Geographers (1984), *Geography and Gender*, Hutchinson, London.

Istat (1996), *Censimento intermedio dell'industria*, Istat, Roma.

Istat (1999), *Commercio estero e attivita' internazionali delle imprese- 1998*, Vol.1, 2, Istat, Roma.

Jackman, J. (1999), Wage Setting Behaviour in a Monetary Union – a Role for the European Social Partnerships, Paper presented for the conference of the National Bank of Austria, Vienna, 10-11 June.

Jessop, B. (1993), 'Towards a Schumpeterian Workfare State? Preliminary Remarks on Post-Fordist Political Economy', *Studies in Political Economy*, n.40, pp. 7-39.

Jessop, B. et al. (1991), *The Politics of Flexibility*, Edward Elgar, Aldershot.

Jones, E. (1983), 'Industrial Structure and Labour Force Segmentation', *Review of Radical Political Economics*, n. 15, pp. 24-44.

Kapp, W. (1968), 'In Defence of Institutional Economics', *Swedish Journal of Economics*, Vol. 70, present in W. J. Samuels (ed.), *Institutional Economics*, Vol. 1, Edward Elgar, Aldershot.

Kapp, W. (1976), 'The Nature and Significance of Institutional Economics', *Kyklos*, Vol. 29, pp. 209-32.

Kaufman, B. (1988), *How Labour Markets Work*, Lexington Books, Massachusetts.

Kaufman, B. (1994), 'The Evolution of Thought on the Competitive Nature of Labour Markets' in C. Kerr and P. Staudohar (eds.), *Labor Economics and Industrial Relations*, Harvard University Press, Cambridge, Mass.

Kerr, C. (1994), 'The Social Economics Revisionists: The 'Real World' Study of Labour Markets and Institutions' in C. Kerr and P. Staudohar (eds.), *Labor Economics and Industrial Relations*, Harvard University Press, Cambridge, Mass.

Kerr, C. and Staudohar, P. (eds.)(1994), *Labor Economics and Industrial Relations*, Harvard University Press, Cambridge, Mass.

Krugman, P. (1994), 'Past and Prospective Causes of High Unemployment' in *Reducing Unemployment. Current Issues and Policy Options*, Federal Reserve Bank of Kansas City.

Labour Studies Group (1985), 'Economic, Social and Political Factors in the Operation of the Labour Market' in B. Roberts et al. (eds.), *New Approaches to Economic Life: Restructuring, Unemployment and the Social Division of Labour*, Manchester University Press, Manchester.

La Malfa, G. and Coppola, P. (1974), *Il futuro dell'industria chimica*, CEEP, F.Angeli, Milano.

Langlois, R. (ed.)(1986), *Economics as a Process*, Cambridge University Press, Cambridge.

Lasch, S. and Friedman, J. (eds.) (1992), *Modernity and Identity*, Basil Blackwell, Oxford.

Lawson, T. (1997), *Economics and Reality*, Routledge, London.

Layard, R. et al. (1991), *Unemployment*, Oxford University Press, Oxford.

Layard, R. et al. (1994), *The Unemployment Crisis*, Oxford University Press, Oxford.

Levine, D. (1998), *Subjectivity in Political Economy*, Routledge, London.

Lindbeck, A. and Snower, D. (1986), *The Insider-Outsider Theory of Employment and Unemployment*, The MIT Press, Cambridge, Mass.

Losch, A. (1954), *The Economics of Industrial Location*, Yale University Press, New Haven.

Low Pay Commision, (1998), *Defining the Minimum Wage*, www.lowpay.gov.uk.

Lukes, S. (1973), *Individualism*, Basil Blackwell, Oxford.

Lunghini, G. (1997), 'Disoccupazione e bisogni sociali' in S. Beretta. and P. Bianchi (a cura di), *Cambiamento delle istituzioni economiche e nuovo sviluppo in Italia e in Europa*, Il Mulino, Bologna.

MacLachlan, I. (1992), 'Plant Closure and Market Dynamics: Competitive Strategy and Rationalisation', *Economic Geography*, n. 68, pp.128-45.

Malinvaud, E. (1994), *Diagnosis Unemployment*, Cambridge University Press, Cambridge.

Mandel, E. (1962), *Marxist Economic Theory*, Merlin Press, vol.1-2, London.

Mandel, E. (1995), *Long Waves of Capitalist Development*, Verso, London.

Martin, R. (1989), 'De-industrialisation and State Intervention: Keynesianism, Thatcherism and the Regions' in J. Mohan, *The Political Geography of Contemporary Britain*, MacMillan, London.

Martin, R. and Rowthorn, B. (eds.) (1986), *The Geography of De-industrialisation*, MacMillan, London.

Martinelli, F. (1998), *The Governance of Post-War Development and Policy in Southern Italy. Notes for a Critical Reappraisal*, Paper presented at the Second European Urban and Regional Studies Conference, 17-20 September, University of Durham, United Kingdom.

Marx, K. (1977), *Il capitale*, Ed. Riuniti, Roma.

Massey, D. (1983), 'Industrial Restructuring: Production Decentralisation and Local Uniqueness', *Regional Studies*, Vol. 17(2), pp. 73-89.

Massey, D. (1985), 'New Directions in Space' in D. Gregory and J. Urry (eds.), *Social Relations and Spatial Structures*, MacMillan, London.

Massey, D. (1995), *Spatial Divisions of Labour*, MacMillan, London.

Massey, D. and Allen, J. (1988), *Uneven Re-Development: Cities and Regions in Transition*, Hodder and Stoughton, London.

Massey, D. and Meegan, R. (1982), *The Anatomy of Job Loss*, Methuen, London.

Massey, D. and Meegan, R. (1985), *Politics and Method*, Methuen, London.

Matzner, E. and Streeck, W. (eds.) (1991), *Beyond Keynesianism*, Edward Elgar, Aldershot.

Meade, J. (1962), *A Neo-classical Theory of Economic Growth*, Unwin University Books, London.

Meade, J. (1995), *Full Employment Regained?*, Occasional Papers, n. 61, Department of Applied Economics, University of Cambridge.

Mele, R. (1975), *L'industria manifatturiera della Puglia*, CESAN, Napoli.

Michie, J. (ed.) (1992), *The Economic Legacy*, Academic Press, London.

Michie, J. and Grieve Smith, J. (eds.) (1994), *Unemployment in Europe*, Academic Press, London.

Michie, J. and Grieve Smith, J. (eds.) (1996), *Creating Industrial Capacity*, Oxford University Press, Oxford.

Michie, J. and Grieve Smith, J. (eds.) (1997), *Employment and Economic Performance*, Oxford University Press, Oxford.

Michie, J. and Wilkinson, F. (1992), 'Inflation Policy and the Restructuring of Labour Markets' in J. Michie (ed.), *The Economic Legacy*, Academic Press, London.

Michon, F. (1992), 'The Institutional Forms of Work and Employment: Towards the Construction of an International Historical and Comparative Approach' in A. Castro et al., *International Integration and Labour Market Organisation*, Academic Press, London.

Miller, S. (1995), *The Chemical Industry*, a Key Note Report.

Minford, P. (1985), *Unemployment: Cause and Cure*, Basil Blackwell, Oxford.

Mingione, E. (1991), *Fragmented Societies*, Basil Blackwell, Oxford.

Mingione, E. (1993), *Labour Market Segmentation and Informal Work in Southern Europe*, Paper presented at the International Seminar: Geographies of Integration, Geographies of Inequality in a Post-Maastrict Europe, 31 August, Greece.

Ministero dell'Industria (1997), *Linee di politica industriale per il sistema Moda"*, Report by the technical staff of the Italian Department of Trade and Industry, Roma.

Morgan, D. (1997), *Focus Groups as Qualitative Research*, Sage Publications, California.

Morgan, D. (1998), *The Focus Groups Guidebook*, Sage Publications, California.

Nelson, R. (1980), 'Production Sets, Technological Knowledge and R&D: Fragile and Overworked Constructs for Analysis of Productivity Growth?', *American Economic Review*, Vol.70, pp. 62-8.

Nelson, R. (ed.)(1993), *National Innovation Systems*, Oxford University Press, Oxford.

Nicholas, K. (1986), *The Social Effects of Unemployment in Teesside*, Manchester University Press, Manchester.

Nichols, T. and Beynon, H. (1977), *Living with Capitalism*, Routledge & Kegan Paul, London.

Nickell, S. (1986), 'Dynamics Models of Labour Demand' in O. Ashenfelter and R. Layard (eds.), *Handbook of Labour Economics*, North-Holland Press, Amsterdam.

Nolan, P. (1994), 'Labour Institutions, Industrial Restructuring and Unemployment in Europe' in J. Michie and J. Grieve Smith (eds.), *Unemployment in Europe*, Academic Press, London.

North, D. (1990), *Institutions, Institutional Change and Economic Performance*, Cambridge University Press, Cambridge.

North, G.A. (1975), *Teesside's Economic Heritage*, County Council of Cleveland, Cleveland.

Northern Region Strategy Team (1976), *The Chemicals Industry in the Northern Region*, Newcastle upon Tyne.

OECD (1994), *The Job Study: Facts, Analysis and Strategies*, OECD, Paris.

OECD (1997), *Employment Outlook*, OECD, Paris.

OECD (1999), *Employment Outlook*, OECD, Paris.

Offe, C. (1985), *Disorganised Capitalism*, Polity Press, Cambridge.

Offe, C. and Heinze, R. (1992), *Beyond Employment*, Polity Press, Cambridge.

Offe, C. and Hinrichs, K. (1985), 'The Political Economy of the Labour Market' in C. Offe, *Disorganised Capitalism*, Polity Press, Cambridge.

Pahl, R. (1984), *Divisions of Labour*, Basil Blackwell, Oxford.

Painter, J. and Goodwin, M. (1995), 'Local Governance and Concrete Research: Investigating the Uneven Development of Regulation', *Economy and Society*, Vol. 24(3), pp. 334-56.

Peck, J. (1996), *Workplace*, Guildford Press, New York.

Peck, J. (1998), *New Labourers? Making a New Deal for the 'Workless Class'*, Paper presented at the annual conference of the RGS\IBG, Guilford, 5-8 January.

Peck, J. and Theodore, N. (1999), *Insecurity in Work and Welfare: Towards a Trans-Atlantic Model of Labour Regulation?*, Paper presented at the annual conference of the RGS/IBG, Leicester, 4-7- January.

Peck, J. and Tickell, A. (1992), 'Local Modes of Social Regulation? Regulation Theory, Thatcherism and Uneven Development', *Geoforum*, n. 23, pp. 347-64.

Peck, J. and Tickell, A. (1995), 'The Social Regulation of Uneven Development: "Regulatory Deficit", England's South East and the Collapse of Thatcherism', *Environment and Planning A*, n. 27, pp. 15-40.

Perrucci, R. (1994), 'Embedded Corporatism', *The Sociological Quarterly*, Vol.35(3), 487-506.

Pettigrew, A. (1985), *The Awakening Giant*, Basil Blackwell, London.

Phelps, E. (1968), 'Money-Wage Dynamics and Labour Market Equilibrium', *Journal of Political Economy*, Vol. 76, pp. 678-711.

Phelps, E. (1972), *Inflation Policy and Unemployment Theory*, MacMillan, London.

Phelps, E. (1994), 'Commentary: Past and Prospective Causes of High Unemployment' in *Reducing Unemployment. Current Issues and Policy Options*, Federal Reserve Bank of Kansas City.

Phillips, J. (1999), *A Brief History of the Chemical Industry on Teesside*, Teesside Chemical Initiative, Middlesbrough.

Picchio, A. (1992), *Social Reproduction: The Political Economy of the Labour Market*, Cambridge University Press, Cambridge.

Pike, A. (1998), *Building a Regional Political Economy Approach to the Geography of Plant Closure*, Paper presented at the Second European Urban and Regional Studies Conference, 17-20 September, University of Durham, United Kingdom.

Pini, P. (1995), 'La disoccupazione nell'area OCSE e in Europa in particolare. E' rilevante il cambiamento tecnologico', *L'Industria*, Vol. XVI(3), pp. 541-605.

Pitelis, C.N. and Wahl, M. W. (1998), 'Edith Penrose: Pioneer of Stakeholder Theory', *Long Range Planning*, Vol. 31(2), pp. 252-61.

Polanyi, K. (1944), *The Great Transformation*, Beacon Paperback, Boston.

Polanyi, K. (1977), *The Livelihood of Man*, Academic Press, London.

Polanyi, M. (1957), *Personal Knowledge: Towards a Post-Critical Philosophy*, Routledge, London.

Pollard, S. (1992), *The Development of the British Economy, 1914-1990*, Edward Arnold, London.

Portes, A., Castells, M. and Benton, L. (1989), *The Informal Economy*, The Johns Hopkins University Press, London.

Powell, W. and DiMaggio, P. (1991)(eds.), *The New Institutionalism in Organizational Analysis*, University of Chicago Press, Chicago.

Prechel, H. (1991), 'Irrationality and Contradiction in Organizational Change: Transformation in the Corporate Form of a US Steel Corporation', *Sociological Quarterly*, Vol. 32, pp. 423-55.

Provincia di Brindisi, (1999), *Rapporto 1998 sull'economia e la societa' della provincia di Brindisi*, Brindisi.

Pugliese, E. et al. (1973), *Mezzogiorno e classe operaia*, Coines Ed.

Rainnie, A. (1989), *Industrial Relations in Small Firms*, Routledge, London.

Ram, M. (1992), 'The West Midlands Clothing Sector: a Suitable Case for Team Working', *Regional Studies*, Vol. 26, pp. 503-9.

Ranci, P. and Vacca', S. (1979), *L'industria petrolchimica in Italia: anatomia di una crisi*, F. Angeli, Milano.

Reich, M. et al. (1973), 'A Theory of Labour Market Segmentation', *American Economic Review*, Vol. 63, pp. 359-65.

Reyneri, E. (1996), *Sociologia del mercato del lavoro*, Il Mulino, Bologna.

Rifkin, J. (1995), *The End of Work*, Putnam & Sons, New York.

Ringen, S. (1987), *The Possibility of Politics*, Oxford University Press, Oxford.

Rubery, J. (1978), 'Structured Labour Markets, Worker Organisation and Low Pay', *Cambridge Journal of Economics*, n. 1, pp. 17-36.

Rubery, J. (ed.) (1988), *Women and Recession*, Routledge, London.

Rutherford, M. (1996), *Institutions in Economics*, Cambridge University Press, Cambridge.

Sabel, C. (1994), 'Learning by Monitoring: The Institutions of Economic Development' in N. Smelser and R. Swedberg, *The Handbook of Economic Sociology*, Princeton University Press, Princeton, NJ.

Sabel, C. and Piore, M. (1984), *The Second Industrial Divide*, Basic Books, New York.

Saint-Paul, G. (1995), 'Some Political Aspects of Unemployment', *European Economic Review*, Vol. 39(1), pp. 575-82.

Saint-Paul, G. (1996), 'Exploring the Political Economy of Labour Market Institutions', *Economic Policy*, n.22-23, pp. 265-315.

Salais, R. (1989), 'L'analyse économique des conventions du travail', *Révue Economique*, n. 2, pp. 199-240.

Salais, R. (1991), 'Flexibilité et conventions du travail: une approche', *Economie Appliquée*, Vol. XLIV(2), pp. 5-32.

Salais, R. (1992), 'Labour Conventions, Economic Fluctuations and Flexibility' in M. Storper and A. Scott (eds.), *Pathways to Industrialisation and Regional Development*, Routledge, London.

Sawyer, M. (1989), *The Challenge of Radical Political Economy*, Harvester Wheatsheaf, London.

Saxenian, A. (1994), *Regional Advantage: Culture and Competition in Silicon Valley and Route 128*, Harvard University Press, Cambridge (Mass).

Sayer, A. and Morgan, K. (1985), 'A Modern Industry in a Declining Region: Links between Method, Theory and Policy' in D. Massey and R. Meegan, *Politics and Method*, Methuen, London.

Sayer, A. and Walker, R. (1992), *The New Social Economy*, Blackwell Publishers, Cambridge, Mass.

Schoenberger, E. (1991), 'The Corporate Interview as a Research Method in Economic Geography', *Professional Geographer*, Vol. 43(2), pp. 180-89.

Schoenberger, E. (1997), *The Cultural Crisis of the Firm*, Blackwell Publishers, Cambridge, Mass.

Schumpeter, J. (1964), *Business Cycles: A Theoretical, Historical and Statistical Analysis of the Capitalist Process*, McGraw-Hill, New York.

Schumpeter, J. (1968), *The Theory of Economic Development*, Harvard University Press, Cambridge, Mass.

Sciberras, E. and Burleigh, D. (1988), *The Clothing Industry in the North-East*, Regional Industrial Research Unit.

Sengenberger, W. (1990), *The Role of Labour Standards in Industrial Restructuring: Participation, Protection and Promotion*, ILO, Geneva.

Sengenberger, W. and Campbell, D. (eds.) (1994), *Creating Economic Opportunities. The Role of Labour Standards in Industrial Restructuring*, ILO, Geneva.

Sestito, P. (1997), 'La questione del lavoro e le interpretazioni proposte' in P. Ciocca (a cura di), *Disoccupazione di fine secolo*, Bollati Boringhieri, Torino.

Shapiro, C. and Stiglitz, J. (1985), 'Equilibrium Unemployment as a Worker Discipline Device', *American Economic Review*, Vol. 74, pp. 433-44.

Silva, F. (1995), 'Vi sono rimedi per l'alta occupazione?', *Economia e politica industriale*, n. 85, pp. 25-43.

Silverman, D. (1993), *Interpreting Qualitative Data*, Sage Publications, London.

Simon, H. (1948), *Economic Policy for a Free Society*, University of Chicago Press, Chicago.

Sinfield, A. (1983), *What Unemployment Means*, Martin Robertson, Oxford.

Snower, D. (1995), 'Evaluating Unemployment Policies: What do the Underlying Theories Tell Us?', *Oxford Review of Economic Policy*, Vol. 11(1), pp. 110-34.

Snower, D. and De La Dehesa, G. (eds.) (1997), *Unemployment Policy: Government Options for the Labour Market*, Cambridge University Press, Cambridge.

Soete, L. (1981), 'Technological Dependency: A Critical View' in D. Seers (ed.) *Dependency Theory: A Critical Reassessment*, Frances Pinter, London.

Solow, R. (1969), *Growth Theory-An Exposition*, Clarendon Press, Oxford.

Solow, R. (1980), 'On Theories of Unemployment', *American Economic Review*, Vol. 70(1), pp. 1-11.

Solow, R. (1990), *The Labour Market as a Social Institution*, Basil Blackwell, Oxford.

Soskice, D. (1990), 'Wage Determination: the Changing Role of Institutions in Advanced Industrialised Countries', *Oxford Review of Economic Policy*, Vol. 6(4), pp. 36-61.

Stigler, G. (1946), 'The Economics of Minimum Wage Legislation', *American Economic Review*, Vol. 36, pp. 358-78.

Storper, M. and Salais, R. (1997), *Worlds of Production*, Harvard University Press, Cambridge (Mass).

Storper, M. and Walker, R. (1989), *The Capitalist Imperative*, Oxford University Press, Oxford.

Streeck, W. (1992), *Social Institutions and Economic Performance: Studies of Industrial Relations in Advanced Capitalist Economies*, Sage, London and Beverley Hills.

Summers, L. (1988), 'Relative Wages, Efficiency Wages and Keynesian Unemployment', *American Economic Review*, Papers and Proceedings, Vol. 78, pp. 383-88.

Svimez (1971), *Gli investimenti industriali agevolati nel Mezzogiorno. 1951-1968*, Giuffre' Ed., Milano.

Svimez (1998), *Rapporto 1998 sull'economia del Mezzogiorno*, Roma.

Swedberg, R. (1995), *Economia e sociologia*, Donzelli Editori, Roma.

Taplin, I. (1995), 'Flexible Production, Rigid Jobs: Lessons from the Clothing Industry', *Work and Occupations*, Vol. 22(4), pp. 412-38.

Tarrow, S. (1979), *Peasant Communism in Southern Italy*, Yale University Press, New Haven.

Tees Valley Joint Strategy Unit (TVJSU) (1995), *Cleveland's Economic Prospects. 1995-2006*, Cleveland.

Tees Valley Joint Strategy Unit (1999), *Developing a Sustainable, Competitive, Diversified Economy*, Cleveland.

Teesside Chemical Initiative (1998), *Teesside Chemical Industry Survey 1997*, Survey and report commissioned by Teesside TEC, Chemical Employers' Group and Teesside Chemical Initiative, Cleveland.

Teesside TEC (1998), *Teesside Chemical Industry Manpower Survey 1997*, Report by Teesside Training and Enterprise Council Chemical Employers' Group and Teesside Chemical Initiative.

Therborn, G. (1986), *Why Some People are more Unemployed than others?*, Verso, New York.

Thomas, R. and Thomas, H. (1994), 'The Informal Economy and Local Economic Development Policy', *Local Government Studies*, Vol. 20(3), pp. 486-501.

Touraine, A. (1971), *The Post-Industrial Society*, Random House, London.

Townsend, A. and Peck, F. (1985), 'An Approach to the Analysis of Redundancies in the UK (post-1976): Some Methodological Problems and Policy Implications' in D. Massey and R. Meegan (eds.), *Politics and Method*, Methuen, London.

Trigilia, C. (1992), *Sviluppo senza autonomia*, Il Mulino, Bologna.

Usui, C. and Colignon, R. (1996), 'Corporate Restructuring: Converging World Pattern or Societally Specific Embeddedness?', *The Sociological Quarterly*, Vol. 37(4), pp. 551-78.

Veblen, T. (1919), *The Place of Science in Modern Civilisation and Other Essays*, New York, Huebsch.

Viesti, G. (1996), 'Modelli e percorsi di sviluppo: alcune riflessioni intorno al caso della Puglia', *Economia Marche*, n. 2, pp. 321-46.

Viesti, G. (1998), 'Sommerso ed emersione nell'industria dell'abbigliamento e delle calzature nel Mezzogiorno', *Meridiana*, n. 33, pp. 37-81.

Viesti, G. (2000), *L'abbigliamento nella Puglia centrale*, Mimeo.

Vivarelli, M. (1991), 'I meccanismi compensativi della disoccupazione tecnologica. Il dibattito classico e I modelli recenti', *Economia Politica*, n.3, pp. 517-57.

Vivarelli, M. and Gatti, D. (1995), 'La disoccupazione tecnologica tra mercato e istituzioni: studi teorici e verifiche empiriche', *L'Industria*, n. 3, pp. 607-25.

Watts, H.D. and Stafford, H.A. (1986), 'Plant Closures and the Multiplant Firm: Some Conceptual Issues', *Progress in Human Geography*, n. 10, pp. 206-27.

Webster, D. (1999), *Unemployment-Research Mailing List*.

Weitzman, M. (1986), *L'economia della partecipazione*, Editori Laterza, Bari.

Wilkinson, F. (1983), 'Productive Systems', *Cambridge Journal of Economics*, n. 7, pp. 413-29.

Wilkinson, F. (1987), 'Deregulation, Structured Labour Markets and Unemployment' in P. Pedersen and R. Lund (eds.), *Unemployment: Theory, Policy and Structure*, De Gruyter, Berlin.

Williamson, O. (1985), *The Economic Institutions of Capitalism. Firms, Markets, Relational Contracting*, MacMillan, London.

Williamson, O. and Winter, S. (eds.)(1993), *The Nature of the Firm*, Oxford University Press, Oxford.

Winter, S. (1993), 'On Coase, Competence and the Corporation' in O. Williamson and S. Winter (eds.), *The Nature of the Firm*, Oxford University Press, Oxford.

Yellen, J. (1984), 'Efficiency Wage Models of Unemployment', *American Economic Review*, Papers and Proceedings, n. 74, pp. 200-205.

Yin, R. (1993), *Applications of Case Study Research*, Sage Publications, London.

Index